Database Management for Microcomputers

Second Edition

Database Management for Microcomputers
Second Edition

Jan L. Harrington
Marist College
Divison of Computer Science and Math

The Dryden Press
Harcourt Brace College Publishers

*Fort Worth   Philadelphia   San Diego   New York   Orlando   Austin   San Antonio
Toronto   Montreal   London   Sydney   Tokyo*

Executive Editor: Richard Bonacci
Project Editor: Cheryl Hauser
Production Manager: Kelly Cordes
Designer: Linda Wooten Miller
Director of Editing, Design, and Production: Diane Southworth
Publisher: Elizabeth Widdicombe

Layout and Design: Black Gryphon® Ltd.
Copy Editor: Matthew Fels
Developmental Editor: Matthew Fels

Address for Editorial Correspondence
The Dryden Press
301 Commerce Street, Suite 3700
Fort Worth, TX 76102

Address for Orders
The Dryden Press
6277 Sea Harbor Drive
Orlando, FL 32887-6777
1-800-782-4479 or 1-800-433-0001 (in Florida)

ISBN: 0-03-031588-3

Printed in the United States of America

3 4 5 6 7 8 9 0 1 2   018   9 8 7 6 5 4 3 2 1

The Dryden Press
Harcourt Brace College Publishers

The Dryden Press Series in Information Systems

Arthur Andersen & Co./Flaatten, McCubbrey,
O'Riordan, and Burgess
Foundations of Business Systems. Second Edition

Arthur Andersen & Co./Boynton and Shank
Foundations of Business Systems: Projects and Cases

Anderson
*Structured Programming Using Turbo Pascal: A Brief
Introduction.* Second Edition

Brown and McKeown
Structured Programming with Microsoft BASIC

Coburn
Beginning Structured COBOL
Advanced Structured COBOL

Dean and Effinger
*Common-Sense BASIC: Structured Programming with
Microsoft QuickBASIC*

Electronic Learning Facilitators, Inc. Series
The DOS Book
The Lotus 1-2-3 Book
Stepping Through Excel 4.0 for Windows
Stepping Through PageMaker 5.0 for Windows
Stepping Through Windows 3.1
Stepping Through Word 2.0 for Windows
*Up and Running with harvard Graphics 1.03 for
Windows*
Up and Running with PageMaker 5.0 for Windows
Up and Running with WordPerfect 5.2 for Windows
Up and Running with Quattro Pro 1.0 for Windows
*Up and Running with Microsoft Works 2.0 for
Windows*
*Up and Running with Lotus 1-2-3 Release 1.1 for
Windows*
Up and Running with Paradox 1.0 for Windows
Up and Running with DOS 6.0
Up and Running with Paradox 4.0 for DOS
Up and Running with Microsoft Works 3.0 for DOS
Up and Running with Excel 4.0 for the Macintosh
Up and Running with Word 5.1 for the Macintosh
*Up and Running with PageMaker 5.0 for the
Macintosh*
*Up and Running with Microsoft Works 3.0 for the
Macintosh*
Working Smarter with DOS 5.0
Working with WordPerfect 5.0
Working with WordPerfect 5.1

Federico
WordPerfect 5.1 Primer

Goldstein Software, Inc.
Joe Spreadsheet, Macintosh Version
Joe Spreadsheet, Statistical

Gray, King, McLean, and Watson
Management of Information Systems. Second Edition

Harrington
Database Management for Microcomputers. Second
Edition

Janossy
COBOL: An Introduction to Software Engineering

Laudon and Laudon
*Business Information Systems: A Problem-Solving
Approach.* Second Edition

Laudon, Laudon, and Weill
The Integrated Solution

Lawlor
Computer Information Systems. Third Edition

Liebowitz
*The Dynamics of Decision Support Systems and Expert
Systems*

McKeown
Living with Computers. Fourth Edition
Living with Computers with BASIC. Fourth Edition
Working with Computers. Second Edition
Working with Computers with Software Tutorials.
Second Edition

McKeown and Badarinathi
*Applications Software Tutorials: A Computer Lab
Manual Using WordPerfect 5.1, Lotus 1-2-3,
dBASE III PLUS and dBASE IV*

McKeown and Leitch
*Management Information Systems: Managing with
Computers*

McLeod
*Systems Analysis and Design: An Organizational
Approach*

Martin
QBASIC: A Short Course in Structured Programming

Martin, Series Editor
Productivity Software Modules
Disk Operating System (DOS) Windows 3.1
Word Processing with WordPerfect 5.0 and 5.1
Word Processing with WordPerfect for Windows 5.2
Spreadsheets with Lotus 1-2-3
Spreadsheets with Quattro Pro 4.0
Database Management with dBASE III PLUS
Database Management with dBASE IV
Database Management with Paradox 4.0
A Beginner's Guide to BASIC

Martin and Burstein
Computer Systems Fundamentals

Martin and Parker
Mastering Today's Software Series
Texts available in any combination of the following:
Microcomputer Concepts
Extended Microcomputer Concepts
Disk Operating System 5.0
Disk Operating System 6.0
WordPerfect 5.1
WordPerfect for Windows 5.2
WordPerfect 6.0
Lotus 1-2-3 (2.2/2.3)
Lotus 1-2-3 (2.4)
dBASE III PLUS
dBASE IV (1.5/2.0)
Paradox 4.0
BASIC

Mason
Using IBM Microcomputers in Business: Decision Making with Lotus 1-2-3 and dBASE III PLUS (or dBASE IV)

Millspaugh
Business Programming in C for DOS-Bases Systems

O'Brien
The Nature of Computers
The Nature of Computers with Productivity Software Guides

Parker
Computers and Their Applications. Third Edition
Computers and Their Applications with Productivity Software Guide. Third Edition
Productivity Software Guide. Fourth Edition
Understanding Computers and Information Processing: Today and Tomorrow. Fifth Edition
Understanding Computers and Information Processing: Today and Tomorrow with BASIC. Fifth Edition

Robertson and Robertson
Microcomputer Applications and Programming: A Complete Computer Course with DOS, WordPerfect 5.1, Lotus 1-2-3, dBASE III PLUS (or dBASE IV) and BASIC
Using Microcomputer Applications (A Series of Computer Lab Manuals)

Roche
Telecommunications and Business Strategy

Simpson and Tesch
Introductory COBOL: A Transaction-Oriented Approach

Sullivan
The New Computer User

Swafford and Haff
dBASE III PLUS

The HBJ College Outline Series

Kreitzberg
Introduction to BASIC

Kreitzberg
Introduction to Fortran

Pierson
Introduction to Business Information Systems

Veklerov and Pekelny
Computer Language C

Preface

There's an old saying that goes "the more things change, the more they stay the same." That saying could easily be applied to what has happened in the database field in the years since the first edition of this book was published. Although the principles of relational database theory have not changed significantly, microcomputer DBMSs have matured considerably. They continue to move closer in power and functionality to products previously found only on larger computers.

The two premises on which the first edition of this book was based haven't changed. If anything, they are even more true today:

- Many small to medium-sized businesses are implementing their database management systems on microcomputers.
- Nearly all microcomputer database management systems are based on the relational model.

In addition, many of those microcomputer systems are being implemented as multiuser systems using a variety of local area network architectures.

This book is primarily intended to be used in a database management course for computer information systems or business that focuses on a microcomputer or client/server environment. It is a theoretically rigorous textbook that keeps a firm eye on how that theory can be applied in practice. The overriding philosophy behind this book is that theory is important in that it gives us a foundation on which to build real-word database applications. However, without seeing how theory translates into practice, all the theory in the world is relatively useless. Given its emphasis on the practical implications of database theory, this book can also be the basis for a short, intensive database design seminar or can be read independently by an individual who wishes to create an effective database system for his or her business.

The first part of the book (Chapters 1 through 5) focuses on the design of relational databases. It has been written to teach readers the following:

- The difference between file and database management systems (Chapter 1)
- The activities that make up the systems development process (Chapter 2)
- The types of relationships found in a database environment (Chapter 3)
- The use of the entity-relationship model to capture the logical structure of a database environment (Chapter 3)
- The details of the relational data model (Chapter 4)
- Techniques for creating relations that will avoid the most common problems of poor relational design (Chapter 5)

Chapter 2 covers material not found in most introductory database texts—the systems development cycle. Too often we forget that database design is only a part of the entire systems development cycle and that it begins with logical data modeling. Chapter 2 is therefore a review of the systems development cycle that reinforces the idea that even the best database design is of little use if it was created without regard for the needs of the users or was part of an ill-conceived implementation plan. Students should preferably have taken a course in systems analysis before coming to a database course. However, students who have only been exposed to systems analysis and design in a freshman computer literacy course should still find Chapter 2 an adequate review. The chapter ends by showing students the needs assessment phase of a case study that appears throughout the book.

The discussion of normalization in Chapter 5 takes students through third normal form, with a nod toward Boyce-Codd normal form. It begins by exploring the connection between a well-drawn entity-relationship diagram and third normal form as a simple, practical technique for good relational design. It then looks at the theory of normalization to help students understand why ER diagrams produce good designs.

Although higher normal forms are of great theoretical interest, they are difficult for students to understand and are of diminishing practical use as they move beyond 3NF. The book, therefore, emphasizes normalization through third normal form, introduces Boyce-Codd normal form, and only briefly mentions fourth, fifth, and Domain Key normal forms.

The second portion of the book focuses on data manipulation. Chapter 6 introduces relational algebra, the operations that provide the theoretical basis for all relational data manipulation. Students need to understand relational algebra because it has significant implications for database query performance.

In Chapter 7, students are introduced to QBE. Chapters 8 and 9 contain in-depth coverage of interactive SQL. Chapter 10 looks at embedded SQL. Because a majority of microcomputer SQL DBMSs support C as a host language, sample programs use C as a host language. In addition to C, Chapter 10 contains SQL embedded in a DBMS's proprietary programming language, emphasizing the differences in programming between a proprietary programming language and a general-purpose host language.

Chapter 11 covers database integrity. It begins with SQL data integrity features including the latest additions for primary key and referential integrity support. It also includes sample SQL programs for enforcing database integrity in environments where the DBMS does not yet fully support it. This emphasis on database integrity is important because many students don't realize the devastating consequences of the introduction of bad data into a database.

The final portion of the book (Chapters 12 and 13) looks at the issues of multiuser databases and data management. Chapter 12 covers such topics as concurrency control and the emergence of database servers and client/server architecture. Chapter 13 looks at both database security and database administration.

Just as Chapter 2 contains something that traditional DBMSs lack, this book also is missing something found in more traditional database texts—a discussion of file and data structures. This omission was made with great care. What this book is trying to do is teach business computing students to view a database as a logical construct, as a shared pool of data, regardless of the physical implementation. Students don't need to know the details of data structures such as linked lists and B-trees to be able to design and implement effective, useful database systems. In fact, teaching file and data structures may make it more difficult for business students to divorce the physical file layouts from the logical database structure.

Choosing software on which to base examples in a book of this type has become a difficult task. When the first edition of this book appeared, there weren't many full-featured DBMSs available for microcomputers; picking the most widely used and influential products was easy. Today the market is crowded with a number of fine products. This book therefore uses several DBMSs, each of which is well suited for demonstrating a given concept. For example, Chapter 7 (QBE) uses *Paradox for Windows.* Although other DBMSs such as *dBASE IV* and *R:BASE* have QBE interfaces for formulating queries, *Paradox* has the most complete implementation, including the ability to use the QBE interface to modify data. Its implementation is closer to that of *DB2* (IBM's flagship relational DBMS for mainframes) than any other found on a microcomputer. It therefore makes *Paradox* the best choice to demonstrate QBE. By the same token, *Oracle 7*'s SQL implementation provides a model that other DBMSs often strive to emulate. It therefore provides an excellent platform for demonstrating the state-of-the-art in interactive SQL, embedded SQL, and SQL data definition capabilities.

Examples throughout the book are taken from two case studies: the relatively simple Small Bank and the more extensive Federated Taxi Company. Two additional case studies, Margaret Holmes, D.M.D. (Appendix A) and East Coast Aquarium (Appendix B) form the basis for the exercises at the end of the chapters.

Each chapter is followed by Things to Think About and/or Exercises. Things to Think About are discussion questions, most of which have no single correct answer. Their intent is to encourage students to view the concepts about which they have been reading in a number of different contexts. The Exercises are included to give students hands-on practice with the concepts presented in the chapters. They will give students practice in assessing user needs, formulating good relational designs, and creating effective queries. The exercises, however, are not tutorial in nature. They assume that students have access to materials that teach the specifics of using a given DBMS.

Acknowledgments

It takes a lot of people to put this kind of book together. I'd like to thank the folks at Dryden who helped make it possible: Richard Bonacci, Matt Fels, Guy Jacobs, Cheryl Hauser, Linda Miller, and Diane Southworth.

Reviewers are also an important part of creating a text. It is therefore my pleasure to acknowledge this edition's reviewers: William Bullers, University of New Mexico; Kenneth Douglas, Southwest Missouri State University; Joseph Franklin, Asheville-Buncombe Technical Institute; Dave Harris, College of the Redwoods; Robert Landrum, Jones Junior College; Robert E. Norton, San Diego Mesa College; Asghar Sabbaghi, Indiana University at South Bend; Dianne Simmons, University of Arkansas–Little Rock; Eugene Stafford, Iona College; Edward L. Summers, University of Texas; Charles Turner, Georgia Southern University; Karen Watterson, San Diego, California; Michael Wybo, McGill University.

People who reviewed the first edition: William Anderson, Montgomery College; Paul Bartolomeo, Community College of Rhode Island; Harvey Blessing, Essex Community College; William Brandt, Defiance College; John Cary, George Washington University; Christopher Carlson, George Mason University; Carl Evert, Xavier University; John Gallagher, Duke University; Alan Hevner, University of Maryland; Wojtek Kozaczynski, University of Illinois–Chicago; Anthony Mann, Sinclair Community College; Albert Napier, Rice University; Ravi Nath, Memphis State University; Richard Scamell, University of Houston; John Windsor, University of North Texas.

People who participated in the marketing survey: Medhi Beheshtian, Loyola University; Glenn B. Dietrich, University of Texas–San Antonio; Don Drake, Seminole Community College; Gordon Everest, University of Minnesota; Nelson Ford, Auburn University; Ella Gardner, George Mason University; Wojtek Kozaczynski, University of Illinois–Chicago; John McCann, Duke University; Joe McGrath, University of Florida; Cameron Mitchell, University of Houston; David Naumann, University of Minnesota; Robert Peterson, Notre Dame University; Dennis Severence, University of Michigan; Charles Snyder, Auburn University; Richard Spinetto, University of Colorado–Boulder; Bin Yao, University of Maryland.

JLH

Contents

Database Management for Microcomputers

Second Edition

1

Introduction

There is probably no more valuable commodity in the business world than information. Information can help us decide when to introduce a new product line, which marketing strategy to adopt, when to attempt a takeover of another company, or even when it's time to close up and declare bankruptcy. However, merely having timely, accurate information is often not enough. An organization must be able to have access to the right information at the right time. In other words, information must be organized in some way so that retrieval is easy and efficient.

This book will introduce you to the principles of one technique for organizing information using a computer as the primary storage device. The technique is referred to as *database management*, and the place where the data are stored is known as a *database*. (This is an extremely simplistic and incomplete definition, which will be expanded later in this chapter.) You will find a discussion of the concepts behind the design of database systems in Chapters 2–5. Chapters 6–12 look at the practical sides of databases. Chapter 13 deals with managing a database installation.

Database systems have largely replaced older forms of mainframe and minicomputer data management known as *file management systems*. However, file management programs are still widely used on microcomputers. File management and database management are fundamentally different. The nature of this difference is essential to an understanding of database systems and why they are now viewed as the best way to manage corporate information. In addition, many microcomputer users are confused about the difference between file and database management and therefore purchase the wrong software for their needs.

Some Introductory Terminology

To understand the differences between file management systems and database systems, there are a few terms you should understand. These are *file, record,* and *field.* Be aware that these definitions come from the realm of computer science; they may not match what you find in the documentation that accompanies the database software you have purchased.

A *file* is a physical entity generally located on either in main memory, on a disk, or on a tape. It has a name and may contain the contents of a document, the code for a computer program, or data organized in some known structure. The latter are often called *data files.* It is important to realize that the term *file* refers to the physical location of data on a physical storage medium. As you will see later in this chapter, it is possible to impose a logical organization on data that bears little resemblance to its physical layout in a file.

The data stored in data files are organized into *records.* A record represents data about a single person, object, or activity. (These are the *entities* about which we are storing data; you will learn a great deal more about entities in Chapter 3.) While it may take more than one record to contain all the data pertaining to any given entity, a single record rarely contains data about more than one entity.

Records can also be viewed as a group of *fields* that describe a single entity. A field is one data item.

To bring these terms into focus, let's look at a simple example—a mailing list. We want to store the name, street address, city, state, and zip code for a group of people. The name, street address, city, state, and zip code are fields, since each represents one piece of data about the entity (a person) described in the mailing list. If we group together the fields for any given individual, we have assembled a record, a complete set of data for that person. The data file that contains the entire mailing list consists of many identical records, each of which describes a different person.

Physical files, made up of records with identical structure, form the basis of traditional file management systems on mainframes and minicomputers and those used on microcomputers today.

File Management Systems

A business that uses file management to process its data maintains one or more files for each data processing application. There will be a separate set of *application programs* associated with each file or group of files. (Application programs are programs that do useful business work.) The programs might print paychecks for an insurance company, record that a video tape has been rented at the local video outlet, print overdue notices for the library, or record an order for ski boots for a mail-order sports company.

As an example of a file processing system, consider Small Bank. This imaginary bank with three branches provides five major services to its customers: interest-paying checking (NOW accounts), passbook savings, certificates of deposit, loans for cars and homes, and safe-deposit boxes. The bank's data processing department therefore maintains five major sets of files and associated programs (see Figure 1.1). These files are stored on a minicomputer housed at Central branch; each branch has terminals that access that minicomputer. At Central branch, the terminals are connected directly to a front-end communications processor. The Eastside and Westlake branches use leased telephone lines to connect to the minicomputer. The system configuration can be found in Figure 1.2.

Table 1.1 shows the data contained in each file and the programs that have been written to maintain it. There are several features of file processing systems that are apparent from this table. Most important, there is a great deal of *redundant data* (the same data about the same entity is stored more than once within the system; multiple copies exist of the same data)—a customer's name, address, phone number, and social security number are repeated for each account of each type that he or she may have. In Table 1.1, the redundant data are highlighted.

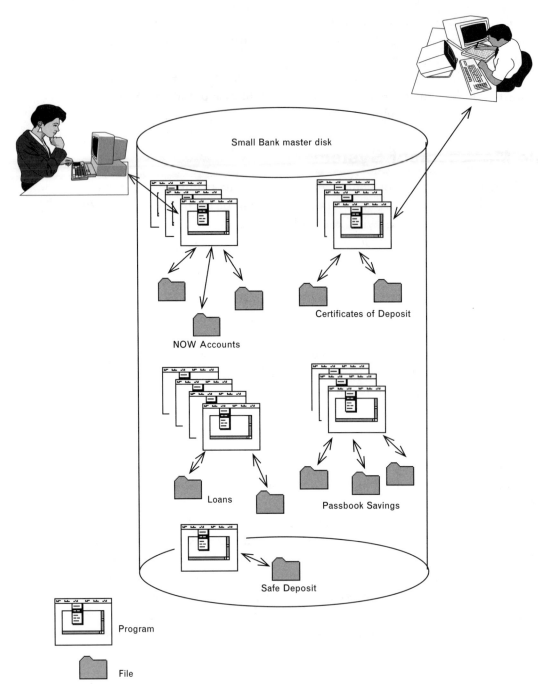

Figure 1.1   Small Bank's file processing system

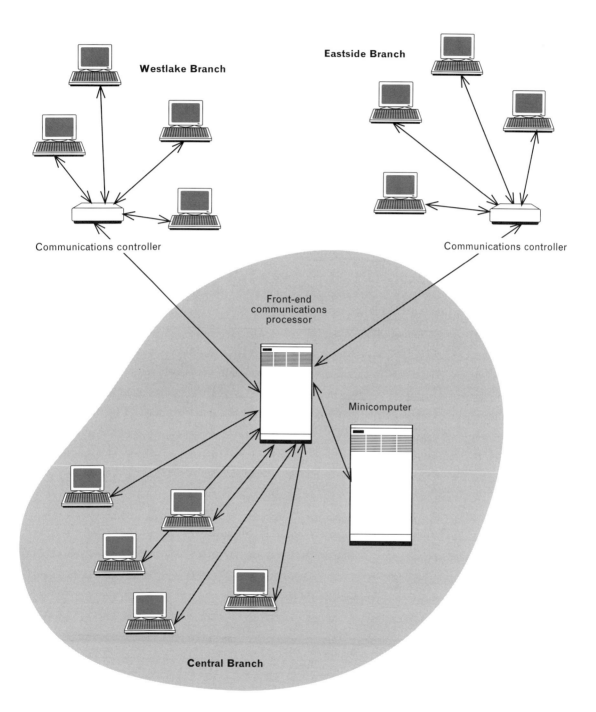

Westlake Branch

Eastside Branch

Communications controller

Communications controller

Front-end
communications
processor

Minicomputer

Central Branch

Figure 1.2 Configuration of the Small Bank computer system

Table 1.1

Data Files, Data, and Application Programs for a Bank Using a File Management System

File	Data	Application Programs
NOW accounts	Customer name Customer address Customer phone number Customer social security number Account number Checks cashed Deposits made Interest earned Service charges Current balance	Credit/debit posting Monthly statement Maintenance (add new accounts, change addresses, etc.)
Passbook savings	Customer name Customer address Customer phone number Customer social security number Account number Withdrawals made Deposits made Interest earned Current balance	Credit/debit posting Interest posting Quarterly statements Maintenance
Certificates of deposit	Customer name Customer address Customer phone number Customer social security number Account number Current balance Date of maturity	Interest posting Quarterly statements Notification of maturity Maintenance
Loans	Customer name Customer address Customer phone number Customer social security number Account number Current balance Payment amount Date payment due Date of last payment	Credit posting Identification of late payments Year-end interest summary Maintenance
Safe deposit boxes	Customer name Customer address Customer phone number Customer social security number Account number Box number Box fee Renewal date	Notice to renew Maintenance

Also notice that each type of account has its own maintenance program to take care of changes in those customer description fields. In fact, because the file that supports each type of account is physically separate from all of the others, there is nothing to ensure that the formats of the customer description fields are the same throughout the system.

Each application program is intimately tied to the file on which it operates. Access to data in that file is based on the program's knowledge of how the data are physically stored (for example, the order, type, and length of each field within its record). Any change in the physical structure of that file will therefore necessitate a change in the application programs that support it.

File management systems generally arise with little overall planning. For Small Bank, it was a seemingly simple matter to accommodate NOW accounts when they became legal by merely creating a new file and the necessary application programs. Certificates of deposit were added into the system in the same manner only a few years earlier. File management systems, especially those that have been in place for a long time, tend to store their files on tape. Using tape is cheaper than using disk, but it has one major restriction in terms of access. Files stored on tape must be processed sequentially, starting at the first record and moving to the second, third, fourth, and so on until the end of the file is reached. There is no way to randomly jump to a specific record without passing over those in front of it. It is therefore more economical to assemble a group of changes or retrieval requests for the file, sort them in the same order as the file, and process them all at once; many modifications and retrievals can then be made with one pass through the file. This particular kind of processing, where activities that affect the file are grouped together, is known as *batch processing*.

Batch processing is generally very fast, especially when there are a large number of changes to be made in the file. Large investment brokers, for example, store data about their clients' stock portfolios on tape. Every morning, before the stock market opens, they update the entire tape to reflect changes based on the previous day's market closing prices. Since every single record on the tape must be updated, batch processing is very efficient. However, a customer wishing to know the current value of his or her portfolio may have to wait until the next business day, until after another batch run has been made, to get that information.

On the surface, a file management system appears simple, logical, and clean. It does, however, present a number of serious problems for the business that uses one and the customers of that business.

Problems with File Management Systems

Consider Jon Dough, the average Small Bank customer. He has a NOW account, a passbook savings account, and a safe deposit box, all at Small Bank. He receives a monthly statement for his NOW account, a quarterly statement for his passbook savings account, and a notice once every two years when the time comes to renew his safe deposit box rental. Small Bank has served Mr. Dough for six years without an error, but now Mr. Dough has moved across town.

Mr. Dough calls the bank to give them his change of address. That one phone call precipitates three computer system actions: Mr. Dough's new address becomes a part of the batch runs that do maintenance on (1) the NOW accounts file; (2) the passbook savings accounts file; and (3) the safe deposit box file. Since Mr. Dough's address is stored in three places, it must be changed in three places. The redundant data does consume disk storage space that could be reclaimed if the data were only stored once and shared by the entire system. However, the inefficient use of disk space is generally not the most serious consequence of redundant data.

Assume that the telephone operator who takes Mr. Dough's message writes it on a slip of paper and gives it to an account clerk. The clerk makes the changes to the NOW account and passbook savings account files. However, the clock strikes noon and the clerk takes off for lunch, leaving the slip of paper lying on the desk. While the clerk is out, several people brush by the desk, producing a gust of wind that swirls the slip of paper off the desk surface and into the wastebasket next to it. The clerk has a busy lunch hour and by the time she returns, she has forgotten all about what she was doing before she left. The result is that Mr. Dough's data is correct in two places; the third—the safe deposit box—has incorrect data (the old address).

As far as Mr. Dough is concerned, all is well with his bank accounts. He receives his NOW account and passbook savings account statements regularly at his new home. Eighteen months after his move, however, Mr. Dough suddenly remembers his safe deposit box—he should have received a renewal notice three months ago. Unfortunately, Mr. Dough's renewal notice went to his old address. Since more than a year had elapsed since his move, the forwarding address he left with the post office had expired and the notice was returned to the bank. When he calls the bank to find out what happened, he learns that the contents of his safe deposit box have been turned over to the state.

File management systems, as Jon Dough found out the hard way, have major problems with data integrity. In the narrowest sense of the term, a system that has *data integrity* can verify that all copies of redundant data items are identical (the problem Jon Dough is facing might be referred to as data distintegrity). Since redundant data in file management systems are stored in physically separate locations, it is exceptionally difficult to ascertain that the contents of those data items are consistent (in other words, the same) throughout all the files in the system.

Data integrity, however, has implications for more than redundantly stored data. Assume for the moment that Small Bank decides to keep a customer master file, one that simply contains a listing of all customers who have any accounts with the bank. There is one record in the file for each customer. If Small Bank's file processing system is to have data integrity, then no person can be entered in any of the account files unless he or she is also entered in the customer master file. In this case, the data integrity is logical, not physical. The customer master file will be of little use if Small Bank can't ensure that every customer in the account files appears in the customer master file.

Verifying this kind of logical data integrity is very difficult in a file processing environment. If verification is to occur, each of Small Bank's account file maintenance programs must at least:

1. Search the customer master file to determine if the customer is already in the file.
2. If the customer has no record in the file (in other words, this is the customer's first account with Small Bank), add the customer to the customer master file.
3. Add the customer to the account file.

File processing systems cannot store data integrity rules. Since data are in separate physical files, there is no way to capture information about relationships between the files or the data in them. If data interity is to be maintained within a file processing system, it must be enforced from within application programs, a procedure that is chancy at best. Even if Small Bank's maintenance programs do verify that a customer appears in the customer master file before adding a new record to an account file, there is nothing to prevent any other application program from modifying the account files in some way that violates the rule that no customer can have an account without first having an entry in the customer master file.

Jon Dough is understandably angry with Small Bank, but he overcomes his anger long enough to apply for a car loan (the interest rate is a half point below the prime rate). To process the loan application, the loan officer needs a history of all of Mr. Dough's accounts with the bank. She therefore asks the data processing department to prepare a single report that summarizes Mr. Dough's data. The data processing manager tells her that it will take at least two days to generate her report. Someone will have to manually search each file in the system; there is no way to know exactly which files contain data pertaining to Mr. Dough.

Small Bank's file management system, like other file management systems, has difficulty processing one-of-a-kind requests. A one-of-a-kind request, sometimes also called an *ad hoc query*, is a requirement for information that arises at the spur of the moment, cannot be predicted, and in all likelihood will never be repeated. Satisfying one-of-a-kind requests is especially complicated when the data are stored in more than one file, since there is generally no easy to way to determine which files contains relevant data; each file must be searched. It is also expensive in terms of programmer resources, especially when files are stored in such a way that a special program must be written to do the data retrieval.

While Jon Dough is wrestling with his problems with Small Bank, the manager is replaced. The new manager sees what appears to be an easy way to save a significant amount of money on postage by switching from five- to nine-digit zip codes. He instructs the data processing department to replace all five-digit zip codes with the appropriate longer code. He's taken a couple of computer courses at night recently and believes that the conversion should be a simple process.

Reality, however, has nothing to do with the new manager's expectations. In the first place, the length and type of the zip code fields are not the same throughout the system; some zip codes are stored as characters, others as numbers. This problem is referred to as a lack of *data consistency*. It means that data that represent the same thing (for example, a zip code) are not stored in the same way throughout the file processing system. Generally this arises because the files were not developed with any consistent, overall plan; each file was created as needed, in complete isolation from other files. As a result, making the same change across all files in the system is very difficult. In our example, changing the size of the zip code field will require:

1. Determining exactly how and where the zip code is stored in each file;
2. Determining what changes must be made to each file to allow the extra space for the expanded zip codes;
3. Writing one or more programs that will make the changes in a manner appropriate to each individual file.

Actually changing the files is only one small part of the problem. Because the application programs are so closely tied to the physical layout of the records in the files, any change in those files will require changes in the application programs that process them. This situation is called a lack of *logical-physical data independence.*

If a system has logical-physical data independence, then it is possible to change the physical structure of the files without changing any application programs that use the data in those files. However, the application programs that use data stored in a file management system must locate the data by their physical position within a file; there is no intermediary program that can translate a more general request (for example, "record number 605" or "Jon Dough's record") into a location within a file. The bank manager's idea to cut costs by using the longer zip codes may well end up costing more in programmer salaries to implement than the savings it would generate.

Small Bank may discover that changing to longer zip codes is only the tip of the iceberg when it comes to problems with the lack of logical-physical data independence. Eventually, Small Bank's files will absorb all the space allocated to them. The data processing department will have to undertake a major reorganization of the entire physical storage system. In most cases this will also require modifications to all application programs.

Database Systems

Database systems arose out of the many difficulties engendered by file management systems. A *database system* logically places all its data in a single, communal pool along with definitions of the relationships that exist between those data. Physically, the data are stored on a disk in one or more files, but the user can think of that data as if they were all in a single location.

The most important implication of this is that data can be shared. For example, Small Bank need only store a customer's name, address, phone number, and social security number once; any application that needs the information can retrieve it from the common data pool (see Figure 1.3). Each

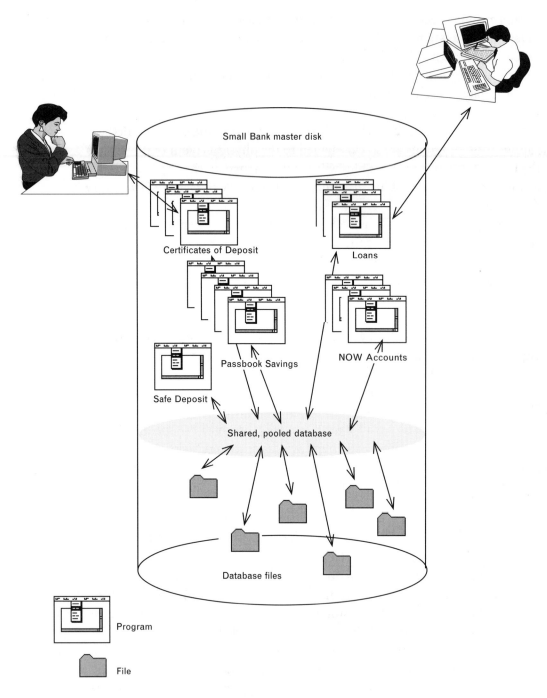

Figure 1.3   A database system for Small Bank

customer's account data can then be related in some way to the customer's name. The nature and structure of data relationships is basic to the design of database systems and forms the topic of Chapter 3.

Access to the data is through a program called a *database management system* or *DBMS*. A DBMS sits between the user and the files where data are physically stored. The user issues requests to the DBMS, which in turn takes care of storing and retrieving the data. DBMSs designed for serious business use support application programs. These programs contain commands to the DBMS embedded within a high-level host language. The host language may be a general programming language like COBOL, C, or BASIC or it may be a language specific to the DBMS, such as the languages that are available with microcomputer DBMSs like *dBASE IV, FoxPro, Paradox, R:BASE,* or *4th Dimension.*

A DBMS user can also search the data directly using an on-line *query language.* An on-line query language is a special set of commands that a DBMS understands. A user enters the commands one at a time from the keyboard; the DBMS executes each command immediately. A full-featured query language allows a user to define database structure, to enter, edit and delete data, to retrieve data, and to format and print reports. While query languages are usually easier to learn than high-level programming languages, their use nonetheless requires specialized user training. Early in 1986, SQL (pronounced "sequel" or "S-Q-L") was accepted by the American National Standards Institute (ANSI) as the national standard query language for relational databases. SQL, which is discussed in Chapters 8–10, has been implemented in many DBMSs. Some DBMSs, however, have their own, proprietary query languages.

> **By the way:** The popularity of graphic user interfaces has given rise to DBMSs that have no command line at which a user types commands. Instead, DBMSs such as *Helix Express* and *4th Dimension* let users perform data manipulation by working with icons, forms, and dialog boxes. The functionality of such products, however, is similar to that provided by traditional query languages.

Unlike file management systems, a well designed database system cannot be developed in bits and pieces; it requires planning. The overall logical organization of a database, as it appears to those who develop and administer the database, is known as a *schema.* A database schema contains definitions of all the data items that the database will contain as well as the relationships between those data. Though database schemas can change, an initial schema must be completely designed before the database system is implemented on a computer. Creating database schemas is discussed in Chapters 4 and 5.

The schema is described in what is known as a *data dictionary*, or *catalog*. In its most primitive form, a data dictionary may be nothing more than a notebook that records information about the schema. More sophisticated systems have on-line data dictionaries. Some are simply text files that record the same information that is kept on paper in a three-ring binder, but others are integrated with the database system itself. In a system with an integrated data dictionary, any change made to the definition of a data item in the data dictionary will cause a corresponding change in the database.

Responsibility for administering and maintaining database schemas falls to a *database administrator* (DBA). The extent of the DBA function within any given organization chiefly depends on the size and complexity of the organization's database system. At the very least, the DBA controls any changes that are to be made to the database schema. In large organizations, the DBA function may be handled by a group of people, working not only to ensure the integrity of the schema, but to manage activities such as application program development and system backup as well. More details about database administration can be found in Chapter 13.

Most applications that use any given database will not need to use every data item in the database. Therefore, many DBMSs allow the user to define a *subschema*, or *view*. A subschema or view is a subset of the schema including only as much of the schema as is needed by a particular application. A subschema or view may also include data elements that aren't actually part of the schema. In particular, these may be summary data, such as the total or average of values stored in the database. The subschema is generally a user or application program's logical view of the database. Theoretically, there is no limit to the number of subschemas that can be defined from any schema.

A database system therefore supports three ways of looking at the data:

1. The schema (the global logical view of the entire system used primarily by system designers and database administrators).
2. The subschema (a logical view of the data related to one particular application used by application programmers and end-users).

3. The physical (the actual way in which data are physically stored in files on a disk—of interest generally to systems programmers and those who write DBMSs).

An easy way to think of this separation can be seen in Figure 1.4. At the "lowest" level are the physical files. In environments where the DBMS is running on a mainframe or minicomputer, only the systems programmers have access to this level; when the DBMS is running on a microcomputer, application programmers may also have access to the physical files. The DBMS acts as an interface between this physical storage and the schema.

The schema, which contains the overall logical view of the database, is used primarily by application programmers who write programs for users and by the database administrator, who is in charge of maintaining the logical relationships in the database. The DBMS also acts as an interface between the schema and any user views (subschemas) that have been defined. This "highest" level is therefore intended for use by the end user.

The diagram in Figure 1.4 represents what is also known as a database system's *three-schema architecture*. User views are called the as *logical schema*, the schema the *conceptual schema*, and physical storage the *physical schema*.

A word of caution is in order about microcomputer database management systems—a great many software packages on the market are advertised as database management systems but are in reality, file management systems. Any piece of software that cannot in some way define a schema based on logical relationships between entities is a file manager, not a database manager. It is important to remember that no matter what the software vendors state in their documentation, *a file is not a database*—a file is a physical entity whereas a database is a collection of files that contain data and definitions of the relationships between the data in those files.

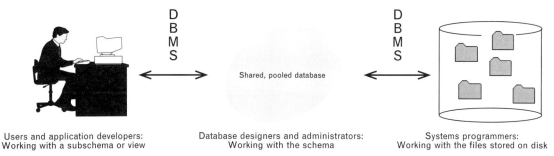

Figure 1.4   The three levels of a database system

Microsoft File, pfs:File, FileMaker Pro, and *PC-File,* for example, are file management programs. While they provide advanced on-line query features, sorting, report generation, and in some cases the ability to look up data stored in more than one file, they cannot represent data relationships. Such software is most useful for stand-alone applications, such as maintaining a mailing list or an inventory list. It cannot, however, efficiently support more complex data processing without encountering one or more of the problems discussed above that are endemic to file management systems.

> **By the way:** The data maintained by a file manager are often called a "flat-file database" in the popular press. However, the term is an oxymoron. If a piece of software handles one flat file at a time, that file simply isn't a data-base.

A spreadsheet package, such as *Lotus 1-2-3,* is also not a database management system. Spreadsheets do allow users to manipulate a block of data and provide some file management capabilities including the ability to sort data on one or more fields. However, like file management software, no spreadsheet has the ability to logically pool data and store information about data relationships.

The Database Advantage

Database systems provide solutions to many of the problems generated by file management systems primarily because of the sharing of data and the common interface provided by the DBMS.

Because data can be shared, database management systems require less redundant data than file processing systems. Database systems do not necessarily eliminate all data redundancy; in some cases, as you will see throughout the first portion of this book, some data redundancy is essential to representing data relationships. In addition, you may decide to retain some duplicated data for performance purposes. On the whole, however, database systems do decrease the amount of duplicated data. While this certainly decreases the amount of disk space that is required, it has far more important consequences.

When data are stored only once, rather than in many different places, the problem of data integrity can be somewhat reduced. For example, if Small Bank had been using a database system when Jon Dough phoned in his address change, Mr. Dough's address would be maintained in only one location (the common data pool used by the entire database system) and therefore changed only once; since each of Mr. Dough's accounts uses the single copy of Mr. Dough's address, there is no chance that any two accounts could have a different address.

Pooling the data to eliminate some redundancy does not, however, solve problems of logical data integrity (think back to the problem caused by the introduction of a customer master file into Small Bank's file processing system). Ideally, a database management system should permit data integrity rules to be stored within its data dictionary. Then, whenever data are modified, the DBMS should automatically consult those rules and take action to ensure that they are enforced. As you will see in Chapter 11, DBMSs vary widely in how well they handle logical data integrity.

Problems with data consistency can also be avoided by reducing data redundancy. Data inconsistency arises when redundantly stored data have incompatible data formats. Therefore, storing a given piece of data only once ensures that there is no possibility of an alternative data format appearing within the database system. When data redundancy is either unavoidable or desirable, data consistency can be maintained by building it into the schema. In other words, since the entire schema is defined before the database is implemented, instances of redundant data items can be identified while the database is still in the planning stages. The designers can then ensure that duplicated data items have identical data formats.

The existence of the DBMS provides solutions to other file management problems. Since the DBMS provides a common access route to data which appears to the user as if the data were in a single pool, one-of-a-kind requests are easy to accommodate. Using the DBMS's query language, a user can formulate a request for data retrieval without having to write an application program. The DBMS will take care of locating the requested data, regardless of where or how it is physically stored.

For example, assume that you have a database that stores the names of all the magazines to which you subscribe (TITLE), the address to which renewals should be mailed, the yearly cost, and the expiration date (EXPIRES). Every so often, you want to see a list of all the magazines that are due to expire shortly. You could certainly write an application program to do the retrieval, but it is simpler to issue a command in whatever query language is being used by your database management system.

For example, if you are using *dBASE IV*'s proprietary query language, the command

LIST TITLE FOR EXPIRES <= 12/31/93

displays the titles of all magazines that have expiration dates before January 1, 1994.

The SQL query might be written as:

SELECT TITLE
FROM   MAGS
WHERE EXPIRES <= '31-DEC-93';

The DBMS also provides logical-physical data independence. Since the DBMS performs the actual storage and retrieval of data, the user of a database management system does not need to be concerned with how the data are stored on disk. A variety of subschemas, for example, can be created off a single database without ever modifying the files that underlie the database system. In other words, the same files can support many different logical views of the data. Conversely, it is possible to modify and even change the physical layout of data files without affecting the schema, subschemas, or application programs. The degree of logical-physical data independence does, however, vary among DBMS packages.

Another advantage of a database system is that it provides many different ways to access data. Application programs are convenient for regular, pre-planned data manipulation. The application developer can often select the programming language that is best suited to a given task. For example, many programmers prefer COBOL for repetitive, day-to-day operations such as entering orders or recording payments. If an application requires extensive arithmetic operations, then an application programmer might choose C or FORTRAN.

Query language, such as SQL and QBE (Query By Example), are better suited for ad hoc queries. In addition, database systems often provide more than one type of user interface for ad hoc queries. For example, SQL is a command-oriented language with which users type data manipulation requests. On the other hand, QBE is a graphic language with which users place data values in the outline of a table. (QBE is discussed in depth in Chapter 7.)

Drawbacks to Database Systems

It would be misleading to think that a database system is the cure for all ills. Database systems bring with them a few problems of their own.

Database systems are more costly in terms of hardware and software than file management systems. Though software prices have dropped dramatically, a DBMS is still the most expensive type of software you can buy for a micro-computer (in other words, a DBMS costs relatively more than a file management program, a word processor or a spreadsheet).

Database systems generally require more hardware than file management systems. While file management systems can operate off floppy disks, perhaps keeping each file on a separate disk, meaningful database applications require both the added storage space and increased speed of a hard disk. DBMS pro-grams tend to be rather large and often require more main memory than file management systems. As hardware prices drop, however, this becomes less and less of a drawback.

Database systems are also more difficult and more costly to develop than file management systems. Because a database system needs a great deal of plan-ning before you ever get to the computer, it absorbs a significant amount of human time, the most expensive part of the typical computer system. The design of database systems requires people with special knowledge and may mean that an organization must hire an outside consultant.

Once they are operational, database systems are more vulnerable to fail-ure than file management systems. If something happens to one file in a file management system, the rest of the system can continue to function. However, if a central database goes down, all data processing within the organization grinds to a halt.

This vulnerability to failure means that database systems must be very careful to keep adequate backup materials and to establish workable recovery procedures. Database backup and recovery does, however, tend to be more complicated than similar procedures in file management systems.

Summary

Database management systems are an alternative to file management systems for the organization, storage, and retrieval of corporate data resources.

File management systems store data for each application within an organization in a separate, physical file. Each file supports its own set of application programs. Because file management systems duplicate and separate data, they are prone to a number of major problems:

1. Lack of data integrity. (Multiple copies of a single data value are not identical and logical cross-references between files are not maintained.)
2. Difficulty handling one-of-a-kind requests. (There is no easy or quick way to answer requests for information that arise on the spur of the moment, that cannot be predicted, and that are not likely to be repeated.)
3. Lack of data consistency. (The same data items in different files are stored with different data formats.)
4. Lack of logical-physical data independence. (Changes to the physical storage of data requires changes in all application programs using those files.)

Database systems provide solutions to these problems by logically viewing the data as if they were stored in a single, unified pool. Database systems therefore provide increased:

1. Data integrity. (When only one copy of a data value is stored, multiple copies that do not agree cannot exist. Since data are logically pooled, integrity rules can be stored in the data dictionary and enforced by the DBMS when data modifications are made.)
2. Ease in handling one-of-a-kind requests. (Since the data are pooled, all data are available to answer unpredictable, spur-of-the-moment requests for information.)
3. Data consistency. (Since a global plan for the database is produced before it is implemented, redundant data items can be identified and the consistency of their formats ensured.)
4. Logical-physical data independence. (DBMS software provides an interface between the user and the physical storage media; it is therefore possible to change the physical storage structures without altering application programs or they way in which on-line queries are formulated.)

Database systems do have a few drawbacks:

1. They require more hardware than file management systems.
2. DBMS software is relatively costly.
3. They are more difficult to develop and cost more to develop than file management systems because they must be thoroughly planned before they are implemented.
4. They are more vulnerable to failure than file management systems; if the database goes down, all processing must stop.

References

Fry, James P. and Sibley, Edgar H. 1976. "Evolution of Database Management Systems." *ACM Computing Surveys.* 8(1).

Holland, R. H. 1980. "Data Base Planning Entails Return to Basics." *Computerworld.* October 27.

Smith, Peter D. and G. Michael Barnes. 1987. *Files and Databases: An Introduction.* Reading, Mass.: Addison-Wesley.

Voell, R. F. 1980. "Data Base Planning." In T. A. Rullo, ed. *Advances in Data Base Management,* Vol 1. Heyden.

Things to Think About

1. Consider your bank. Do you get a single statement for your checking account and another for your savings account? Or do you get one integrated statement for all of your accounts at the bank? What clues do these different kinds of statements give you about the type of system the bank might be using (i.e., file management versus database management)?
2. Of all the problems associated with file management systems, which do you consider to be the most devastating for an organization? Why? When formulating your answer, consider the impact of the problems in terms of tangibles such as hardware costs, software costs, and programmer salaries. Then look at their implications for intangibles such as customer satisfaction.

3. A large insurance company is considering exchanging its current file processing system for a database system. The managers' major concern in making the change is the volume of data that must be processed every day (thousands of separate activities). They are worried that a database system will be too slow. What arguments might you make to the managers to convince them that they will gain more by living with the decrease in speed than by staying with their file processing system?

4. A lumber mill has hired you to evaluate its information system. You discover that a file management system is used to keep track of inventory. The inventory is updated once a week. The manager says that this works just fine, since even though the mill produces cut lumber throughout the work week, all orders are shipped on Mondays. What advantages does the file management system afford the lumber mill? What might they it by switching to a database system?

5. File management software can be a useful business tool for managing stand-alone applications like a mailing list. What other application areas can you think of that might be adequately handled by a file manager rather than a DBMS?

6. Some file management software packages support an on-line query language. Can an on-line query language be used if files are stored on tape? Why or why not? By the same token, is it possible to use a DBMS without disk storage? Why or why not?

7. The introduction of a database system into a large organization has often frightened the application programmers in the organization's data processing department. They fear that the DBMS's on-line query language will mean that there will no longer be a need for as much application programming and they will either lose their jobs or be downgraded. What arguments might you make to calm their fears?

2

The Design Process

There are really two ways to view the problem of designing a database system. In its narrowest sense, database design is concerned with creating the "best" logical structure for a given set of data items. In fact, Chapters 3 and 4 of this book deal with just exactly that. However, to assume that database design means merely putting data items together in some optimal way is somewhat shortsighted.

To take a broader, more complete view of database design, the designer must investigate the environment which the database system will serve. In other words, it is difficult to create a useful, efficient logical design for data storage and retrieval without knowing the requirements of the people who will be using the database. By the same token, someone must select and purchase hardware and software for the system. Someone must implement the database and train the users. Together, these activities are part of what is known as the *systems development cycle*.

When a database system is the intended product of a systems development project, the entire project is often referred to as a database design project. Therefore, to avoid confusion between the logical design of a database schema and the overall development of an information system, we will refer to the former as *database design*, and the latter as *systems development*. The purpose of this chapter is to review the systems development cycle and to show you where database design fits within it.

The Systems Development Cycle

The systems development cycle (Figure 2.1) is a set of procedures used by organizations to develop computer information systems. While there are many schemes for describing the steps in the cycle, they usually include the following:

1. Performing a needs assessment.(The purpose of the needs assessment is to identify the strong and weak points of the current system and to define what improvements should be made, either by designing a completely new system or by modifying the old, to create a system that meets the current needs of the organization. The result of this phase is a document that details the requirements of the new or improved system.)
2. Generating alternative proposals for the new or improved system (These are not specific design proposals, but general strategies for meeting the requirements of the organization as identified during the needs assessment.); evaluating and selecting the most cost effective strategy.
3. Creating the detailed system design.
4. Implementing the system. (This includes acquiring and testing the necessary hardware and software as well as actually putting the system to work within the organization.)

Figure 2.1 is drawn as a circle for a very important reason. The four steps above are part of a continuous process that, once begun, should be continued indefinitely by an organization. Good systems designs contain provisions for re-doing the needs assessment at regular intervals. If the system is satisfactory, then no further action is required until the next scheduled needs assessment. However, if the needs assessment indicates that the system should be modified, the organization follows the remaining steps in the cycle. The database design itself fits within step 3 of the systems development cycle.

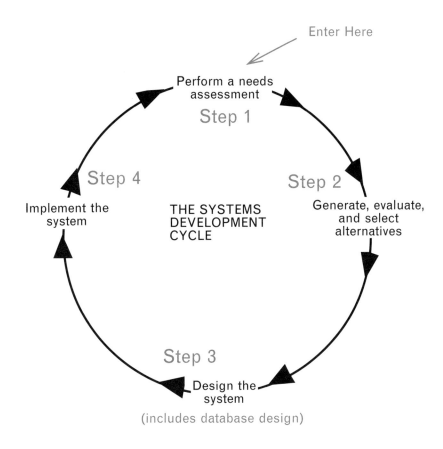

Figure 2.1   The systems development cycle

Working from the document prepared at the end of step 1 and with details of the implementation alternative selected at the end of step 2, designers create the database schema, create user views, and design application programs to manipulate the data. Though it is not necessarily part of the database design process, step 3 may also include the design of the physical storage mechanisms needed to support the database system. The development of a computer-based information system can be a complex task. If you wish to explore the process in greater depth, see the sources in the reference list at the end of this chapter.

The Needs Assessment

Another term for the needs assessment phase of the systems development process is *systems analysis.* The person who coordinates and/or performs the analysis is a *systems analyst.* Systems analysts are trained in interviewing and other data gathering techniques, which they use to form a picture of an organization's current information system and to identify how well that system is meeting the organization's information needs. In particular, a systems analyst will attempt to create a picture of how information moves through an organization. A data flow diagram (discussed later in this chapter) is often used as a summary tool.

When approaching a systems development project, it is essential to realize that developing an information system is really solving a business problem. It is therefore possible to use a general problem-solving model as a framework for conducting the needs assessment. A model commonly used by systems analysts and computer programmers alike is the *input-process-output* model (IPO).

IPO assumes that most information processing activities involve taking some input, processing it in some way, and producing some desired output. An analyst working with this model first identifies the output of an information system. During the needs assessment phase, the analyst will identify both current outputs and outputs that the organization currently doesn't have but would like to have. Once he or she knows what the outputs are or should be, the analyst can identify the input needed to produce those outputs. The final step is to describe the process that transforms the input into output.

Identifying output before specifying input and how that input should be processed may seem a bit backwards. Consider, however, this simple analogy: You want to make some dessert to serve after dinner. The problem you are solving is "making dessert." Since you have few groceries in the house, you will have to go to the market regardless of what dessert you choose to make. Before you can go to the market, you must decide what dessert you will make; otherwise, how can you know what items to purchase? The part of the recipe that governs the transformation of raw ingredients (even if it means merely opening a box and mixing) is the last detail with which you will be concerned. In other words, if you don't know what you want out of a project, how can you possibly know what should go in?

The first step in a systems analysis using the IPO model is therefore to specify the output that the current system produces. Usually, this involves spending time with the people who are using the system. The systems analyst asks those individuals to identify the results of information handling procedures currently in place. Often, this means looking at forms, reports, and files. Then the analyst gathers data on what input is used to produce the output. He or she attempts to identify which input documents, along with other sources of input (for example, data files kept on disk), contribute to the production of each individual output. Finally, the analyst asks current system users to demonstrate and/or describe the procedures they follow to transform input into output.

The movement of data from input, through processing, to output is often summarized in a data flow diagram. While there is more than one way to draw a data flow diagram, commonly they have three symbols: squares for sources of input (people or departments, not the input itself), round-cornered rectangles for processes, and open-ended rectangles for places where data are stored. Arrows connect the symbols to show the way in which data move from one to the other. Labels are added to the diagram to identify symbols. Specific inputs and outputs are identified by labeling the data flow arrows, showing exactly what is traveling along a given path.

Figure 2.2 contains a data flow diagram that shows Small Bank's procedure for establishing a new NOW account using its file processing system. At the top of the diagram, the New Accounts Clerk is the source of input that initiates the entire process. The New Accounts Clerk transmits new account forms, which are then used in a data entry process that builds a transaction file. The transaction file is a place for data storage (it appears in a rectangle). The transaction file and the existing NOW accounts file are both used to create an updated NOW accounts file. The process also produces another output—the New Accounts Summary Report—which is transmitted back to the New Accounts Clerk.

The data flow diagram shown in Figure 2.2 is a picture of Small Bank's current system. Once it has been completed, the analyst must identify where this system works well and where it doesn't. He or she asks those who are using the system to specifically evaluate their current system. What does it do right? What output would they like to retain in the new system? Where does the current system fall down? What output would they like to see added to the new system? In situations where new outputs are requested, the analyst must also identify the input needed to produce those outputs and at least get a general overview of the processes needed to create them. The analyst can then modify, or perhaps completely redraw, the data flow diagram to show new patterns of information flow.

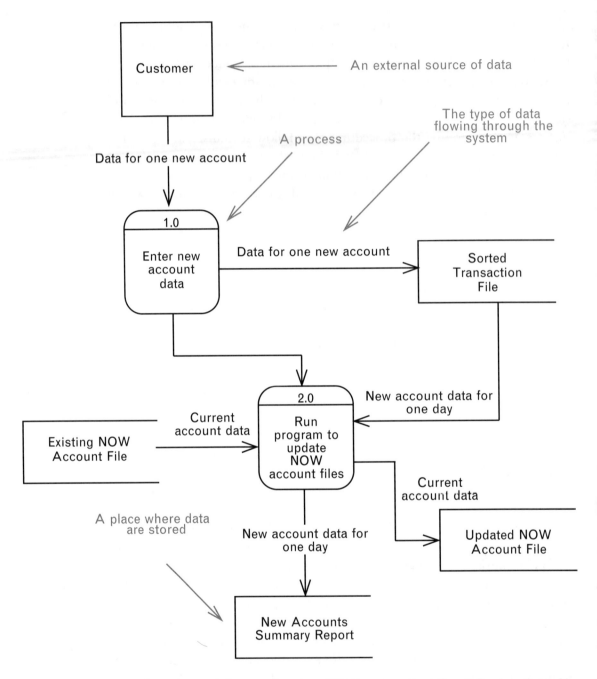

Figure 2.2   A data flow diagram for creating new NOW accounts at Small Bank using a file processing system

Figure 2.3 presents a data flow diagram that might be created to show how accounts could be created if Small Bank were to upgrade to a database system. The New Accounts clerk still completes a new account form. However, the update requests are no longer batched. In fact, they are sent directly to an update program that operates on the existing database to produce an updated database. The system continues to produce a paper summary of new accounts which is returned to the New Accounts clerk.

After completing a data flow diagram of a new or improved system, the analyst reports to corporate management. Together, they rank the outputs that the system might provide in order of importance (this is often referred to as "prioritizing"). Generally, the database designer proposes a set of priorities which are then taken to management for approval. The database designer must

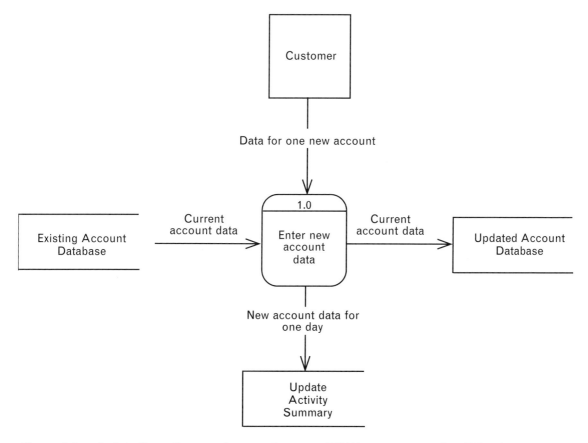

Figure 2.3   A data flow diagram for creating new **NOW** accounts at Small Bank using a database system

be familiar enough with databases in general, with the limitations placed on data retrieval by existing software, and with the environment in which the database will operate to justify his or her recommendations.

The issue of communication between the person doing the systems development and management cannot be overemphasized. There are many horror stories in the business world about system development projects that have gone awry and cost organizations hundreds of thousands of dollars. The common denominator in most of these tales is a lack of communication between those developing the system and the people who will benefit from the information the system is expected to provide. At the very least, a systems developer should present his or her proposals for system output for management approval before proceeding any further with system development.

Finally, using all the data he or she has gathered, the analyst prepares a *requirements document* that will be transmitted to management for approval. This extensive report includes details of all outputs that the new or improved system must provide. It may also specify the inputs associated with each output, the processes for transforming input to output, and the resources (people, time, and money) needed to implement various outputs. The requirements document may include paper samples of all reports (information-bearing documents) the system should produce to formalize the hard copy output which the new system will provide. It may also contain paper samples of CRT screen formats for data display to define the on-line output that the new system will provide.

It is important to realize that a database system will not be able to provide every output that every user desires; some types of output may simply not be feasible. Infeasible types of output generally include those things that consume amounts of resources disproportionate to their value. In other words, they may require excessive development time in terms of the current goals set for database implementation or they may be tasks with limited usefulness that consume large quantities of database processing time. Note that "infeasible" isn't the same as "impossible"; impossible output is output that cannot be generated from the database, regardless of how much time or effort is expended.

There are no hard-and-fast guidelines as to what constitutes feasible and infeasible output. The decision must be based on factors unique to each particular database environment. In most cases, however, output that users have requested will be evaluated in terms of the ratio between the importance of the particular output to the organization as a whole and the cost of creating the particular output.

Generating and Evaluating Alternatives

There will always be more than one way to implement the specifications delineated in a given requirements document. Any systems development process will have at least two design alternatives:

1. Keep the old system (this is always a possibility)
2. Install a new or modified system

More often, however, the systems analyst will present management with several ways in which the old system can be changed to better meet the needs of the organization. The alternatives will include various types of hardware (e.g., one size of computer versus another or one brand of computer versus another) and various sources for software (e.g., purchased off the shelf or custom-programmed specifically for the organization). The alternatives will also deal with which of the feasible outputs should be developed and in which order they should be developed; a development timeline may also be included.

Each alternative has a variety of costs associated with it. Costs for hardware and software can be estimated relatively easily. The difficult portion of the analysis is trying to assign values to the benefits each alternative will bring to the organization. Often, affixing dollar values to intangible benefits (e.g., better customer satisfaction) is based on the knowledge of experienced managers. The final decision is made by comparing costs to benefits and then applying human judgment. Many decisions about the type of system to be implemented are made on "gut feelings," a process that is not necessarily wrong; experienced managers often have knowledge about their market which cannot be easily expressed in words, much less quantified.

Detailed System Design

It is at this point in the development cycle—once a general design strategy has been approved—that the actual design of a database begins. If not included in the requirements document, paper samples of output formats can be used to identify the data items that are necessary to produce each individual output; these form the pool of data upon which the database system will be built.

However, knowing the types of data that need to be stored in the database is not enough to produce an effective design. A database schema not only consists of the pool of data items, but contains definitions of the relationships between those data. Therefore, the systems designer must be able to assemble a set of rules that describe how the data interact; these are known as *constraints*. Constraints emerge as the systems analyst conducts interviews with an organization's personnel. Further information about database constraints appears throughout the rest of this book.

Having both a pool of data items and a set of constraints, the database designer is ready to create an effective logical organization for the data. Keep in mind that this logical design is independent of any application programs that might be written to interact with the database; designing programs is not a part of the logical database design. While most database design textbooks begin their discussions of database design at this point in the systems development process, it is important to remember that the needs assessment, alternative generation, and alternative selection must be performed before schema creation is possible.

Separate from the logical database design, system designers plan and design the application programs that will be written to interface with the database. In doing so, they use the sample screens that are part of the requirements document. They also consider issues such as user-interface design to develop programs that are easy to learn and use.

During the design phase, system designers must also plan for data conversion. Regardless of whether the new system is replacing a paper-based system or a computer-based system, some historical data will need to be transferred from the old system to the new. For example, Small Bank would need to transfer its customer and account data; they may choose not to transfer transaction data.

If the old system is paper-based, data conversion may require a significant amount of data entry time. If the old system is computer-based, then data conversion may require programming to translate the current data format to that required by the new system.

Implementation

The implementation of an information system generally involves the following activities:

1. Purchasing, installing, and testing hardware
2. Purchasing off-the-shelf software (If the information system includes a database, then the major software item will be the DBMS. An organization

may also decide to purchase application or utility programs which have been written specifically for their DBMS.)

3. Tailoring off-the-shelf-software (In some cases, it may be necessary to modify off-the-shelf software to better meet the needs of the organization.)
4. Writing application programs
5. Testing all software
6. Writing documentation
7. Converting data from its existing format so that it can be imported into the new system
8. Training users
9. Final implementation of the system

While the activities above are listed as if they were a series, they do not always occur in sequence. Steps 1 and 2 can occur simultaneously. Once the hardware and purchased software are available, steps 3–8 can be performed concurrently. Step 9, placing the system in actual use, cannot begin until all other activities are completed.

Even if a system has been superbly designed, its software tailored perfectly to the organization, and all hardware and software thoroughly tested, it can still fail if the implementation is not handled properly. The most successful implementation schemes are based on the premise that if something can go wrong, it will. Therefore, most new computer systems are implemented using a parallel approach.

With the parallel approach to implementation, the new system is run along with the old system (in other words, the two systems are run in parallel). This continues through at least one complete business cycle. There are two major advantages to this strategy that offset the additional effort of doing everything twice:

1. Output from the new system can be checked against output from the old to verify that the new system is performing accurately.
2. If for some unforeseen reason it becomes necessary to shut down the new system, the organization still has an operational, up-to-date old system which can be used until the new system is repaired.

There is also one major drawback to the parallel approach. Unless the process is carefully scheduled and dates for shutoff of the old system strictly enforced, users may postpone cutover to the new system. Users have a tendency to stay with what is comfortable; an old system that they know may be more comfortable than a new system, even if the old system was fraught with problems that are solved by the new system.

The opposite of the parallel approach is often referred to as the plunge approach, since an organization plunges into the new system, completely discontinuing the old. A plunge is often an invitation to disaster, since any failure of the new system may cause major disruption in the operation of the organization. A plunge can be very successful in an organization that has no computerized system; it is also used successfully to introduce replacement systems. However, it can be risky and usually shouldn't be undertaken without some sort of fall-back position such as manual data processing procedures.

Conducting a Needs Assessment

To better understand the idea of a needs assessment, imagine that you have been hired to develop a database system for the Federated Taxi Company. FTC is owned and operated by Joe and Mary Kelly. Until recently, the business has been profitable but small. However, the City Council has just made 100 more taxi licenses available, 30 of which were acquired by FTC. With the added taxis on the road, FTC's manual record keeping has become unwieldy and therefore inaccurate. The Kellys are astute businesspeople and realize that computerizing their record keeping is the only realistic answer to their problem. They are also intelligent enough to recognize that they don't have the necessary computer skills to handle the project themselves. Therefore, they decided to seek the help of an outside consultant—you.

Conducting the Interviews

On your first visit to FTC you are met by Mrs. Kelly. Once the two of you are comfortably seated in the office, you ask her to describe for you in general terms how the company operates:

"FTC owns all of its cabs," Mrs. Kelly explains. "We have a full-time maintenance staff that handles all repairs except major body work. However, our drivers are not on the FTC payroll. A driver rents a cab from us for a fixed fee for each shift; the fee for a given shift is based on the earning potential for that time period. For example, fees for a day shift—8 a.m. to 4 p.m.—are higher than those for the graveyard shift—midnight to 8 a.m. Drivers also pay for all their own gas. In order to make a profit, then, a driver must take in more money than the rental fee and the cost of the gas. This arrangement benefits a driver who consistently finds fares and who can drive economically.

"For new drivers, the rental fee is due before the driver takes the cab out on the road. We allow drivers who have been with us for a while to pay when they return from their shift.

"The rental arrangement also simplifies management of the company. Our payroll is small; we pay the three-person office staff, a janitor for the garage and the office, our five mechanics, and the six dispatchers. We make our profit by keeping as many cabs on the road as we can. Therefore, adding all these new cabs hasn't placed much of a strain on our payroll system—the current 'one-write' system is still working pretty well—but handling information about the cabs has become a nightmare.

"We keep records on each of the cabs, both to make sure they get regular preventative maintenance and to identify any cabs that are being mistreated by their drivers. Every so often we do have to refuse a driver's request for cab rental because of a poor driving record. Therefore, we also keep records on each of the drivers—which cab they rented, how far they drove, and so on. One of the things we need to be able to do with our new record keeping system is to match up drivers with cabs that develop major problems so we can identify which driver is responsible.

"We're also having trouble with our parts inventory. You can't buy the big 'Checker' cabs any more, so the new cabs aren't the same make as the older cabs. This means that we now have to stock two sets of everything. And by the same token, our accounts payable systems are overwhelmed by the new work-load. The bookkeeper says she's nearly ready to quit, but I don't think it's quite that bad. The clerk who schedules drivers for cabs isn't particularly happy either.

"Like most cab companies, ours are radio dispatched. We have three dis-patchers that work a regular five-day week, one on each shift, and three part-timers for the weekends. The dispatchers are responsible for checking drivers in and out, answering phone calls, and sending cabs to make pick-ups. When a dispatcher comes in for a shift, we give him a list of the cabs that are scheduled to be driven that shift. He then uses a grid on the office whiteboard to keep track of where each cab is at any time. It's been working quite well while the number of cabs has been small, but some days now there isn't room on the board to list all the cabs on the road. However, I'm concerned that our dis-patchers won't take to a computer easily; most of them are retired people. I'm

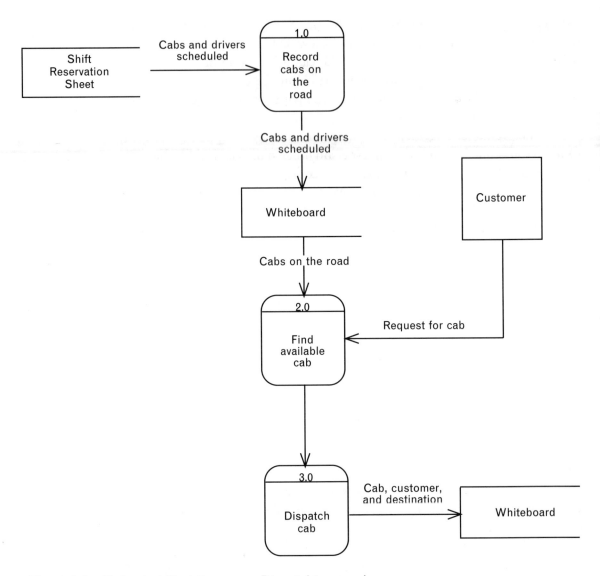

Figure 2.4   Federated Taxi Company: Dispatching a cab

also afraid that a computer won't be fast enough for them, that it won't give them an overview of all the cabs at once. I think a bigger whiteboard is the answer, at least for the time being." (The data flow diagram that you draw for cab dispatching can be found in Figure 2.4.)

While the conversation you had with Mrs. Kelly was a great start, it didn't give you enough detail to create a requirements document. You need to make another visit to FTC so that you can talk to some of the employees. Cab scheduling and maintenance records are handled by two people, an office clerk and the chief mechanic. To understand how they interact and share data, you must speak with both of them.

The chief mechanic shows you a 5" x 8" card file that is kept on the ledge of a pass-through (a window without a window pane) between the office and the garage. Noting the physical placement of the file may at first seem like an unnecessary detail, but it is important in terms of who has access to the data. The chief mechanic and the office clerk both need to use the data in that card file regularly and any computer system that ultimately replaces the card file must provide the same sort of access.

The card file is divided into two sections. In the first section is one card for each cab. The data on the card includes:

- Cab number
- Manufacturer
- Model
- Year
- License number
- Date of last tune-up
- Mileage at last tune-up

The cards are kept in order by the date of last tune-up. In order to determine which cars are due for regular maintenance, the chief mechanic merely checks those cards at the front of the box. He orders tune-ups for any car whose date of last tune-up is more than three months prior to the current date. He decides on any further required maintenance by checking the cab once it is in the garage. Cabs are also scheduled for maintenance whenever a driver reports a specific problem.

The back portion of the card file also contains one card per cab, but these are kept in order by cab number. Each card contains the cab's maintenance record and the result of random inspections of the cab's condition. The last entry on the card is always a short statement of the cab's present condition.

The chief mechanic has no set procedure for deciding which cabs will be inspected. In most cases, it depends on who is driving the cab. In other words, cabs driven by new, inexperienced drivers will be inspected far more frequently than cabs driven by drivers whom the chief mechanic knows and trusts. He relies on experienced drivers to report mechanical problems as they arise.

The clerk who actually schedules drivers uses two loose-leaf notebooks in addition to the card file. One notebook contains one or more sheets for each driver, listing the driver's history with the company. The sheets of paper are kept in alphabetical order by driver name, and data pertaining to individual drivers are kept in chronological order. The clerk records:

- Date the activity occurred
- Type of activity (for example, the shift for which a cab is rented, any traffic tickets received, any accidents in which the driver was involved)
- Additional notes and comments (in the case of a traffic ticket or accident, the clerk includes details of the incident)

Unless something unusual occurs, such as a serious accident, the driver history notebook is reviewed by Mr. or Mrs. Kelly once a week. The owners make decisions on how specific drivers should be handled. For example, they may decide that a particular driver has established a safe record and is no longer required to pay the cab rental prior to taking a cab out onto the street.

Cab scheduling is done in the second loose-leaf notebook. The notebook, so crammed full of paper that the rings barely stay closed, is divided into two sections. The first section has one page for each shift in the next three months (there are three shifts per day), organized by shifts within a day. The second section contains one page for each cab, organized by cab number. The clerk established the notebook in this manner so that it was possible to not only assign drivers to cabs, but to know which cabs and drivers were on the street for any given shift.

The clerk handles the cab reservation process as follows:

1. A driver requests a cab for a specific shift on a specific day (a number of drivers have standing reservations; they drive the same cab for the same shift five or six days a week).
2. The clerk turns first to the driver history notebook. If the driver's status has changed in any way, the driver is informed. If the Kellys have decided that the driver's record is unsatisfactory, the request for a reservation will be refused.

3. Unless the driver has requested a specific cab, the clerk assigns the driver to a cab. In either case, the driver's name, the date and the shift are written in the notebook. Before assigning a cab, however, the clerk must check the back portion of the chief mechanic's card file to ensure that the cab is in working condition. Since there is a maximum number of cabs that can be on the road during any given shift, the clerk must also check the front portion of the notebook to be sure that the day and shift in question aren't completely filled. When selecting cabs for drivers who do not request a specific vehicle, the clerk makes an effort to rotate the cabs, ensuring that usage is spread evenly throughout the fleet. Decisions on which cab to assign are generally made by looking at which cab has logged the fewest miles in the given week.

4. Assuming that the reservation can be made, the cab number and driver are transferred to the sheet in the front portion of the notebook corresponding to the appropriate day and shift. The data are also written on the driver's sheet in the driver history notebook.

At this point, you quickly sketch a data flow diagram for the shift reservation process (Figure 2.5).

Each morning the clerk checks the reservation sheets to determine if enough cabs are scheduled to be on the streets. If the number of cabs is too low, the clerk will begin to call drivers to see if any are interested in working.

When a driver comes in before a shift, he or she requests the keys for the cab from the dispatcher. The dispatcher verifies the reservation by checking the appropriate sheet in the front of the schedule notebook, collects the prepaid cab rental if required, and hands over the keys. The dispatcher must then indicate that the driver has shown up for a reserved shift. The notation is made in three places: on the page for the specific shift for the specific day, on the page for the cab, and on the driver history page. (The data flow diagram that you draw to summarize issuing a cab to a driver appears in Figure 2.6.)

When a cab is returned the dispatcher does very nearly the opposite of issuing a cab. He or she collects the keys, asks the driver for the cab's odometer reading, and collects any rental fee due. Then, the dispatcher enters the odometer reading in three places: on the page for the specific shift for the specific day, on the page for the cab, and on the driver history page. (The data flow diagram that you draw to summarize the return of a cab appears in Figure 2.7.)

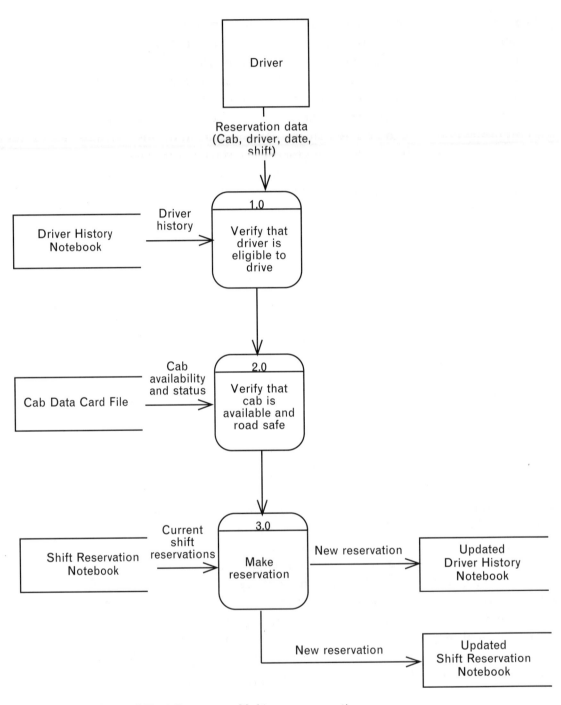

Figure 2.5   Federated Taxi Company: Making a reservation

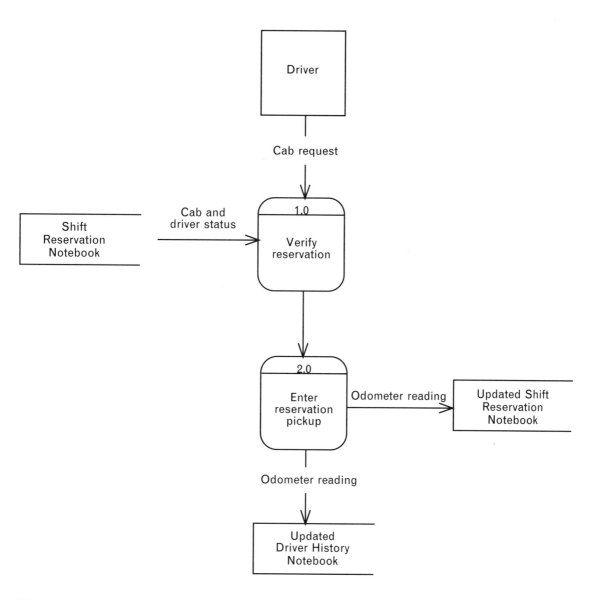

Figure 2.6   Federated Taxi Company: Issuing a cab to a driver

Listening to the clerk's description of this procedure, two things occur to you in your role as a systems analyst. First of all, this procedure has been very well thought out. Whoever designed it paid special attention to the ways in which people needed to access the data. On the other hand, while this manual system worked well when the number of cabs was small, the sheer volume of

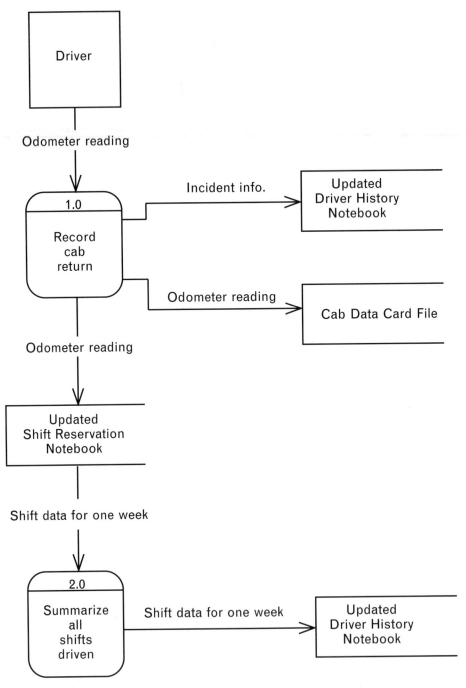

Figure 2.7   Federated Taxi Company: Recording the return of a cab

paper required to cope with the increased fleet and increased pool of drivers has made the entire process unmanageable. The process suffers from those problems generally associated with data redundancy—increased storage space and more importantly, a lack of data integrity.

Meeting with Management

While FTC is a small business, its information needs are nonetheless complex. Before you write a requirements document, you would really like some information of what parts of the system are most important to the management. Therefore, you schedule a meeting with Mr. and Mrs. Kelly. At that meeting you identify the major modules within FTC's information system:

- Payroll
- Cab/driver scheduling
- Cab maintenance
- Driver history
- Cab dispatching
- Spare parts inventory
- Accounts payable
- Accounts receivable

Not all of these areas are of equal priority in terms of computerized implementation. From what Mrs. Kelly said during your interview with her, payroll is probably the least important at the current time. While dispatching probably could benefit from being computerized, the Kellys seem to be reluctant to proceed in that area at this time. Cab maintenance, driver history, and the spare parts inventory would appear to be the most important, while accounts payable and receivable are of slightly less importance.

There is a very important issue that should be considered at this point. One way to ensure that a computerization project will fail is to attempt to computerize an entire organization at one time. Successful system designers propose implementation plans that introduce computers in successive phases. In the case of the Federated Taxi Company, the applications that lend themselves to computers fall into five broad groups: (1) cab scheduling and maintenance, including driver history; (2) cab dispatching; (3) spare parts inventory; (4) accounting; and (5) payroll.

Considering the priorities set by the company's owners, the cab scheduling and maintenance is by far the most important, and therefore should be implemented first. A computerized inventory system should not be installed until the cab scheduling and maintenance system has been implemented successfully. The accounting functions can be computerized after the inventory. Logically, the cab dispatching should be computerized immediately after the cab scheduling and maintenance functions. However, until the Kellys change their minds about wanting it on the computer, there is nothing that you can do.

Unless the owners come to feel that payroll is not being handled adequately by their manual system, there is no need to include plans for payroll in an implementation schedule. It is essential to realize that sometimes there are processes within an organization that do not need to be computerized. Successful system developers try to be aware of processes that are functioning optimally without computers and generally will propose no modifications in those processes. The old aphorism—"if it ain't broke don't fix it"—applies in full measure to systems development.

You discuss the problems with attempting to implement the entire system with the Kellys. They agree with your recommendation that cab scheduling and maintenance be implemented first. Your requirements document will therefore be limited to the specifics for these two modules, though it will consider carefully where the cab scheduling and maintenance modules will interface with those parts of the system that will be implemented at a later date.

Putting Together the Requirements Document

You've decided to organize your requirements document by drawing sample output formats. Along with each desired output, you'll list the inputs needed to produce that output. To organize the document, outputs are documented by the person who will be their primary users.

Outputs and Data for the Chief Mechanic

The chief mechanic needs the following:

- Screen display of the current status and/or history of a specific cab (Figure 2.8)

```
Cab Number: 106        Make/Model: Checker       Model year: 1968

Plate: 496 AAA         Odometer: 206777          Status: road-safe



                          MAINTENANCE


DATE               TYPE OF SERVICE                 ODOMETER READING
06/12/94           Standard tune-up                200115
06/10/94           Repair right rear tire          199580
03/10/94           Standard tune-up                190442
02/17/94           Replace master brake cylinder   187111
12/11/93           Standard tune-up                185225
12/11/93           Replace seat covers             185225
09/11/93           Standard tune-up                180991
06/15/93           Standard tune-up                175224

                          -MORE-
```

Figure 2.8   Sample "cab info" screen

DATA ITEMS:

- Cab number
- Make
- Model
- Year of manufacture
- Date of purchase
- License number
- For each time maintenance is done on the cab,
    - date of work
    - type of work
    - odometer reading
- Cab status (e.g., road-safe or not road-safe)
- Current odometer reading

```
                    MAINTENANCE LIST

                       07/15/94


                 LAST       TYPE OF        LAST
      CAB#  PLATE#  MAINT.     WORK           TUNE-UP

      104   356 QLT  06/23/94  New windshield  04/12/94
      105   111 ABC  04/12/94  Tune-up         04/12/94
      144   290 AAQ  04/14/94  Tune-up         04/14/94
      238   980 JAM  07/03/94  New wiper blades 04/12/94
      278   771 TOW  04/14/94  Tune-up         04/14/94
      404   206 TTL  04/14/94  Tune-up         04/14/94
```

Figure 2.9   Sample printed output of cabs needing regular maintenance

- Paper listing of those cabs needing regular maintenance (Figure 2.9).

DATA ITEMS:

- Cab number
- License number
- Date of last maintenance
- Type of work last performed
- Date of last tune-up

The chief mechanic has also indicated that he wants to be able to retrieve information about the incidents in which a cab was involved, although no specific screen layout has been requested. The data to provide that information include:

- For each accident in which the cab has been involved,
  - date of accident
  - description of damage incurred
- Summary of condition of the cab

```
┌─────────────────────────────────────────────────────────────────────┐
│                                                                       │
│    Driver: Aaron Wells                          Phone: 555-5151       │
│   Address: 291 W. 51st, Anytown 10051       License #:   US5151       │
│    Status: pay after                        Exp. date: 12/15/95       │
│                                                                       │
│                                                                       │
│                             SHIFTS                                    │
│                                                                       │
│                                                                       │
│           Date        Shift      Cab#       Driven                    │
│                                                                       │
│          Ø7/14/94      day        2Ø5         no                      │
│          Ø7/13/94      day        2Ø5         yes                     │
│          Ø7/12/94      day        387         yes                     │
│          Ø7/11/94      day        2Ø5         yes                     │
│          Ø7/Ø8/94      day        2Ø5         yes                     │
│          Ø7/Ø7/94      day        2Ø5         yes                     │
│          Ø7/Ø7/94      eve        387         yes                     │
│          Ø7/Ø6/94      day        2Ø5         yes                     │
│          Ø7/Ø5/94      day        2Ø5         no                      │
│                                                                       │
│                            -MORE-                                     │
│                                                                       │
└─────────────────────────────────────────────────────────────────────┘
```

Figure 2.10   Sample "driver info" screen

Outputs and Data for the Scheduling Clerk

The scheduling clerk needs several predefined screens of data:

- Screen display of the current status and/or history of a specific driver (Figure 2.10).

DATA ITEMS:

- Driver name
- Driver address
- Driver phone number
- Chauffeur's license number
- Date chauffeur's license expires

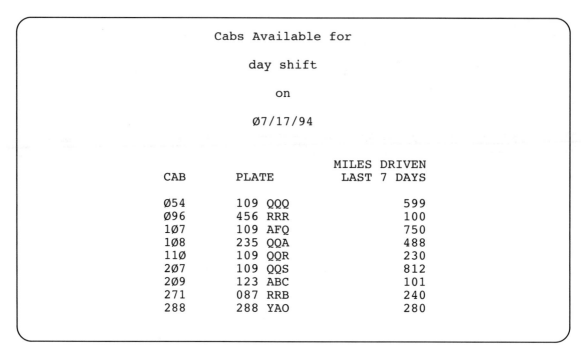

Figure 2.11   Sample display of cabs available for a single date and shift

- For each time the driver rents a cab,
  - Date and shift
  - Cab number
  - A flag that indicates whether or not the driver actually drove a reserved shift
- For each incident in which the driver is involved,
  - Date
  - Nature of incident (e.g., traffic ticket or accident)
- Driver status

- Screen display of the cabs available for a given shift on a given day (Figure 2.11).

DATA ITEMS:

For each cab with a status of "road-safe" and no reservation for the requested day and shift:

```
                          CAB#  Ø51              Miles  last
                                                seven  days:  2292


                       SHIFT  AVAILABILITY

     DATE           DAY        EVENING        NIGHT

     Ø7/12/94        x            x             x
     Ø7/13/94                     x
     Ø7/14/94                     x
     Ø7/15/94                     x             x
     Ø7/16/94                     x             x
     Ø7/17/94        x
     Ø7/18/94        x            x             x
     Ø7/19/94        x            x
     Ø7/2Ø/94        x                          x


                          -MORE-
```

Figure 2.12 Sample cab-availability screen

- Cab number
- License number
- Number of miles driven in the past week (Note that this is a computed data item. It assumes that the database stores odometer readings for each cab taken at the start of each shift for which the cab is in use.)

- Screen display of days and shifts available for a specific cab (Figure 2.12)

DATA ITEMS:

Assuming the cab has a status of "road-safe"
- Cab number
- Date of each available shift in the next three months
- Number of miles driven in the past week

```
    SHIFT: Evening        Date: Ø7/17/94


DRIVER                 CAB#     PLATE#          COMMENTS

Bailey, Max            ØØ2      345 YAO         pay before
Daker, MaryAnn         ØØ6      997 IUF         pay after
Lewis, John            Ø45      867 POP         pay before - ticket Ø7/14/94
Miller, Pat            1Ø8      76Ø PLP         pay after
Miller, Phyllis        215      776 IKL         pay before
Phong, Quen            318      333 IPO         pay after
Wong, David            341      285 KKN         pay after
Young, Leslie          49Ø      249 LKL         pay before
Zilog, Charlie         492      888 IOA         pay after
```

Figure 2.13   Sample cab schedule screen

- Screen display of the cabs and drivers scheduled for a given shift on a given day (Figure 2.13)

DATA ITEMS:

- Date and shift number
- For each cab that has been reserved,
  - Cab number
  - Cab license number
  - Driver name
  - Comments about driver

Output for the Dispatchers

Because the dispatchers won't be using the computers, the output they receive from the system will be a paper report:

- Paper listing of the cabs and drivers scheduled for a given shift on a given day (Figure 2.14)

```
                        Shift Schedule for
                         August 12, 1994
                             Evening


Cab#       Plate        Driver#              Notes

023        256 POZ      Erlich, Martin       2 tickets last week—give warning
025        808 IIK      Kowalski, Pete       pay after
045        008 IKL      French, Janice       first shift—pay before
106        802 UWQ      Thieu, Lin Van       pay after
277        172 OIY      Jackson, Rafael      pay before
318        181 JHG      Kolson, Jan          pay after (status change)
```

Figure 2.14 Sample printed shift schedule

DATA ITEMS:

- Date and shift number
- For each cab that has been reserved,
    - Cab number
    - Cab license number
    - Driver name
    - Comments about driver

Summary Output for the Kellys

While there are many kinds of summary output that can be created from the database under design for Federated Taxi, the weekly driver summary report examined by the owners is of vital importance. Since that information is used for decision making on a regular basis, it should be included in the original design. The report might appear as in Figure 2.15. The data items required to construct it are:

- Driver name
- For each shift the driver has completed,
    - Date and shift number
    - Cab number
    - Miles driven
    - Comments (e.g., notes about incidents, excessive cab wear noticed by maintenance personnel, etc.)

```
                         Driver Summary
                      06-20-94 to 06-26-94


Driver              Date    Shift    Cab#    Miles  Comments

Abelman, John       06-20   day      356     204
                    06-21   day      256     287    speeding ticket
                    06-22   day      356     225
                    06-23   day      356     305
                    06-24   day      356     287

Erlich, Martin      06-20   eve      244     256
                    06-22   eve      244     297
                    06-23   eve      244     106    rear-ended a bus
                    06-24   eve      018     288
                    06-25   eve      018      57    stuck on freeway

Jackson, Rafael     06-20   eve      013     242
                    06-21   eve      013     233    seat fabric cut
                    06-22   eve      013     211
                    06-23   eve      013     525    out-of-town run
                    06-24   day      029     106    too tired
```

Figure 2.15 Sample printed weekly summary report

Other Data Items

The data items listed for each of the eight outputs that Federated Taxi's database system will provide are only those that will be visible on either a CRT screen or a piece of paper. However, there are "hidden" data items that, while they may not appear as an output item, must be retained in the database in order to produce visible outputs. For example, in order to maintain a driver's history record and to compile the driver history summary report, there must be a data item that indicates whether or not a driver actually drove a shift for which he or she reserved a cab. In order to compute the number of miles a cab travels in each shift or in a given week, the database must also store the odometer readings of each cab at the beginning of each shift.

Table 2.1
Data items describing cabs for the Federated Taxi Company

Data Item Name	Contents
Cab #	Unique number assigned to a cab and painted on its side
Make/Model	Name of manufacturer/model name
Year	Model year
Plate	License plate
Current Odom.	Odometer reading at end of last shift
Maint. Date	Date some type of maintenance was performed
Maint. Type	Type of maintenance performed
Maint. Odom.	Odometer reading when maintenance was performed
Inci. Date	Date of incident (traffic citation or accident) in which cab was involved
Inci. Time	Time incident occurred
Inci. Type	Type of incident
Inci. Details	Details about an incident
Condition	Summary of condition of cab
Cab Status	Status of cab (either "road-safe" or "not-road-safe")

The definition of the output formats and the identification of the additional "hidden" data items needed to create those outputs provides enough information for you, the systems analyst, to describe the pool of data items that will form the shared data pool upon which the database system will be based. There are three general groups of data:

1. Data items that describe a cab (Table 2.1)
2. Data items that describe a driver (Table 2.2)
3. Data items that describe cab reservations (Table 2.3)

Note that while the same data items may appear in more than one of the three data item groups, this does not mean that the data must be stored redundantly. Rather, this only indicates data that will be shared.

The outputs which have been described above are predictable outputs which will be used repeatedly. However, there will certainly be times when either the chief mechanic or the scheduling clerk has a need for information which either cannot be predicted or which may never be needed again. If the Kelly's wish these two employees to be able to satisfy such ad hoc information needs on their own, then the mechanic and the clerk must be trained in the syntax of whatever query language their DBMS supports.

Table 2.2
Data items describing drivers for the Federated Taxi Company

Data Item Name	Contents
Driver #	Unique number assigned to each driver
Driver name	Driver's name
Driver address	Driver's address
Driver phone	Driver's phone number
License #	Chauffeur's license number
Exp. Date	Date chauffeur's license expires
WkDate	Date for which a cab is reserved
Shift name	Shift for which a cab is reserved
Cab #	Cab number for which a reservation has been placed
WkFlag	"True" if driver works a reserved shift, "False" if he or she does not
Inci. Date	Date on which a driving incident occurred
Inci. Time	Time at which a driving incident occurred
Inci. Type	Description of a driving incident
Inci. Details	Specific information about an incident
Driver Status	Driver status (generally either "pay first," "pay after," or "do not reserve")

Table 2.3
Data items describing cab reservations for the Federated Taxi Company

Data Item Name	Contents
Cab #	Cab number
Plate	Cab license plate
WkDate	Date for which the cab is reserved
Shift Name	Shift for which the cab is reserved
Driver #	Number of driver who reserved cab
WkFlag	"True" if the driver shows up to drive the shift, "False" if he or she does not
Starting Odom.	Odometer reading at the beginning of the shift
Ending Odom.	Odometer reading at the end of the shift

The Kellys must also be told that the system will work most efficiently if the dispatchers are trained to input data indicating which drivers have driven their shifts, the odometer readings at the start and end of shifts, and the amount of cab rental paid. If they are still adamant that the dispatchers not interact with the computer at all, then some alternative procedure must be established to ensure that the data are captured on paper and kept for the clerk to handle during normal business hours.

Summary

Database design is more than identifying an optimal way of arranging the data items in a database. It is part of a larger set of activities known as the systems development cycle. The systems development cycle is used by organizations to implement successful computer systems.

The steps in the systems development cycle can be described as:

1. Conduct a needs assessment (systems analysis) which includes evaluating the current system and identifying how it should be modified to meet the needs of the organization;
2. Generate general alternative strategies for remedying the weaknesses identified during the needs assessment; evaluate the alternatives and select one for implementation;
3. Create a detailed systems design based on the selected alternative (including database design);
4. Implement the system.

Once an organization begins the cycle, it should continue indefinitely. Effective systems designs include provisions for periodic re-evaluation.

Systems development projects are usually coordinated by systems analysts. Systems analysts use interviewing and data gathering techniques during the needs assessment to create a picture of the current system, to identify where it succeeds and where it should be modified to better meet the organization's information needs.

A systems analysis is really solving a business problem. The process is therefore amenable to a general problem solving model like IPO (Input-Process-Output). A designer using IPO will first identify the outputs the system should provide. He or she will then determine what input is necessary to produce the desired outputs. Finally, the designer specifies the process to be used to transform the inputs to the outputs.

Successful systems development projects include open lines of communication between the person or people developing the system and corporate management. They do not attempt to implement an entire system at once, but instead assign priorities to parts of the system. The small parts of the systems are implemented in order of their assigned priority. Successful projects also employ the parallel method of implementation; the new system is run in tandem with the old until it is clear that the new system is accurate and reliable enough to discontinue the old.

References

Aktas, Ziya 1987. *Structured Analysis and Design of Information Systems.* Prentice-Hall.

Alter, Steven. 1992. *Information Systems: A Management Perspective.* Reading, Mass.: Addison-Wesley.

Anthony, R. 1965. *Planning and Control Systems: A Framework for Analysis.* Division of Research, Graduate School of Business Administration, Harvard University.

DeMarco, T. 1978. *Structured Analysis and System Specification.* Yourdon Press.

Embley, David W., Barry D. Kurtz, and Scott N. Woodfield. 1992. *Object-Oriented Systems Analysis.* Yourdon Press.

Holland, R. H. 1980. "Data Base Planning Entails Return to Basics." *Computerworld.* October 27.

McKeown, Patrick G. and Robert A. Leitch. 1993. *Managing with Computers.* Dryden Press.

Voell, R. F. 1980. "Data Base Planning." In T. A. Rullo, ed. *Advances in Data Base Management*, Vol. 1. Heyden.

Things to Think About

1. You have been hired as a consultant by an independent drug store to help computerize a pharmacy. The owner doesn't know anything about the systems development cycle. In your own words, explain to the owner the steps you will take to design his system.

2. The owner of the local fish store has been shopping. She has purchased a microcomputer with four megabytes of RAM and a 200-megabyte hard drive. For software, she has purchased a word processor, a spreadsheet, and a relational DBMS (the dealer told her those were the most widely used business applications). After making the purchases, she has asked you to use the DBMS to computerize her business. What problems does this situation present to a systems designer? What kind of mistake has the fish store owner made?

3. The owner of the drug store in question 1 above has asked you to design and implement a database system for his accounts receivable, his accounts payable, his inventory, and his prescription records. He wants the entire system installed at the same time. Is this a good idea? Why or why not?

4. Many systems development projects fail because of a lack of communication. In what phases of a systems development project is communication an essential element? Between which groups of people should the communication occur?

5. Not everyone is cut out to be a systems analyst. Make a list of the skills and personality traits that, in your opinion, characterize the ideal systems analyst. Is this a job you would like? Why or why not?

6. IPO (Input-Process-Output) is a general problem solving model; it doesn't apply only to the design of a database system. To what activities in your daily life might you apply IPO to help you solve a problem or achieve some goal?

Exercises

In Appendix A and Appendix B you will find transcripts of interviews conducted during the needs assessment phase of a systems development project for two different organizations—the East Coast Aquarium and the office of Margaret Holmes, D.M.D. Using the information contained in the interviews, do the following:

1. Identify the major application areas where a database system will be useful.
2. Assign developmental priorities to the application areas.
3. Design output formats for the major applications.
4. List the data items that must be stored in the database in order to produce the outputs you have designed.

Data Relationships

The essence of a database system is its ability to depict data relationships. In most cases, a database schema represents relationships between data objects, or *entities.* An entity is anything about which an organization wishes to store data, such as Small Bank's customers or the Federated Taxi Company's cabs. Each DBMS uses a *data model* to express the schema. (The relational data model is discussed in Chapter 4.) However, before you can capture data relationships in a formal data model, you must identify those relationships. In the process of database design, this step occurs after the requirements document has been written but before the schema is written. This chapter looks at the type of data relationships that can be represented in a database system and at a method for documenting them independent of any data model—the *entity-relationship model.*

When thinking about data relationships, it is important to remember that schemas deal with theoretical, or possible, relationships between entities. However, a database stores actual data occurrences. An *occurrence*, or *instance*, of an entity refers to actual data values describing the data object that are stored in a database. Data relationships within the database are therefore between specific occurrences of data.

For example, assume there are six divisions in a corporation. There are between 20 and 100 employees working for each division. In the database itself, data about each employee is related to the specific division for which that employee works. Any given division is related to between 20 and 100 individual employees. However, the database schema only indicates that there is some relationship between employees and divisions.

Nonetheless, before any data can be stored, you must identify the types of data relationships that your database will be able to represent. In addition, you must identify the pieces of data (the *attributes*) that describe each entity.

Entities and Attributes

As you have read, an entity is something about which an organization stores data. It can be a person, a physical object, a place, or an event. When diagramming relationships between entities in an entity-relationship (ER) diagram, an entity is represented as a rectangle containing the entity's name. For example,

```
┌─────────────────────┐
│                     │
│      Employee       │
│                     │
└─────────────────────┘
```

represents an entity from a personnel database. This particular entity describes people who are employed.

Attributes are typically shown in an ER diagram by placing them in bubbles that are connected to the entity with a line. There are a number of attributes that might be used to describe an employee, for example, including an employee number, name, social security number, and birthdate.

Notice in Figure 3.1 that each attribute has a name (the word that appears inside the bubble). Below each attribute is the attribute's *domain*. A domain is an expression of the possible values that can be assigned to an attribute. Domains can be very broad (for example, "dates") or very specific (for

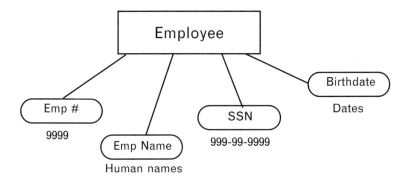

Figure 3.1   An employee entity and its attributes

example, "9999," which stands for four numbers). When attributes are actually defined using a DBMS, *domain constraints* can be established to ensure that stored data are taken only from each attribute's domain.

There is more than one way to draw an ER diagram. However, to ease translation of that diagram into a data model a DBMS can use, there is a rule that must be observed about attributes: *attributes must be single-valued.* In other words, each occurrence of an entity has only one value for each attribute associated with it. The employee entity, for example, has only one value for employee number, name, social security number, and birthdate.

However, what should you do if you want to store the names and birthdates of an employee's children? Because an employee can have more than one child, the attributes for child's name and child's birthdate would be *multivalued* (have more than one value, as they do in Figure 3.2). The presence of such multivalued attributes indicates that another entity is required. In this case, the entity might be called Child and would have the child's name and birthdate as attributes (see Figure 3.3). Each occurrence of the Child entity represents one child, with one value for child's name and birthdate. You would then indicate a relationship between the Employee entity and the Child entity, using the technique described in the following section.

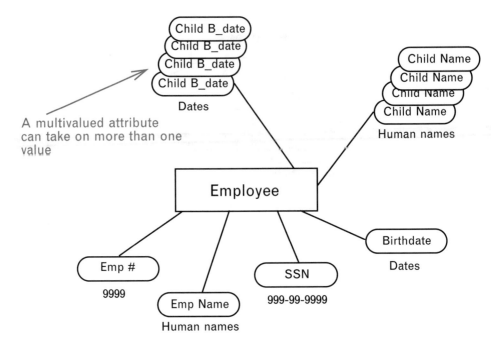

A multivalued attribute
can take on more than one
value

Figure 3.2   Multivalued attributes

Types of Data Relationships

Each relationship between two entities can be one-to-one, one-to-many, or many-to-many. More than one relationship may be identified between the same two entities; when that occurs, each relationship has a different meaning in the database environment.

One-to-One Relationships

If a *one-to-one relationship* exists between two entities, then each occurrence of each entity is related to zero or one occurrence of the other entity. In Western cultures, for example, at any given time each man has only one wife; each woman has only one husband. The relationship is therefore between the Man entity and the Woman entity.

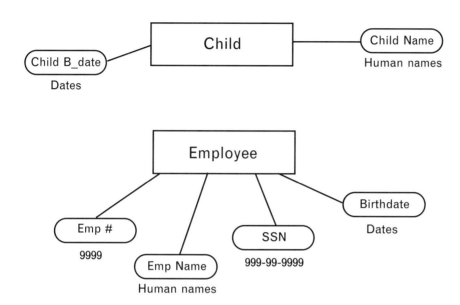

Figure 3.3   Taking care of a multivalued attribute by creating a new entity

ER diagrams use a combination of a diamond, a line, and some letters and/or numbers to indicate relationships between entities. In the examples that follow, attributes have been omitted to help you focus on relationships between entities. However, in a complete ER diagram, attributes and their domains are included; you will see them in examples later in this chapter.

A one-to-one relationship, for example, is often drawn as:

The diamond on the line between the boxes contains an action phrase describing the relationship. Numbers above the line show the type of relationship. (They are also often written 1:1.) In this case, the relationship can be read: "One man is married to no women or to one woman; one woman is married to no men or one man."

The one-to-one relationship above is very unusual. In general, true one-to-one relationships do not occur in the real world. Most one-to-one relationships are actually special cases of one-to-many relationships.

One-to-Many Relationships

If a *one-to-many relationship* exists between two entities, then an occurrence of the entity on the "one" end of the relationship may be related to zero, one, or more occurrences of the entity on the "many" end. For example, a man may have zero, one, or more daughters but a woman can have only one father. This type of relationship is often drawn:

This diagram looks very similar to the diagram of the one-to-many relationship. The difference is in the letter that appears next to the Woman box. The N means that many women are related to one man. The relationship is also often written 1:N.

The relationship above represents a second type of relationship between the entities Man and Woman. Keep in mind that there is no reason that two entities in the same database system cannot have more than one relationship between them. Each relationship will be described separately and will have a different meaning, just as the two relationships between Man and Woman.

The one-to-many relationship is very common in database environments. It describes the nature of the relationship between the Employee and Child entities in the personnel database described earlier. Each employee can be related to zero, one, or more children; each child can be related to one employee. Small Bank's database also contains several one-to-many relationships. For example, the bank carries each account at one branch (although customers can access their accounts at any branch):

Many-to-Many Relationships

If a *many-to-many relationship* exists between two entities, then each occurrence of an entity in the relationship may be related to zero, one, or more occurrences of the other. A man, for example, may have zero, one, or more sisters; a woman may have zero, one, or more brothers:

The letters that identify the type of relationship are M and N, often written M:N. This indicates that one man is related to zero, one, or more women and that one woman is related to zero, one, or more men. Although this relationship is between the same two entities as the two preceding types of relationships, it has a different meaning.

Many-to-Many Relationships and Composite Entities

Like one-to-many relationships, many-to-many relationships are common in database schemas. However, in practice they present two major problems. First, the formal data models used by today's DBMSs to represent database schemas cannot handle many-to-many relationships directly. In addition, a database may need to store attributes that don't describe an entity, but that instead apply to the many-to-many relationship between two entities. What makes this a problem is the rule that relationships can't have attributes; only entities can have attributes.

To better understand this second problem, assume that Small Bank wants to store data about the office supplies it purchases. Each office supply item can be purchased from many vendors; each vendor sells many supply items. The relationship could be diagrammed:

The vendor entity can have attributes such as the vendor's name, address, and phone number. The supply item entity can have attributes such as the item number, description, color, and weight. However, the price of the item varies, depending on the vendor from which the item is purchased. The price therefore can't be stored with either vendor entity or the supply item entity. Instead, the price applies to the *relationship* between vendor and supply item. Unfortunately, as you have just read, the relationship "sells" can't have attributes.

The solution to the problem is to create an entity that represents the relationship between two entities. Such an entity, created from a many-to-many relationship, is called a *composite* entity. It is drawn as a rectangle with a diamond inside it:

For this particular example, the composite entity has been given the name "Catalog Entry" to indicate that it represents one entry in a vendor's office supply catalog. Each catalog entry has a price associated with it; in other words, it represents the price charged by one vendor for one supply item.

To see how the Catalog Entry entity replaces the many-to-many relationship, take a look at Figure 3.4. Notice that there is a one-to-many relationship between the Vendor and Catalog Entry entities, indicating that a vendor sells many different items. In other words, each occurrence of the Catalog Entry entity represents one entry in a vendor's supply catalog. There is also a one-to-many relationship between the Supply Item and Catalog Entry entities. This means that a supply item is listed in many catalogs. As you can see, a composite entity replaces a many-to-many relationship with two one-to-many relationships.

Another characteristic of an ER diagram can be seen in Figure 3.4. Notice that the Catalog Entry entity has only two attributes, the catalog number and the price. However, by themselves these attributes aren't enough to identify the item being sold or the vendor from which it comes. To completely identify the catalog entry, you need to know which vendor (the Vendor # attribute from the Vendor entity) and which item (the Item # attribute from the Supply Item entity). Nonetheless, the Vendor # and Item # attributes aren't duplicated on the Catalog Entry entity.

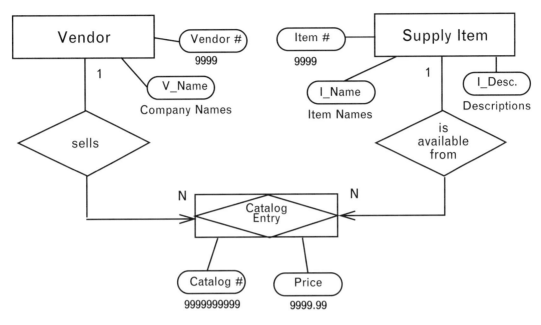

Figure 3.4   Using a composite entity to replace a many-to-many relationship

When a one-to-many relationship exists between two entities, the entity at the "many" end *inherits* the attributes that belong to the entity at the "one" end. In this case, the Catalog Entry entity inherits all the attributes for the vendor in whose catalog it appears as well as all the attributes for the supply item that the catalog entry describes.

An ER Diagram for Small Bank

An entity-relationship diagram that documents the relationships between Small Bank's branches, customers, accounts, and transactions appears in Figure 3.5. As you can see from the diagram, there are five entities.

Because a customer may have opened accounts at more than one branch, there is a many-to-many relationship between a branch and a customer. The composite entity Branch Patronage has therefore been created to reduce that many-to-many relationship to two one-to-many relationships. This composite entity has no attributes of its own, but instead inherits the attributes of both branch and customer. Notice that the remainder of relationships are all one-to-many.

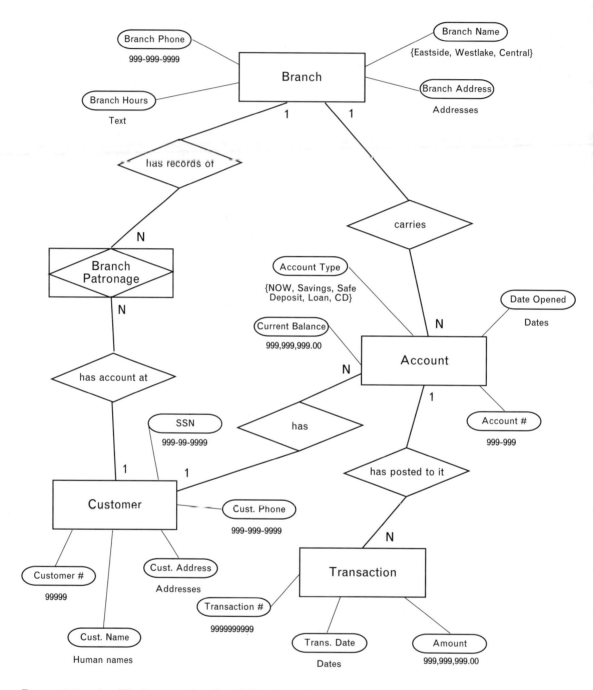

Figure 3.5   An ER diagram for Small Bank

Some of the attributes in Figure 3.5 have a very small domain. For example, consider the Branch Name attribute. Since Small Bank has only three branches, the domain of that attribute is three very specific values: Eastside, Westlake, and Central. The values are placed on the ER diagram, surrounded by braces ({}).

Relationships Between More than Two Entities

The ER diagram for Small Bank contains relationships that involve only two entities. However, you may occasionally encounter situations where three or more entities participate in one relationship. As an example, consider the relationships between the Federated Taxi Company's cab, driver, and shift entities. Note that the Federated Taxi Company defines a "shift" as an eight-hour period (*day*, *eve*, or *ngt*) on one specific date. There is a many-to-many relationship between a cab and a driver (over time, a driver can drive many different cabs and the same cab can be driven by many drivers). There is a second many-to-many relationship between a cab and a shift (a cab can be driven during many shifts and many cabs are driven during a shift). The relationship between driver and shift is also many-to-many (a driver drives many shifts and many drivers work any given shift).

The relationships between cab, driver, and shift could be diagrammed as in Figure 3.6. (Attributes have been left out to emphasize the relationships between entities.) Notice that a composite entity has been introduced to reduce each many-to-many relationship to two one-to-many relationships.

The diagram in Figure 3.6 is technically correct. However, it presents a significant problem: there is no way to determine who drove which cab when. The Driver in Cab composite entity indicates which driver drove which cab, but not *when* it was driven; the Cab on Shift composite entity indicates when a cab was driven, but not *who* drove it; the Driver on Shift composite entity indicates when a driver drove, but not *which* cab was driven. This situation arises because the relationship is not between any two entities, but between all three of them. In other words, who drove what cab when is a joint relationship between cab, driver, and shift.

When a relationship exists between more than two entities, use a single composite entity to represent that relationship, just as you would for a many-to-many relationship between two entities. For example, Figure 3.7 includes one composite entity—Shift Driven—that represents one driver who will take,

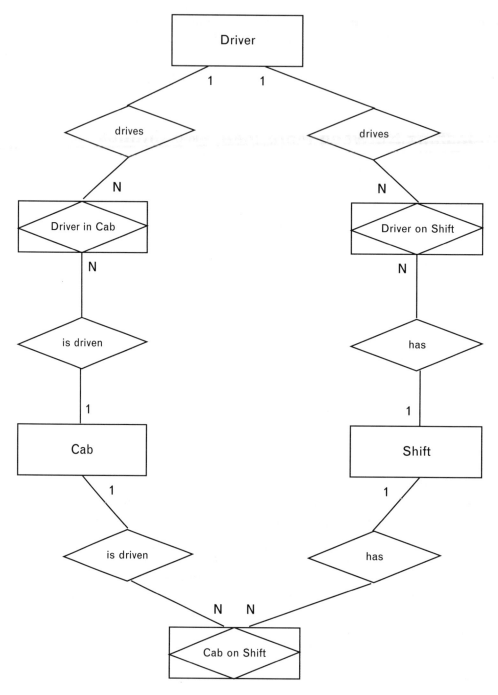

Figure 3.6   One way of representing the relationships between cab, driver, and shift

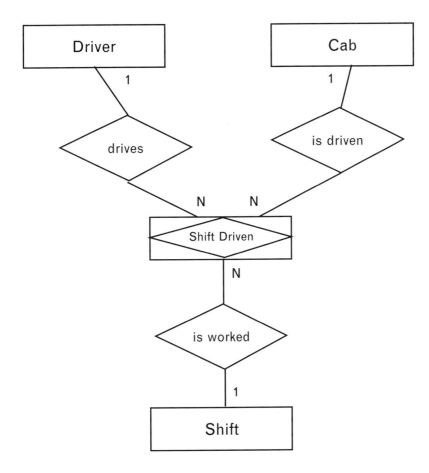

Figure 3.7 Handling a relationship between three entities

or has taken, one cab on the road for one shift. For each time a driver has driven or plans to drive, the database contains one occurrence of the shift driven entity.

A Complete Entity Relationship Diagram for the Federated Taxi Company

A complete entity-relationship diagram for the Federated Taxi Company can be found in Figure 3.8. This diagram captures the relationship between shift, driver, and cab that you saw in Figure 3.7.

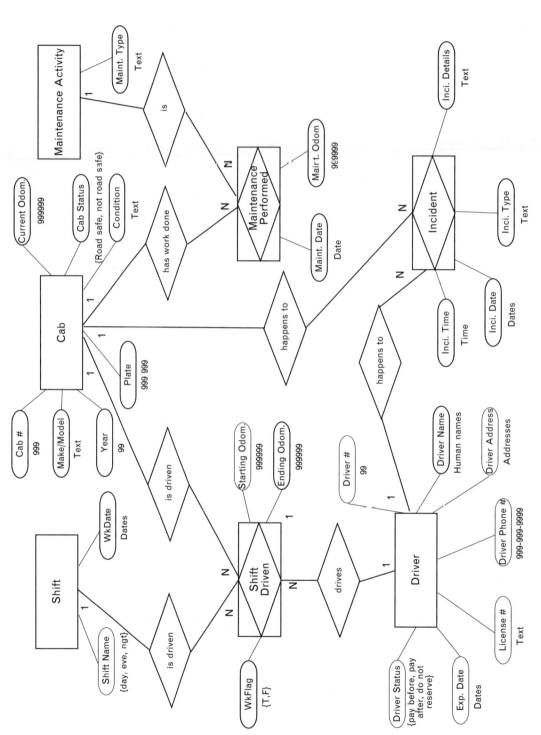

Figure 3.8   The complete ER diagram for the Federated Taxi Company

In addition, it documents incidents that occur when a cab is on the road. (Incidents include such things as traffic tickets and accidents.) Because the same cab and driver can be involved in many incidents, the incident entity is a composite entity that reduces the many-to-many relationship between cab and driver to two one-to-many relationships.

The diagram also includes entities for maintenance performed on cabs. The maintenance activity entity represents a type of maintenance that might be performed on a cab, such as an oil change or a tune-up. There is therefore a many-to-many relationship between a cab and a maintenance activity. The composite entity maintenance performed has been created to replace the many-to-many relationship and provides a place for storing data about when the maintenance was performed and the cab's odometer reading at that time.

A Final Note: The Art of Identifying Data Relationships

The usefulness of a database system is in large part determined by how closely the data relationships described in the database schema match the actual relationships between data objects in the real world. However, there is no formula or set procedure for identifying those relationships and their meaning. For that reason, many people consider this part of database design more of an art than a science.

Much of the information needed to identify entities and their relationships can be found in the system requirements document. However, there is no substitute for in-depth knowledge of the database environment, the entities within it, and how they interact. This type of information usually surfaces during systems analysis interviews. If it does not, the person performing the database design must return to people actually working in the database environment to gather additional information.

> **By the way:** As frustrating as it may seem, there is no formula for quickly understanding a database environment so that you can identify the data relationships. You must spend enough time in the environment, interviewing and observing people, so that you personally understand what data are used and how they relate.

Summary

Three types of relationships can be defined between data objects:

- One-to-one: When a one-to-one relationship exists between data object A and data object B, zero or one occurrences of B will be associated with each occurrence of A.
- One-to-many: When a one-to-many relationship exists between data object A and data object B, zero, one, or more occurrences of B will be associated with each occurrence of A.
- Many-to-many: When a many-to-many relationship exists between data object A and data object B, zero, one, or more occurrences of B will be associated with one or more occurrences of A.

The Entity-Relationship model is a graphic technique that is used to represent relationships between data objects in a database environment. Entity-relationship diagrams are general expressions of data relationships that do not rely on any formal data model. The major elements of an entity-relationship (ER) diagram are:

- Entity: An entity is a data object. It is represented in an ER diagram as a rectangle.
- Attribute: An attribute is a data item that describes an entity.
- Relationship: A relationship between two entities is represented as a diamond. Relationships cannot have attributes.
- Composite entity: A composite entity is an entity that is created from the relationship between two simple entities. Composite entities can have attributes. They are therefore created whenever attributes apply to the relationship between two entities rather than to the entities themselves.

References

Chen and Associates. 1988. *E-R Designer Reference Manual.* Chen and Associates.

Chen, Peter P-S. 1976. "The Entity-Relationship Model—Toward a Unified View of Data." *ACM Transactions of Database Systems.* 1:9-36.

Chen, Peter P-S. 1977. *The Entity-Relationship Approach to Logical Data Base Design.* Q.E.D. Information Sciences, Data Base Monograph Series no. 6.

Fleming, C. C. and B. von Halle. 1990. "An Overview of Logical Data Modeling." *Data Resource Management.* 1(1):5–15.

Sandifer, Alice and Barbara Von Halle. 1991 "Business Rule Modeling: An Elusive Yet Powerful Asset." *Database Programming and Design.* 4(1):11–14.

Teory, Tobey J. 1990. *Database Modeling and Design: The Entity Relationship Approach.* Morgan Kaufmann.

Exercises

Look again at the interview transcripts in Appendixes A and B (East Coast Aquarium and the Office of Margaret Holmes, D.M.D.). Create an entity-relationship diagram for each organization. (It will almost certainly be necessary to break the diagrams onto more than one page.) Each diagram should include:

- Simple entities (represent each entity as a labeled rectangle)
- Attributes (show all attributes that describe data objects)
- Attribute names (give each attribute a descriptive name)
- Attribute domain (indicate the type of data to be stored in a given attribute)
- Relationships (represent relationships between entities as labeled diamonds)
- Relationship types (indicate the direction of all one-to-many relationships)
- Composite entities (create a composite entity for each many-to-many relationship to reduce it to two one-to-many relationships)

4

The Relational Data Model

A *data model* is a formal way of describing the relationships in a database to a database management system. With only one or two exceptions, microcomputer DBMSs are based on the relational data model.

This chapter looks at the fundamental concepts behind the relational data model. In it, you will see how data relationships are represented and be introduced to how those relationships are used to gain access to data. You will also learn about rules placed on data to help maintain data integrity. The chapter ends by considering exactly what qualifies as a relational database management system and what impact those criteria should have on your choice of software.

The relational model was first proposed by E. F. Codd in 1970 (Codd, 1970). Codd took most of his ideas from mathematics. In mathematics, a *relation* is a table with a very precise definition. For most people, however, knowledge of the rigorous math isn't essential to being able to design good databases.

Relations

A relational database views all data as if they were stored in two-dimensional tables comprised of columns and rows. As an example, consider Figure 4.1. The table in that figure contains data about Small Bank's branches, customers, accounts, and account transactions. The table itself—not the data it holds—is the relation. When a table holds data, it is called an *instance* of a relation, since any given relation can theoretically hold an infinite variety and volume of data values.

Primary key

Branch	Customer #	Account #	Transaction #	Trans. Date	Amount
Central	10010	000-001	3333333001	02/01/93	+100.00
Central	10010	000-002	3333333002	02/01/93	-25.00
Central	10010	000-002	3333333003	02/01/93	-52.50
Central	10010	000-002	3333333004	02/02/93	+1500.00
Central	10010	000-003	3333333005	02/02/93	+100.00
Eastside	10020	000-009	3333333006	02/02/93	+2599.00
Eastside	10020	000-009	3333333007	02/02/93	-25.00
Eastside	10020	000-009	3333333008	02/03/93	-10.00
Central	10030	000-006	3333333009	02/03/93	+525.00
Central	10040	000-010	3333333010	02/03/93	-824.00
Central	10040	000-010	3333333011	02/03/93	-115.00
Westlake	10010	000-004	3333333012	02/03/93	+190.25
Westlake	10050	000-018	3333333013	02/03/93	-190.25
Westlake	10050	000-018	3333333014	02/03/93	-165.99
Westlake	10050	000-005	3333333015	02/04/93	+25.00
Eastside	10060	000-012	3333333016	02/04/93	-40.99
Eastside	10070	000-017	3333333017	02/04/93	-886.00
Eastside	10070	000-017	3333333018	02/04/93	+1920.23

Figure 4.1   A relation containing Small Bank's transaction data—transaction numbers are unique

A relational database is made up of a collection of relations. Logically, each table is a separate entity. (Some relational DBMSs store each relation as a separate file. Others put the data for all relations in the database in a single file or in a set of files completely unrelated to the logical structure). Regardless of how the data are physically stored, the relations are logically separate tables.

The tables that are actually stored by a relational database are called *base tables*. During processing, the DBMS may create other tables that are not stored on disk, but are retained in main memory only until the application using them finishes. These temporary tables are often referred to as *virtual tables*.

Relations have a number of distinguishing characteristics. First of all, each relation has a name. In Figure 4.1, the relation is called *Activity*, since it contains data on activity against Small Bank's accounts. Relation names are arbitrary, but generally they reflect the type of data stored in the relation.

A relation is made up of a collection of attributes. Like an attribute in an ER diagram, an *attribute* in a relation is a data item that describes an entity about which data are to be stored. When you look at a relation, the attributes form the columns. In Figure 4.1, *Branch, Customer #, Account #, Transaction #, Transaction Date*, and *Amount* are attributes. Each attribute has a name which is generally suggestive of the data that attribute will contain and a domain that specifies the possible values for that attribute. Attribute names must be unique within each relation but can be repeated in different relations in the same database.

> **By the way:** A domain is an example of a *constraint* on a relation. A constraint is a restriction, or rule, that governs which data can be stored in a relation. You will be introduced to other constraints in this chapter.

The order in which attributes are defined is irrelevant. Attributes can be viewed in any order without changing the meaning of the data. By the same token, you don't need to view every attribute in a relation; you can view any subset of attributes at any time.

Each row in a relation is called a *tuple*. Duplicate tuples are not permitted. It is important to realize that while the rule against duplicate tuples exists as part of relational database theory, that does not mean that relational database management systems will automatically ensure that each tuple is unique; it may be up to the user or application programmer to enforce this constraint.

Although new rows are typically added to the bottom of a relation, they can be viewed in any order without changing the meaning of the data. A subset of rows can also be viewed without affecting stored data.

By the way: There are two sets of terminology commonly used to describe relations and tables. You can use the theoretical terms *relation, attribute,* and *tuple* or the equivalent practical terms *table, column,* and *row.* Both sets of terms are used interchangeably in the database world, although *table, column,* and *row* are becoming more common in practice because most people find them more intuitive than the older, theoretical terms.

Primary Keys

Each relation in a relational database has a *primary key.* A primary key is a single attribute or a combination of attributes whose values uniquely identify each tuple in the relation. In other words, while the values of other attributes may be repeated in the relation, primary keys must be unique.

For an example, refer again to Figure 4.1. The *Customer #* attribute cannot serve as a primary key. Customer numbers are repeated each time an account belonging to that customer records some activity. *Account #* also cannot serve as the primary key, since the account number is repeated for every action posted to that account. However, if we know that Small Bank never reuses transaction numbers, then the *Transaction #* attribute can be designated as the primary key.

What if Small Bank's transaction numbers are duplicated? Assume, for example, that transaction numbers are unique only within one single account (see Figure 4.2). In that case, *Transaction #* is not sufficient to uniquely identify each tuple in the relation. Instead, it is the combination of *Account #* and *Transaction #* that is not repeated. The primary key for the relation must then consist of the *concatenation* of the two attributes. Concatenation simply means that the value of one attribute is viewed as if it were pasted on the end of the other to form a single value. Most DBMSs do not physically concatenate the values of multiple attributes that form primary keys; rather, they logically view the values as if they were one.

You may have noticed that which attribute or combination of attributes are needed to form the primary key depends a great deal on the database environment. It is often very difficult to decide which attributes will contain unique

Primary key = Account # + Transaction #

Branch	Customer #	Account #	Transaction #	Trans. Date	Amount
Central	10010	000-001	3333333001	02/01/93	+100.00
Central	10010	000-002	3333333055	02/01/93	-25.00
Central	10010	000-002	3333333056	02/01/93	-52.50
Central	10010	000-002	3333333057	02/02/93	+1500.00
Central	10010	000-003	3333333057	02/02/93	+100.00
Eastside	10020	000-009	3333333006	02/02/93	+2599.00
Eastside	10020	000-009	3333333007	02/02/93	-25.00
Eastside	10020	000-009	3333333008	02/03/93	-10.00
Central	10030	000-006	3333333012	02/03/93	+525.00
Central	10040	000-010	3333333010	02/03/93	-824.00
Central	10040	000-010	3333333011	02/03/93	-115.00
Westlake	10010	000-004	3333333081	02/03/93	+190.25
Westlake	10050	000-018	3333333013	02/03/93	-190.25
Westlake	10050	000-018	3333333014	02/03/93	-165.99
Westlake	10050	000-005	3333333014	02/04/93	+25.00
Eastside	10060	000-012	3333333044	02/04/93	-40.99
Eastside	10070	000-017	3333333017	02/04/93	-886.00
Eastside	10070	000-017	3333333018	02/04/93	+1920.23

Duplicate transaction numbers

Figure 4.2   A relation containing Small Bank's transaction data—transaction numbers are not unique

values without knowing the rules under which the data operate. For example, there is no way to determine a primary key for Small Bank's data without knowing how transaction numbers are assigned. For the remaining examples from Small Bank's database, however, we will assume that transaction numbers are unique.

Figure 4.3 contains another version of a relational database for Small Bank (this happens to be a "better" design than that in Figure 4.1 and Figure 4.2; you'll understand why later). It consists of five tables: Branch, Customer, Branch Patronage, Account, and Transaction.

Branch

Branch Name	Branch Address	Branch Phone	Branch Hours
Eastside	4232 E. 44th, Newtown 02311	555-4232	0900-1200 M-S
Westlake	109 Lake Street, Newtown 02315	555-0109	0830-1630 M-F
Central	100 Central Square, Newtown 02311	555-0100	0830-1800 M-S

Customers

Customer #	Customer Name	Customer Address	Customer Phone	SSN
10010	Jones, Samuel	105 W. 99th, Newtown 02899	555-0105	123-45-6789
10020	Abrams, Max	2204 Nox Hill, Newtown 02845	555-2204	234-56-7890
10030	Cohen, Esther	39 Summer, Newtown 02845	555-0039	345-67-8901
10040	Khan, Satya	1001 N. 54th, Newtown 02898	555-1001	456-78-9012
10050	Brown, Judith	RR1 Box 99C, Rural City 02811	555-9900	567-89-0123
10060	Wales, Miranda	33 Summer, Apt # 18, Newtown 02945	555-0033	678-90-1234
10070	Smith, Samuel	RR6 Box 125, Rural City 02811	555-1250	789-09-2345

Account

Account #	Customer #	Branch	Account Type	Date Opened	Current Balance
000-001	10010	Central	NOW	10/10/82	2568.12
000-002	10010	Central	CD	02/02/92	10520.00
000-003	10010	Central	Safe Deposit	05/15/56	NULL
000-009	10020	Eastside	NOW	10/21/89	512.89
000-006	10030	Central	NOW	06/30/91	3888.00
000-010	10040	Central	Savings	01/05/51	25.00
000-004	10010	Westlake	Loan	11/25/92	15085.85
000-018	10050	Westlake	NOW	10/31/87	2500.12
000-005	10050	Westlake	CD	04/18/92	5012.89
000-012	10060	Eastside	NOW	10/10/90	386.00
000-017	10070	Eastside	NOW	07/16/92	259.00

Branch Patronage

Branch Name	Customer #
Central	10010
Eastside	10020
Central	10030
Central	10040
Westlake	10010
Westlake	10050
Eastside	10060
Eastside	10070

Transaction

Transaction #	Account #	Trans. Date	Amount
3333333001	000-001	02/01/93	+100.00
3333333002	000-002	02/01/93	-25.00
3333333003	000-002	02/01/93	-52.50
3333333004	000-002	02/02/93	+1500.00
3333333005	000-002	02/02/93	+100.00
3333333006	000-009	02/02/93	+2599.99
3333333007	000-009	02/02/93	-25.00
3333333008	000-009	02/03/93	-10.00
3333333009	000-006	02/03/93	+525.00
3333333010	000-010	02/03/93	-824.00
3333333011	000-010	02/03/93	-115.00
3333333012	000-004	02/03/93	+190.25
3333333013	000-018	02/03/93	-190.25
3333333014	000-018	02/03/93	-165.99
3333333015	000-005	02/04/93	+25.00
3333333016	000-012	02/04/93	-40.99
3333333017	000-017	02/04/93	-886.00
3333333018	000-017	02/04/93	+1920.23

Figure 4.3   Another version of Small Bank's Transaction data

The Account relation contains data that describes each account: the customer that owns it, the branch at which it is carried, the date it was opened and its current balance. The primary key is *Account #*, an arbitrary unique identification number assigned to each account when it is opened.

The Branch relation describes each of Small Bank's three branches. Because the branch names are unique, the *Branch Name* column can be used as the primary key.

The Branch Patronage relation pairs customers and the branches at which they have opened accounts. Because each customer can have many account at many branches and each branch carries accounts for many customers, the primary key can't be either *Customer #* or *Branch Name*. (Notice in Figure 4.3 that there are duplicate values in each column.) The primary key must therefore be the concatenation of the two attributes. This relation is what is known as *all-key*, since no attributes exist in the relation that are not part of the primary key.

The Transaction relation describes activity posted to accounts. Its primary key is *Transaction #*, an arbitrary sequence number assigned to transactions as they occur.

The choice of a primary key for the Customers relation is not so clear. *Customer #* alone would be acceptable as a primary key; it is an arbitrary, unique identifier. So might the social security number. By the same token, a concatenated key, consisting of *Customer #* and *SSN* also meets the requirement of uniquely identifying each tuple.

The concatenated key is *redundant*. In other words, it contains more attributes than are absolutely necessary to make a valid primary key; if you remove either attribute from the key, the key will still be valid. Primary keys, however, must be nonredundant. That means that they must include the fewest number of attributes needed to uniquely identify a tuple. The concatenated key is therefore not an acceptable primary key.

Customer # and *SSN* are what is known as *candidate keys*, since either could serve as the primary key. In a situation where more than one candidate key exists in a relation, select the key which consists of the fewest number of attributes and which is least likely to be *null* (which designates an unknown value). In this case, *Customer #* is the better choice. Some people may not have social security numbers, in which case the *SSN* attribute might be null.

> **By the way:** In general, social security numbers make lousy primary keys. Not only can they be null, but they aren't necessarily unique. The Social Security Administration has been known to issue duplicate social security numbers. In addition, people often make errors when giving their social security numbers.

Null is a value. It is not the same as zero or a blank. Rather, it means that the value of an attribute is unknown. If one instance of an attribute that is part of a primary key is null, there's no problem. However, if some other instance also has an unknown value, then the primary key loses its property of uniqueness. Therefore, the relational model states that "no part of a primary key can be null." This rule is an example of an integrity constraint. This particular integrity constraint is known as *entity integrity* (the other major integrity constraint—referential integrity—is discussed shortly).

If you think again about the primary keys in Small Bank's relations, you will notice that there are three arbitrary primary keys: the customer number, the account number, and the transaction number. Small Bank assigns values to these keys sequentially as customers, accounts, and transactions are added to the database. The numbers that make up these keys have absolutely no meaning; they are simply unique identifiers.

However, it is often tempting to use meaningful data as primary keys. For example, many mail-order firms use your telephone number as your customer number. Such a primary key is *information-bearing* and in most cases should not be used. There are several problems with information-bearing keys. First, the value of an information-bearing key can change. If you move, your phone number is likely to change. A mail-order firm that uses your phone number as your customer number is faced with either changing all the data it has stored about you to match the new phone number or accidentally entering you as a new customer. Second, an information-bearing key over time may not always identify the same occurrence of an entity. After a while, the telephone company reuses phone numbers. Your new phone number may be the same as the previous phone of another customer of the same mail-order firm. If the company hasn't changed the phone number of the other customer, then you may accidentally become associated with data that relate to the other customer.

Finally, information bearing keys may be null. For example, a mail-order firm often does business with people who mail, rather than telephone, their orders. Such orders may not be accompanied by a phone number.

Foreign Keys and Referential Integrity

In Figure 4.1 and Figure 4.2, it is very easy to see which transaction is related to which account and which account belongs to which customer. The relationships in Figure 4.3 may not appear so obvious. Consider, however, that if you look at pairs of relations in Figure 4.3, some have attributes in common. For example, the attribute *Account #* appears in Account and Transaction; *Customer #* appears in Customers, Account, and Branch Patronage.

This duplication is no accident. It is the technique used by relational databases to show relationships between entities. If, for example, customer number 10010 has four accounts, each of which appears in Account, then the data associated with customer number 10010 in Customers applies to each account in Account. In other words, if the attribute *Customer #* has duplicate values in both Account and Customers, we can assume that all data values in tuples with the same customer number refer to the same individual, regardless of the relation in which they appear.

The attribute *Customer #* in Account is a *foreign key.* A foreign key is an attribute (or the concatenation of two or more attributes) in one relation that is defined on the same logical domain as the primary key in some other relation. This means that the columns in the tables do not necessarily need the same names; they need only contain logically equivalent data. A foreign key can be a nonkey attribute (in other words, it isn't part of the primary key of its table) or it can be part of a concatenated key; however, it is not the entire primary key of its table.

For example, if a column called *Cust #* contains customer numbers for Small Bank in relation A, and if the *Cust_Numb* column of relation B also contains customer numbers for Small Bank, a primary key-foreign key relationship could exist between them. Matching values between foreign and primary keys represent the relationships between the entities described in relations. In a fully relational database, there are no physical connections between relations (in other words, no pointers), just the logical connections made by duplicate values.

To get a listing of a customer's name, address and account numbers, a relational database uses the Customers relation to retrieve the customer's name and address. Although the customer number is not a part of the output, it must also be retrieved. That number is then used to search the Account relation to find all accounts belonging to the specific customer.

There are a number of foreign keys in Figure 4.3:

- Branch patronage
  - *Branch name* is a foreign key that references the primary key of Branch.
  - *Customer #* is a foreign key that references the primary key of Customers.
- Account
  - *Customer #* is a foreign key that references the primary key of Customers.
  - *Branch* is a foreign key that references the primary key of Branch.
- Transaction
  - *Account #* is a foreign key that references the primary key of Account.

Because foreign keys reference primary keys, it is essential that a primary key value exist somewhere in the database for every foreign key value. This is known as *referential integrity*. The constraint is usually stated as: "every non-null foreign key value must reference an existing primary key value."

> **By the way:** As long as a foreign key isn't part of the primary key of its table, it can be null.

Referential integrity is essential to the logical consistency of a database. Consider, for example, what would happen if a row containing a customer number of 10090 were inserted into the Account table in Figure 4.3. When the time came to prepare monthly account statements, an application program would attempt to match 10090 with a row in Customers to retrieve the name and address of the account owner. Because no matching row exists in Customers, Small Bank has no way to know to whom the account statement should be sent. To prevent this problem from arising, Small Bank places a referential integrity constraint on the Account table. Each time someone attempts to add a row to Account, the DBMS verifies that a matching customer number exists in Customers before permitting the addition.

> **By the way:** Not all DBMSs can store primary key–foreign key relationships in their data dictionary. Handling data integrity (including referential integrity) is discussed in Chapter 11.

A Notation to Describe Relations

There is a simple notation that is often used to describe a relation. For example, the Customers relation from Figure 4.3 would be written:

    Customers (Customer #, Customer Name, Customer Address,
       Customer Phone, SSN)

The name of the relation is written first, followed in parentheses by the names of the attributes which make up the relation. Although the order of the attributes in a relation is unimportant, the attributes that form the primary key are usually listed first. The primary key attributes are also underlined.

The other four relations from Figure 4.3 are written:

    Branch (Branch name, Branch Address, Branch Phone, Branch Hours)
    Branch Patronage (Branch Name, Customer #)
    Account (Account #, Customer #, Branch, Account Type, Date Opened,
       Current Balance)
    Transaction (Transaction #, Account #, Trans. Date, Amount)

Relations for the Federated Taxi Company

Data to monitor Federated Taxi Company's cab scheduling and maintenance might be stored in the following set of relations:

    Cab (Cab #, Make/Model, Year, Plate, Current Odom., Cab Status,
       Condition)
    Driver (Driver #, Driver Name, Driver Address, Driver Phone #,
       License #, Exp. Date, Driver Status)

Shift (<u>Shift name</u>, <u>Wkdate</u>)
Shift driven (<u>Shift name</u>, <u>Wkdate</u>, <u>Cab #</u>, Driver #, Wkflag,
    Starting Odom., Ending Odom.)
Incident (<u>Inci. Date</u>, <u>Inci. Time</u>, <u>Driver#</u>, Cab #, Inci. Type,
    Inci. Details)
Maintenance activity (<u>Maint. Type</u>)
Maintenance performed (<u>Cab #</u>, <u>Maint. Date</u>, <u>Maint. Type</u>,
    Maint. Odom.)

The relation Cab stores basic information about each vehicle. This is information that doesn't change very often. The one exception is the current odometer reading (*Current Odom.*); this is updated every time a cab returns from a shift. The primary key in this relation is *Cab #*. These are numbers assigned to each cab when it is purchased. The cab numbers are also painted on the side of each cab.

At first glance, it might appear that *Plate* is a candidate key for the relation Cab. Each cab has only one plate number and no two cabs have the same plate. However, in FTC's operations there is a chance that the value of *Plate* could be null. If a cab is badly damaged and requires extensive repairs for which maintenance must wait for parts, the cab will sit in the garage unregistered, without a license plate. (In the state where FTC is located, a vehicle's license plates must be turned in to the Motor Vehicles Division if the car isn't going to be registered and insured; in fact, the only way to cancel insurance is to turn in the plate.) Therefore, since the value of *Plate* may be null, it is not suitable as a primary key.

To make matters worse, occasionally license plates change; it's not unusual for a state to replace all license plates. Although there is nothing that says a primary key value shouldn't change, changing the value of a primary key that has foreign key references to it throughout the database forces all those foreign keys to be updated when the primary key changes. Therefore, using a primary key whose value is likely to change opens up the possibility of major referential integrity problems.

Static information about drivers is stored in the relation Driver. Since two drivers could have the same name, each is assigned a unique driver number (*Driver #*). That number, which consists of only one attribute, makes a far more convenient key than, for example, name and address.

The Shift relation describes the date and shifts on which FTC sends or will send cars on the road. Because there are up to three shifts each day, the primary key must be the concatenation of the date (*WkDate*) and the shift (*Shift Name*).

The relation Shift Driven stores data about which drivers have driven or are scheduled to drive a shift. There are two candidate keys in the relation: the concatenation of *Shift Name, WkDate*, and *Cab #* or the concatenation of *Shift Name, WkDate*, and *Driver #*. If we assume that a driver drives only one cab during a shift and that a cab is driven by only one driver during a shift, then either candidate key works as the primary key. Nonetheless, one of the candidate keys must be designated as the primary key.

The attribute *WkFlag* is what is known as a *Boolean*. It can take only one of two values—*true* or *false*. When a driver reserves a cab for a shift, *WkFlag* is set to *false*. If the driver reports for the shift, then *WkFlag* is changed to *true*. Then, to discover which drivers failed to show up for their scheduled shifts, FTC's scheduling clerk can ask the DBMS to retrieve all rows from Shift Driven with a date and shift that have already passed and a *WkFlag* value of *false*.

The relation Incident contains one row for every traffic citation and accident that occur. Since it is important to FTC to know exactly when incidents occurred, the relation includes not only the number of the cab involved, but the associated driver, date, and time. Because it is possible for more than one cab to be involved in an incident on any date and time, the primary key consists of the three attributes *Inci. Date, Inci. Time*, and *Cab #*. Note, however, that the concatenation of *Inci. Date, Inci. Time,* and *Driver #* is an equally valid candidate key.

The relation Maintenance Activity stores a list of all the types of maintenance that can be performed on a cab. The actual maintenance done to cabs is recorded in Maintenance Performed. Since more than one type of maintenance can be performed on a single cab on a single day, the primary key must consist of the three attributes *Cab #, Maint. Date*, and *Maint. Type*.

There are several foreign keys in this set of relations, some of which are concatenated:

- Shift Driven
  - The concatenation of *Shift Name* and *WkDate* is a foreign key that references the concatenated primary key of Shift.
  - *Cab #* is a foreign key that references the primary key of Cab.
  - *Driver #* is a foreign key that references the primary key of Driver.

- Incident
    - *Cab#* is a foreign key that references the primary key of Cab.
    - *Driver #* is a foreign key that references the primary key of Driver.

> **By the way:** Logically, whenever a row is inserted into Incident, the DBMS or an application program should verify that the concatenation of *Inci. Date, Driver #*, and *Cab #* matches an existing row in Shift Driven; this ensures that the driver and cab were indeed on the road when the incident occurred. However, because this concatenation isn't the primary key of Shift Driven, the reference doesn't represent referential integrity. In this case, it's a very good thing. That means FTC can every so often delete rows from Shift Driven and still retain incident data, without violating referential integrity.

- Maintenance performed
    - *Cab #* is a foreign key that references the primary key of Cab.
    - *Maint. Type* is a foreign key that references the primary key of Maintenance Activity.

User Views

Relational DBMSs typically allow application programmers and users to create customized subsets of the base tables that contain only the parts of the relational schema that a given application will use. These subsets are known as *views.*

A view consists of a query that, when executed, creates a virtual table. The query that defines a view may select and rearrange the attributes in the base tables in any way that makes logical sense to the user. It is therefore possible to use views as a security device. By including only non-sensitive attributes and/or rows in a particular view and restricting a group of users to that view, users can be prevented from gaining access to data to which they have no rights.

The data in a view table are not stored on disk; they exist only as a virtual table kept temporarily in main memory. View definitions, however, are stored. Then, whenever a user invokes a view, the virtual table to support that view is created from the base tables. Because a user has only one virtual table in his or her work area at a time, the view's table is replaced when the user issues another data manipulation command to the DBMS. The beauty of a view is that it is always current—the DBMS reassembles its contents from current data each time it is used.

The "Fully Relational" DBMS

If you spend a bit of time looking at software ads in computer and business publications, you'll notice that virtually every software package that handles data in tables claims to be a relational DBMS. Some even claim to be "fully relational." None, however, conform to the theoretical definition of a "fully relational" DBMS.

The criteria which a DBMS must meet in order to be considered fully relational were explained in an important two-part article written by E. F. Codd (Codd, 1985). The criteria include 12 rules which describe how a fully relational DBMS should define, store, retrieve, and otherwise manage data.

Rule 1: The information rule

> "All information in a relational data base is represented explicitly at the logical level in exactly one way—by values in tables."

On the surface, Rule 1 seems relatively simple—the major characteristic of the relational model is the tabular representation of data. However, Rule 1 contains the phrase "all information." This implies that not only must data be stored in tables, but any other information used by the DBMS as well. This includes the description of the schema (table and attribute definitions), integrity constraints, actions to be taken when constraints are violated, and security information (descriptions of which users have what rights to which data objects within the database). Users, assuming they have the appropriate security clearance, should be able to query these tables in the same way that they query tables that store data.

Microcomputer DBMSs that claim to be relational do store data in tables. However, many generally fail to meet this rule for two reasons: they don't store other aspects of the database environment in tables, and they rely on data structures other than tables to represent data relationships. In particular, many microcomputer DBMSs require the user to set up pointers between tables to indicate a one-to-many or many-to-many relationship. Although the relational data model allows a DBMS to use pointers to implement data relationships, such pointers should be "under the covers"; users and application programmers should be unaware of such data structures. The only data structure users and application programmers should handle is tables.

On the other hand, a DBMS that uses SQL as its query language does adhere to rule 1. All information, even security information, is stored in tables in the data dictionary. Any authorized user can query the data dictionary using standard SQL syntax.

Rule 2: Guaranteed access rule

> "Each and every datum (atomic value) in a relational data base is guaranteed to be logically accessible by resorting to a combination of table name, primary key value and column name."

Rule 2 simply states that it is possible to retrieve each individual piece of data stored in a relational database by specifying the name of the table in which it is stored, the column in which it is stored (in other words, the attribute name), and the primary key that identifies the row in which it is stored.

The important consequence of this rule is that primary keys must be unique. If they are not, then we cannot be certain that a primary key value will identify the precise row in a table that we wish to retrieve. Instead, we could only be assured of retrieving any row that contained given primary key values. Therefore, any microcomputer DBMS that does not somehow enforce the requirement that primary keys be unique will violate Rule 2.

Rule 3: Systematic treatment of null values

> "Null values (distinct from the empty character string or a string of blank characters and distinct from zero or any other number) are supported in the fully relational DBMS for representing missing information in a systematic way, independent of data type."

An attribute is given a value of null to indicate that its value is unknown. A fully relational DBMS permits the inclusion of null as a value for non-primary-key attributes regardless of data type. It will also have some scheme for handling the nulls when a user retrieves data.

At first it may not be apparent why the handling of nulls is important, but consider the situation where a user formulates a SQL query against the FTC database that is based on a negative:

```
SELECT Driver_Name
FROM Driver
WHERE Driver_Status <> "do not reserve";
```

This query retrieves the names of all drivers who are eligible to reserve cabs (in other words, the value of Driver_Status is something other than "do not reserve"). What should the DBMS do with tuples that have a value of null for Driver_Status? Null is not equal to "do not reserve." Should those tuples be retrieved by this query, or should they be excluded? Rule 3 makes no statement about exactly how the nulls should be handled, but insists that the DBMS have some policy about them. It is equally valid to include or exclude nulls from retrievals. Whichever the DBMS designers decide to do, it must be consistent and it must be coded into the DBMS itself.

Many microcomputer DBMSs do not support nulls. However, any DBMS that supports SQL as its query language does recognize and handle columns containing null values.

Rule 4: Dynamic on-line catalog based on the relational model

> "The data base description is represented at the logical level in the same way as ordinary data, so that authorized users can apply the same relational language to its interrogation as they apply to regular data."

Rule 4 reiterates the idea that all information in a relational database, in this case the catalog (the relational term for a data dictionary), must be stored in tables that can be queried in the same way as tables that store data. It also specifies that the catalog must be on-line and dynamic. That means that when an authorized user makes some change to the schema, that change will be automatically propagated into the structure of the base tables. For example, to add an attribute to a base table, the user simply issues a command which adds a row to one of the relations in the catalog, indicating that another attribute is part of the table in question. The user does not need to issue another command to add a column to the base table; that action is initiated by the DBMS when the change is made to the catalog.

Many microcomputer DBMSs do not support true relational catalogs. However, SQL-based DBMSs do maintain a set of data dictionary tables. Such DBMSs are called *data-dictionary driven*, because all changes to the structure of the database and all requests for data access require access to the data dictionary tables before any action is performed against the base tables.

Rule 5: Comprehensive data sublanguage rule

"A relational system may support several languages and various modes of terminal use (for example, the fill-in-the-blanks mode). However, there must be at least one language whose statements are expressible, per some well-defined syntax, as character strings and that is comprehensive in supporting all of the following items:

- data definition
- view definition
- data manipulation (interactive and by program)
- integrity constraints
- transaction boundaries (begin, commit and rollback)"

Rule 5 requires a fully relational DBMS to support a command-driven query language, regardless of any other types of command structure present in the DBMS. SQL docs meet this requirement. However, the requirement of a command-line syntax excludes any DBMS that has a graphic, as opposed to text-based, interface. Many of today's microcomputer DBMSs (in particular, those written specifically for the Macintosh), provide the functionality of a text-based DBMS, but do so using icons, windows, and other graphic tools. In the strictest sense, DBMSs with graphic user interfaces do not meet this rule, although some might argue that they nonetheless meet the spirit of the rule.

Rule 5 requires that a DBMS's query language be able to handle data definition (the definition of the base tables that make up a database's schema) and view definition (the definition and storage of the queries that define views). In addition, it should be able to perform data manipulation (storing, modifying, deleting, and retrieving data), both from the command line and embedded in a program.

A database designer must also be able to use the DBMS's query language to define integrity constraints. Keep in mind, however, that this rule doesn't specify exactly which constraints must be supported.

Rule 5 also mentions something called a *transaction*. In a multi-user environment, actions against a database performed by application programs may be contained within transactions. A transaction is defined as a unit of work presented to a database. A DBMS query language that adheres to Rule 5 supports statements that indicate where a transaction begins and where it should end. Transactions can end in one of two ways. If they end in an expected manner, then they are *committed* (all changes to the database are made permanent); if they end in an unexpected or undesirable manner, then they are *rolled back* (all changes to the database are undone and the database is restored to the state it was in before the transaction began). Transactions are discussed in more detail in Chapter 12.

Most single-user microcomputer DBMSs are not transaction-based. Therefore, their query languages do not contain syntax to mark transaction boundaries. SQL, however, provides statements to explicitly end transactions (the start of a transaction is implicit in a number of SQL commands).

Rule 6: View updating rule

> "All views that are theoretically updatable are also updatable by the system."

Rule 6 states that whenever a user creates a view that meets the criteria for updatability, the DBMS must be able to propagate those updates into the base tables. However, not all views can be used to modify data. Each DBMS that supports views has criteria that define a theoretically updatable view. For most of today's DBMSs, updatable views must be based on only one base table and must include all columns that have been defined as "not null" (primary key columns and any other columns that must have a value before a row is stored).

> **By the way:** The criteria for an updatable view vary from one DBMS to another. A very few are beginning to support updating on multi-table views. Consult your product documentation for details.

Some microcomputer DBMSs fail to adhere to this rule simply because they don't allow views. SQL, however, supports views that conform to relational database theory. Views are defined with a single SQL command and implemented as virtual tables. View definitions are stored within the data dictionary.

Rule 7: High-level insert, update and delete

> "The capability of handling a base relation or a derived relation as a single operand applies not only to the retrieval of data but also to the insertion, update and deletion of data."

Rule 7 states that a fully relational DBMS must support syntax for adding, modifying, and deleting data that operate on an entire table. The DBMSs that use SQL as a query language adhere to this rule. DBMSs with proprietary query languages and graphic user interfaces vary in the extent to which they can update more than one row at a time.

Rule 8: Physical data independence

> "Applications programs and terminal activities remain logically unimpaired whenever any changes are made in either storage representation or access methods."

Rule 8 requires that the operation of applications programs and interactive commands be unaffected by any changes made in the way data are physically stored. When microcomputer DBMSs fail this rule, they tend to fail spectacularly. Some store each table in a single physical file. To locate the file, a user or application program must know the file's path name. If the file is moved to another disk directory, a user or application program won't be able to find it. Microcomputer DBMSs that store all their data in one file, however, do adhere to this rule.

Rule 9: Logical data independence

> "Application programs and terminal activities remain logically unimpaired when information-preserving changes of any kind that theoretically permit unimpairment are made to the base tables."

A DBMS that adheres to Rule 9 permits changes to the schema without affecting activities that make no use of the portion of the schema that was changed. For example, adding an attribute to a base table should not disrupt programs or interactive commands that have no use for the new attribute.

In some circumstances most DBMSs fail this rule. All the DBMSs with command-line interfaces support retrieval syntax to display all the attributes from a relation with a single keyword. If an attribute is added to a relation, then re-issuing the same command displays the additional attribute as well, regardless of whether it is actually required. A programmer can get around the problem by avoiding the use of the "display all attributes" syntax and always specifying exactly which attributes should be displayed. However, this ability to enforce Rule 9 in applications software does not mean that the DBMS meets the rule; logical data independence must be enforced by the DBMS.

Rule 10: Integrity independence

> "Integrity constraints specific to a particular relational data base must be definable in the relational data sublanguage and storable in the catalog, not in the application programs."

> "A minimum of the following two integrity constraints must be supported:
>
> • Entity integrity: No component of a primary key is allowed to have a null value.
> • Referential integrity: For each distinct nonnull foreign key value in a relational data base, there must exist a matching primary key value from the same domain."

As you will see later in this book, it is possible to enforce integrity constraints by using applications programs and other tricks. However, doing so does not meet Rule 10. To meet Rule 10, a DBMS must permit the integrity constraints (and actions to be taken when the constraints are violated) to be stored in the catalog.

Microcomputer DBMSs vary considerably in how well they support integrity rules, from absolutely no support for integrity rules to a flexible syntax for defining any rules a user might need. The SQL standard has no syntax for referential integrity, although many implementations have added syntax to support it. SQL also does not fully support primary keys. Columns can be designated "not null" (a value is required), but tables can be created without any "not null" columns.

Rule 11: Distribution independence

"A relational DBMS has distribution independence."

A distributed database is one where the data are stored at more than one physical location. This is different from a multiuser database, where remote users access a database stored in a single, centralized location. Rule 11 indicates that whenever a database is distributed, users should be unaware of that fact. They must be able to work with the database as if it were centralized.

There is little microcomputer software to fully support a distributed database. Although it is relatively easy to retrieve data from a distributed database (even those with pieces that come from different vendors), updating distributed data presents significant problems.

Rule 12: Nonsubversion rule

"If a relational system has a low-level (single-record-at-a-time) language, that low-level language cannot be used to subvert or bypass the integrity rules or constraints expressed in the higher level relational language (multiple-records-at-a-time)."

Rule 12 states that a DBMS musn't permit integrity constraints to be bypassed through use of a data manipulation language that operates on a single row at a time. The major implication of this rule is that all access to a relational DBMS must be through the data dictionary, regardless of whether the access is requested with a query language or with some other low-level access language. The data dictionary must enforce integrity constraints regardless of how the user or application program requests actions against the database.

Finally, there is a caveat to the 12 relational rules known as "Rule Zero":

> "For any system that is advertised as, or claimed to be, a relational data base management system, that system must be able to manage data entirely through its relational capabilities."

In other words, regardless of how well a DBMS meets the twelve relational criteria discussed above, it isn't relational if it "cheats" by performing even one data management function in a manner not described by those rules.

At the time he wrote his 12 rules, Codd believed that there weren't any "fully relational" DBMSs on the market. The same appears to hold true today, especially for microcomputer DBMSs. Nonetheless, in 1989 Codd extended the relational data model to include 333 rules (Codd, 1989).

The Theory Versus Implementation Question

As you were reading the theoretical rules for a fully relational DBMS, you may have begun to wonder about the relationship of those rules to the effectiveness of database software and whether all the rules were really necessary. The publication of Codd's article stirred up a controversy over just that issue, much of which was conducted in the computer industry press, as seen in Crawford (1986), Gallant (1986a), and Gallant (1986b). The question posed by software developers was: "If product meets the needs of our customers, does it really matter if it doesn't meet the theoretical criteria for a fully relational DBMS?"

There is no easy or straightforward answer. The debate between database theorists and those who write DBMS software has been going on for years and is likely to continue for some time. Before you make up your own mind, however, there are some things on both sides of the argument that you should consider.

From the perspective of the business using a DBMS, the bottom line has always been: "Does it get the job done accurately, within our time constraints and within our budget?" The business purchaser isn't concerned about whether or not the software meets a series of theoretical rules, but only about whether the software performs as advertised. Certainly, microcomputer DBMSs that do not adhere strictly to Codd's rules are powerful, effective data management tools, most of which will perform satisfactorily in a business environment.

The performance issue underlies much of software developers' reluctance to implement strict adherence to Codd's rules in their products. It is true that adding code to a DBMS to verify and enforce integrity constraints—to maintain an on-line, dynamic catalog, for example—slows down the performance of the system. Software developers prefer to market a faster product, leaving the enforcing of constraints to applications programs written by the customer.

On the other hand, a database created by a DBMS that adheres to Codd's rules will contain far less bad data than a database that doesn't systematically enforce integrity and primary key constraints. It will be easier to maintain, since changes to the schema are made only once (in the catalog) and changes in physical storage methods don't require modifications at the applications level.

Summary

The relational model, used for most microcomputer DBMSs, views data as a set of two-dimensional tables known as relations. The relations are logically separate entities. A relation has the following characteristics:

- A name
- A set of attributes that define the columns in the table
- A unique, non-null primary key (one or more attributes whose value or values uniquely identify each row in the table)

The relationships between tables in a relational database are established through the presence of foreign keys. A foreign key is one or more attributes in one relation that are defined on the same logical domain as a primary key in another relation. The foreign key-primary key reference logically links the two tables. Rows with matching foreign key-primary key values contain data describing the same entity.

The formal theoretical criteria for a fully relational DBMS were defined in October, 1985 by E. F. Codd, the theorist who originally proposed the relational model. To be considered fully relational, a DBMS must meet 12 criteria:

1. All information in the database must be stored in tables.

2. All information in the database must be retrievable by using only a table name, a column name, and a primary key value.
3. NULL values must be handled in a systematic manner.
4. The DBMS must support an on-line, dynamic catalog.
5. The DBMS must have a query language that handles data definition, view definition, data manipulation, integrity constraints, and transaction boundaries.
6. The DBMS must be able to update any theoretically updatable views that a user can create.
7. Insert, update, and delete commands must work on entire tables.
8. Changes in physical storage methods must not affect applications activities.
9. Logical changes to the schema must not affect applications that do not use the portion of the database affected by the changes.
10. The DBMS must support definition of integrity rules and consequences to be taken when rules are violated within the catalog; the DBMS must automatically check for adherence to those rules.
11. If the database is distributed, it should appear to users as if it were centralized.
12. There must be no way to get around the integrity rules specified in the catalog.

A fully relational database must also be able to manage all of its activities through its relational capabilities (Rule Zero). A controversy has arisen between those whole believe that it is important to adhere to the strict theoretical model and those who believe that it is enough to write software that meets a user's needs.

References

Babad, Y. M. and J. A. Hoffer. 1984. "Even No Data Has a Value." *Communications of the ACM.* 27:748–756.

Codd, E. F. 1970. "A relational model of data for large shared data banks." *Communications of the ACM.* 13(6):377-387.

Codd, E. F. 1979. "Extending the database relational model to capture more meaning." *ACM Transactions on Database Systems.* 4(4):397-434.

Codd, E. F. 1982. "Relational Database: A Practical Foundation for Productivity." *Communications of the ACM.* 25:109–117.

Codd, E. F. 1985. "Is Your DBMS Really Relational?" *Computerworld.* (October 14):ID/1–ID/9.

Codd, E. F. 1989. *The Relational Data Model, Version 2.* Addison-Wesley.

Crawford, Douglas B. 1986. "Can one size fit all?" *Computerworld Focus.* (February 19):13-16.

Gallant, John. 1986a. "Strained relations: DBMS debate turns bitter." *Computerworld.* (January 13):1+.

Gallant, John. 1986b. "Sideline view: users want resolution to relational debate." *Computerworld.* (January 20):1+.

Kemm, Tom. 1990. "Relational Integrity." *DBMS.* 3(12):69–75.

Laborde, Dominique. "Putting Relational to Work: Why Is It Taking So Long?" *Database Management.* 1(3):29–32.

Olle, T. W. 1975. "A Practitioner's View of Relational Data Base Theory." *ACM-SIGMOD FDT-Bulletin.* 7(3–4):29–43.

Navathe, S., R. Elmasri, and J. Larson. 1986. "Integrating User Views in Database Design." *Computer.* January:50–62.

Storey, V. C. and R. C. Goldstein. 1988. "A Methodology for Creating User Views in Database Design." *ACM Transactions on Database Systems.* 13(3):305–338.

Wood, D. 1990. "A Primer of Features and Performance Issues of Relational DBMSs." *Data Resource Management.* 1(1).

Exercises

1. Below you will find groups of relations that might be used to represent data for Margaret Holmes, D.M.D. and East Coast Aquarium. For each set of relations, do the following:

   - Underline the primary key attributes in each relation;
   - List each foreign key and the primary key it references;
   - For each attribute, indicate a reasonable domain.

   When necessary, refer back to the interview transcripts in Appendixes A and B to clarify the meaning of data relationships in the context of a specific database environment.

   A. For the office of Margaret Holmes, D.M.D.

   Patients (Patient #, Patient Name, Patient Address, Patient Phone, SSN, Birthdate, Sex, Bill Payer, Rel. to Bill Payer)
   Payer (Bill Payer, Payer Address, Payer Home Phone, Payer Emp., Payer Work Phone, Insurer, Amount Owed)
   Appointment (Patient #, Appointment Date, Appointment Time)
   Treatment (Patient #, Appointment Date, Procedure, Comments)
   Cost (Procedure, Price)
   Income (Payment Date, Payment Source, Payment Amount, Payer)

   Attributes:

Patient #	Unique number assigned to each patient
Patient Name	Patient's name
Patient Address	Patient's address
Patient Phone	Patient's home phone
Birthdate	Patient's birthdate
Sex	Patient's sex
SSN	Patient's social security number
Bill Payer	Person responsible for the bills (may be the same as Patient Name)
Rel. to Bill Payer	Relationship between patient and whoever pays the bills

Payer Address	Address of Payer
Payer Home Phone	Home phone of Payer
Payer Emp.	Where Payer works
Payer Work Phone	Work telephone of Payer
Insurer	Insurance company covering Payer and dependents
Appointment Time	Time of an appointment
Appointment Date	Date when a patient received treatment
Procedure	Treatment given to a patient
Comments	Text of any notes the treatment provider wishes to record
Price	Normal cost of a procedure
Payment Date	Date a payment is received
Payment Source	Type of payment—cash, personal check, insurance check, etc.
Payment Amount	Amount of payment
Amount Owed	Amount owed by Payer at any given time

B. For the East Coast Aquarium

Animal (Species #, English Name, Latin Name)
Possible Homes (Species #, Habitat)
Tank (Tank #, Place in Building, Size, Master Keeper)
Population (Species #, Tank #)
Feeding (Species #, Type of Food, Food Amount, Feeding Interval)

Species #	Unique number assigned to a species
English Name	English name of a species
Latin Name	Latin name of a species
Habitat	Type of habitat in which a species can live
Tank #	Unique number assigned to a tank
Place in Building	Location of tank in building
Size	Size of a tank (in gallons)
Master Keeper	Keeper in charge of a tank
Type of Food	A type of food fed to an animal
Food Amount	Amount of food fed to an animal
Feeding Interval	How often animal should be fed a given food

2. Take a good, hard look at the DBMS you are using for this class.

    a. How does it measure up to the 12 rules for a fully relational database? Which rules does it meet completely? Which rules does it meet part-way? Which rules doesn't it meet at all? (If you aren't sure exactly what your DBMS can do, check with your instructor.)

    b. Of the rules that it only meets part-way or not at all, which will have the most impact on the implementation of a good database (e.g., one with the least bad data, such as foreign keys that don't reference existing primary keys)?

3. In your opinion, how important are the 12 rules for a fully relational database? Should people who write DBMS software be attempting to adhere to those rules? Or should they simply be attempting to write software that works? Why?

5

Normalization

For any given set of attributes that form the central pool of data for a database, there are many different ways that those attributes can be assembled into a set of relations. Some arrangements are "better" than others. The theory behind the arrangement of attributes into relations is known as *normalization* theory. The set of rules that govern the ways in which attributes can be arranged are called *normal forms*.

This chapter first looks at the reasons why we bother to normalize relations. It then presents both practical and theoretical techniques for creating good relational designs.

Normal forms provide an increasingly more stringent set of design rules that relations must meet. The least stringent is first normal form (often written 1NF); the most stringent is domain-key normal form. The full range of normal forms recognized by database theorists appears in Figure 5.1. They are nested in this way to indicate that if a relation, or set of relations, meets the criteria for an inner normal form, it is also in all the normal forms outside it. For example,

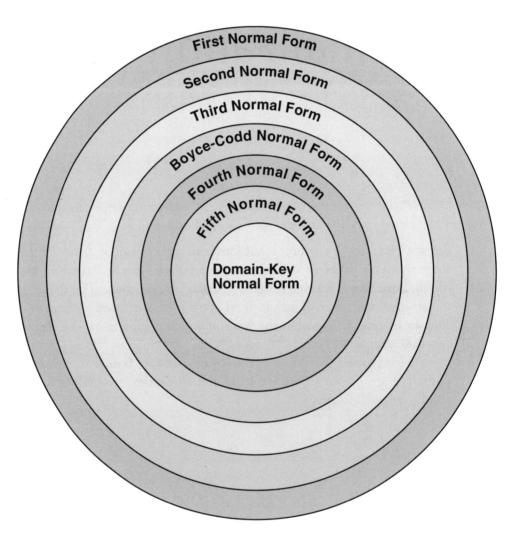

Figure 5.1　The relationship of normal forms

if a relation is in Boyce-Codd normal form, then it is also in third, second, and first normal forms. The higher a normal form that a database can meet, the theoretically "better" the design.

To be honest, if you can design and implement your database as a set of 3NF relations, then you will have avoided the large majority of database design problems. Boyce-Codd and fourth normal forms were created to handle special situations that occasionally arise in relations and are less frequently considered in practice. However, fifth normal form and domain-key normal form are usually only of theoretical interest and are not considered as practical design objectives. Because a third normal form design is the most common way in which relational databases are designed, this chapter focuses on normalization to that point. However, it also introduces Boyce-Codd normal form.

This chapter begins by looking at first normal form and the problems it presents. Then, to give you a feeling for where you are heading, it looks at how a third normal form design avoids those problems. (There doesn't seem to be much point in going to all the effort of learning to design third normal form relations if you don't know why they matter!)

There are many ways to arrive at a third normal form relational design. One way is to take a well-designed ER diagram and translate it into relations. Because you are already familiar with ER diagrams and how they represent data relationships, this is the first design technique to which you will be introduced. However, there is a large body of theory behind the design of relations. You will therefore also read about the theory behind normal forms from first through Boyce-Codd. (Some people do find using the theoretical criteria for normalization easier than working from ER diagrams.)

First Normal Form and Its Problems

A first normal form relation is a two-dimensional table with only one value at the intersection of a column and a row (in other words, no "repeating groups"). Figure 5.2 contains a first normal form relation that captures Small Bank's transaction data. (As you will soon see, this is *not* a good way to design a database.) Putting all the attributes into a single relation is conceptually simple; however, first normal form relations are prone to several significant problems.

Bank

Customer #	Customer	Customer Address	Customer Phone	Transaction #	Account #	Trans. Date	Amount
10010	Jones, Samuel	105 W. 99th, Newtown 02899	555-0105	3333333001	000-001	02/01/93	+100.00
10010	Jones, Samuel	105 W. 99th, Newtown 02899	555-0105	3333333002	000-002	02/01/93	-25.00
10010	Jones, Samuel	105 W. 99th, Newtown 02899	555-0105	3333333003	000-002	02/01/93	-52.50
10010	Jones, Samuel	105 W. 99th, Newtown 02899	555-0105	3333333004	000-002	02/02/93	+1500.00
10010	Jones, Samuel	105 W. 99th, Newtown 02899	555-0105	3333333005	000-002	02/02/93	+100.00
10020	Abrams, Max	2204 Nox Hill, Newtown 02845	555-2204	3333333006	000-009	02/02/93	+2599.99
10020	Abrams, Max	2204 Nox Hill, Newtown 02845	555-2204	3333333007	000-009	02/02/93	-25.00
10020	Abrams, Max	2204 Nox Hill, Newtown 02845	555-2204	3333333008	000-009	02/03/93	-10.00
10030	Cohen, Esther	39 Summer, Newtown 02845	555-0039	3333333009	000-006	02/03/93	+525.00
10040	Khan, Satya	1001 N. 54th, Newtown 02898	555-1001	3333333010	000-010	02/03/93	-824.00
10040	Khan, Satya	1001 N. 54th, Newtown 02898	555-1001	3333333011	000-010	02/03/93	-115.00
10010	Jones, Samuel	105 W. 99th, Newtown 02899	555-0105	3333333012	000-004	02/03/93	+190.25
10050	Brown, Judith	RR1 Box 99C, Rural City 02811	555-9900	3333333013	000-018	02/03/93	-190.25
10050	Brown, Judith	RR1 Box 99C, Rural City 02811	555-9900	3333333014	000-018	02/03/93	-165.99
10050	Brown, Judith	RR1 Box 99C, Rural City 02811	555-9900	3333333015	000-005	02/04/93	+25.00
10060	Wales, Miranda	33 Summer, Apt. #18, Newtown 02945	555-0033	3333333016	000-012	02/04/93	-40.99
10070	Smith, Samuel	RR6 Box 125, Rural City 02811	555-1250	3333333017	000-017	02/04/93	-886.00
10070	Smith, Samuel	RR6 Box 125, Rural City 02811	555-1250	3333333018	000-017	02/04/93	+1920.23

Figure 5.2   A first normal form relation for Small Bank

The primary key for the relation in Figure 5.2 is *Transaction #*. What happens, then, when a customer opens a new account and no transactions have yet been posted? Is there any way to insert the customer number, customer name, and account number into the relation? In other words, is it possible to record data about a customer and account before there has been activity against the account? No, because there isn't enough data to form a complete primary key. The *Transaction #* attribute is null (unknown), yet entity integrity specifies that no part of a primary key can be null. This situation is known as an *insertion anomaly*. It arises whenever a user wishes to insert data into a relation and cannot do so because it isn't possible to assemble a complete primary key.

Consider, now, what happens when Small Bank decides to purge the relation in Figure 5.2, transferring all the transaction data to archival tape storage. Not only are the data about the transactions removed from the relation, but information about customers, their names, addresses, and accounts must be deleted as well. Why? Removing the transaction number causes the primary key to become null, making it impossible to leave the row in the relation. However, Small Bank needs to retain the customer and account data; an account doesn't cease to exist if there are no transactions posted against it during any given period. This problem is what's known as a *deletion anomaly*. Whenever the deletion of a row causes the accidental loss of data that should be retained, the relation has a deletion anomaly.

The underlying practical cause of insertion and deletion anomalies is the inclusion of data for more than one entity in a single table. In fact, although insertion and deletion anomalies arise when part of the primary key is null, they affect *all* the data that describe an entity and are therefore discussed in terms of entities rather than attributes. The table in Figure 5.2, for example, contains a customer entity, an account entity, and a transaction entity. An insertion anomaly forces you to insert data about an unrelated entity before you can store data about an entity in which you are interested. In this case, Small Bank must insert data about a transaction entity before it can store any customer or account data. By the same token, a deletion anomaly forces you to delete data about an entity that you would like to retain when you delete data about an unrelated entity. Small Bank, for example, must delete customer and account data when deleting transaction data.

The relation in Figure 5.2 also contains a great deal of redundant data. For example, a customer's name is stored once for every transaction posted to every account the customer has. What happens if the customer changes his or her name? The DBMS must locate every occurrence of the customer name and change it. First normal form relations, which by nature contain a great deal of redundant data, are therefore prone to the problems that arise from redundant data, such as data inconsistency and a lack of data integrity. The problems that arise from such unnecessary duplicated data are often called *update anomalies* or *modification anomalies.*

Looking At Third Normal Form

As you read earlier, third normal form is generally considered a good relational database design objective. This is because in most cases, placing relations in third normal form provides a design that eliminates most relational design problems. (You will be introduced to second normal form on page 120. However, it is easier to understand the theory behind the normalization process if you first see how the target of the process—third normal form—solves problems.)

If the relation from Figure 5.2 is transformed into a set of third normal form (3NF) relations, then we can avoid insertion and deletion anomalies as well as many of the problems arising from redundant data. (Second normal form, which is discussed later in this chapter in terms of normalization theory, also helps remove some anomalies.) Figure 5.3 contains just such a design. It contains the same attributes as the relation in Figure 5.2, yet is free of insertion and deletion anomalies. It also contains much less redundant data than Figure 5.2.

Before examining 3NF relations for anomalies, first identify their primary keys. In this example, the Customers relation can use *Customer #* as its primary key; the Account relation can use *Account #*. Because transaction numbers are arbitrary unique numbers, *Transaction #* serves as the primary key for Transaction.

To see why the design in Figure 5.3 is "better" than the first normal form design, consider again the situation where a customer opens a new account. With the 3NF design, data about the customer can be inserted into the Customers relation without knowing a transaction number; all you need to form a primary key is the customer number. Data about an account can be inserted into the Account relation without knowing a transaction number; all you need to form a primary key is the account number. Therefore, the insertion anomaly

Customers

Customer #	Customer Name	Customer Address	Customer Phone
10010	Jones, Samuel	105 W. 99th, Newtown 02899	555-0105
10020	Abrams, Max	2204 Nox Hill, Newtown 02845	555-2204
10030	Cohen, Esther	39 Summer, Newtown 02845	555-0039
10040	Khan, Satya	1001 N. 54th, Newtown 02898	555-1001
10050	Brown, Judith	RR1 Box 99C, Rural City 02811	555-9900
10060	Wales, Miranda	33 Summer, Apt. # 18, Newtown 02945	555-0033
10070	Smith, Samuel	RR6 Box 125, Rural City 02811	555-1250

Account

Account #	Customer #
000-001	10010
000-002	10010
000-003	10010
000-009	10020
000-006	10030
000-010	10040
000-004	10010
000-018	10050
000-005	10050
000-012	10060
000-017	10070

Transaction

Transaction #	Account #	Amount
3333333001	000-001	+100.00
3333333002	000-002	-25.00
3333333003	000-002	-52.50
3333333004	000-002	+1500.00
3333333005	000-002	+100.00
3333333006	000-009	+2599.99
3333333007	000-009	-25.00
3333333008	000-009	-10.00
3333333009	000-006	+525.00
3333333010	000-010	-824.00
3333333011	000-010	-115.00
3333333012	000-004	+190.25
3333333013	000-018	-190.25
3333333014	000-018	-165.99
3333333015	000-005	+25.00
3333333016	000-012	-40.99
3333333017	000-017	-886.00
3333333018	000-017	+1920.23

Figure 5.3   A third normal form design for the relation in Figure 5.2

that existed in the first normal relation—which required that at least one transaction be posted before the customer and account could be entered—is not present.

The deletion anomaly discussed earlier is also not present in the 3NF design. If the Transaction relation is completely purged of data, or even deleted from the database, the relations Customers and Account are untouched. Information about customers and accounts is therefore left unaltered in the database.

If a customer closes all of his or her accounts with Small Bank, it is still possible to retain demographic data about that person in the database. It works in this way: Every time an account is closed, the row in Account that describes that account is deleted. However, the row in Customers that describes the customer is not deleted. Therefore, even if a given customer has no rows in Account, he or she can still appear in Customers.

It is important to recognize that the reverse is not true. While a customer number can exist in Customers without having any matching rows in Account, a customer number cannot exist in Account without having a matching customer number in Customers.

The latter situation would be a violation of referential integrity. In other words, the customer number in Account is a foreign key referencing the primary key in Customers. Primary key values do not need to have existing foreign key values that reference them, whereas foreign key values must reference existing primary key values.

The relation Customers eliminates much of the redundant data that could cause integrity and consistency problems. The demographic data about a customer is stored only once. Therefore, whenever a person changes an address or phone number, it only needs to be retrieved and modified once in the database.

Creating Third Normal Designs From ER Diagrams

There is a direct correspondence between a database whose tables are in third normal form and a properly constructed ER diagram. To use an ER diagram for 3NF design, the ER diagram must include only one-to-many relationships; all many-to-many relationships must have been replaced by a composite entity and one-to-many relationships. In addition, there should be no duplicated attributes.

Assuming that an ER diagram is properly constructed, then a 3NF database contains one table for each entity. Each entity's attributes become attributes in the table. An entity on the "many" end of a one-to-many relationship also inherits the primary key of the entity on the "one" end of the relationship. The inherited attribute (or attributes, in the case of a concatenated primary key) therefore becomes a foreign key referencing the primary key of the table at the "many" end of the relationship. As you know, this duplication of attributes is the way in which relationships are represented in a relationship database.

When the entity inheriting an attribute is a composite entity, its primary key becomes the concatenation of the inherited attributes (the primary keys of its "parent" entities). The only exception to this rule occurs when a composite entity is given an arbitrary unique key. The primary keys of the parent entities are still part of the table, but not part of the primary key.

Third Normal Form for Small Bank

To better understand how this works, look again at the ER diagram for the complete Small Bank database (Figure 5.4). There are five entities in the diagram, one of which is composite. The 3NF database therefore contains five tables:

- Branch (<u>Branch Name</u>, Branch Address, Branch Phone, Branch Hours)

   The Branch table uses *Branch Name* as the primary key (there are only three branches). Because the Branch entity isn't at the "many" end of any relationships, it has no inherited attributes and therefore no foreign keys.

- Customer (<u>Customer #</u>, Cust. Name, Cust. Address, Cust. Phone, SSN)

   The Customer table uses *Customer #* as the primary key (it is an arbitrary unique identifier). Because the Customer entity isn't at the "many" end of any relationships, it has no inherited attributes and therefore no foreign keys.

- Branch Patronage (<u>Branch Name</u>, <u>Customer #</u>)

   The Branch patronage relation is a composite entity representing the many-to-many relationship between the Customer entity and the Branch entity. It has no attributes of its own. However, it inherits the primary keys of its two parent entities. The primary key of the table is the concatenation

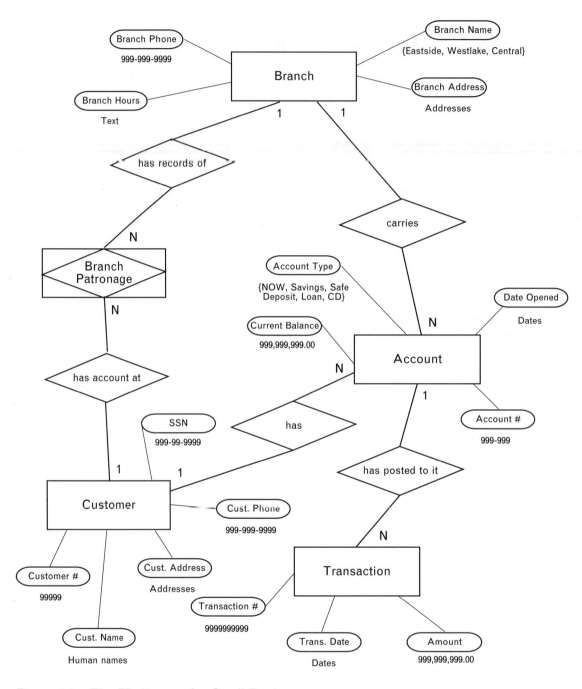

Figure 5.4   The ER diagram for Small Bank

of the two inherited attributes. *Branch Name* is a foreign key referencing the primary key of Branch; *Customer #* is a foreign key referencing the primary key of Customers.

- Account (<u>Account #</u>, Branch Name, Customer #, Date Opened, Account Type, Current Balance)

Third Normal Form for the Federated Taxi Company

A third normal form database for the Federated Taxi Company can also be created directly from its ER diagram (reprised in Figure 5.5. The ER diagram contains seven entities, producing seven tables:

- Cab (<u>Cab #</u>, Make/Model, Year, Plate, Current Odom., Cab Status, Condition)

  The Cab table uses *Cab #* as the primary key. Because the cab entity isn't at the "many" end of any one-to-many relationships, it doesn't have any inherited attributes or foreign keys.

- Driver (<u>Driver #</u>, Driver Name, Driver Address, Driver Phone #, License #, Exp. Date, Driver Status)

  The Driver table uses *Driver #*, an arbitrary unique identifier, as its primary key. There are no inherited attributed or foreign keys.

- Shift (<u>Shift Name</u>, <u>WkDate</u>)

  Because the same three shifts (day, eve, ngt) are repeated each day, the primary key of the Shifts table is the concatenation of *Shift Name* and *WkDate*. There are no inherited attributes or foreign keys.

- Shift Driven (<u>Shift Name</u>, <u>WkDate</u>, <u>Cab #</u>, Driver #, WkFlag, Starting Odom., Ending Odom.)

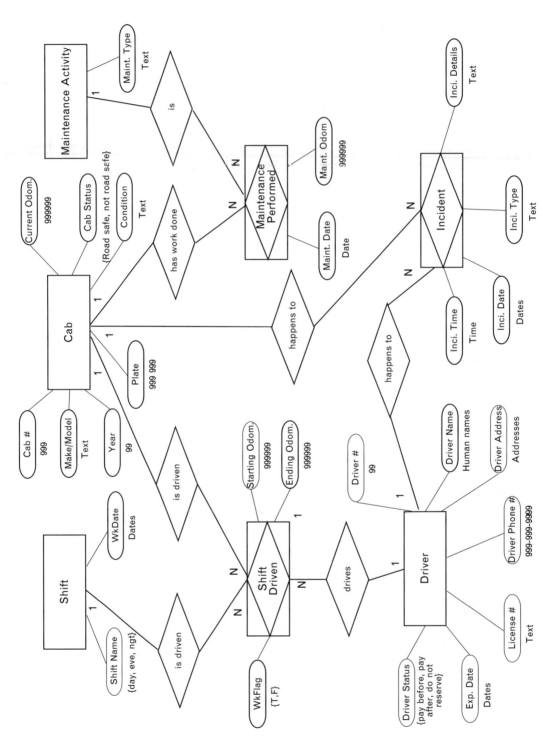

Figure 5.5   The ER diagram for Federated Taxi Company

The Shift Driven table represents a composite entity. Its primary key is therefore the concatenation of the simple entities from which it is created. Because Shift Driven could be defined by either the Shift and Driver entities or the Shift and Cab entities, the relation has two candidate keys: *Shift Name + WkDate + Cab #* and *Shift Name + WkDate + Driver #*. Whenever a row is added to Shift Driven, we always know the shift, the cab, and the driver. Either candidate key can therefore be selected as the primary key.

Shift Driven contains four inherited attributes, comprising three foreign keys. *Cab #* is a foreign key that references the primary key of the Cab table. *Driver #* is a foreign key that references the primary key of the Driver table. The concatenation of *Shift Name* and *WkDate* form a foreign key that references the primary key of the Shift table. (Keep in mind that when a table has a concatenated primary key, any foreign key that references it must be the concatenation of the same attributes.)

- Incident (<u>Inci. Date</u>, <u>Inci. Time</u>, <u>Driver #</u>, <u>Cab #</u>, Inci. Type, Inci. Details)

An incident is a composite entity related to the driver and cab involved in the incident. It therefore inherits the primary keys of the Driver and Cab relations (*Driver #* and *Cab #*). Because the same driver and cab might be involved in more than one incident, the primary key must also include the date and time the incident occurred.

Driver # is a foreign key that references the primary key of the Driver relation; *Cab #* is also a foreign key, referencing the primary key of the Cab relation.

- Maintenance Activity (<u>Maint. Type</u>)

The Maintenance Activity table provides a reference list for the types of maintenance that can be performed on a cab. Because it has only one attribute, it is all-key. It also has no inherited attributes and no foreign keys.

- Maintenance Performed (<u>Cab #</u>, <u>Maint. Date</u>, <u>Maint. Type</u>, Maint. Odom)

  The Maintenance Performed table is a composite entity formed from the Cab and Maintenance Activity entities. Its primary key therefore includes the primary keys of the entities from which it was created (*Cab #* and *Maint. Type*). Because the same type of maintenance can be performed more than once on a given cab, the primary key must also include the date on which the work occurred (*Maint. Date*). The inherited attributes—*Cab #* and *Maint. Type*—are foreign keys that reference the primary keys of their respective tables.

The Theory Behind Normalization

Developing a third normal form database from an ER diagram is an easy, effective way to get a good relational design. At the same time, there is a body of relational design theory that stringently defines normal forms. Understanding the concepts behind this theory will help you understand *why* well-constructed ER diagrams produce third normal form. It also provides an alternative to ER diagrams for creating third normal form designs.

Understanding Second Normal Form

Second normal form is a midway point between first and third normal form, although it is virtually never a design objective. A relation is in 2NF if:

- It is in 1NF; and
- All non-key attributes are *fully functionally dependent* on the primary key.

There is one very important new term in the preceding definition—fully functionally dependent. Understanding functional dependence is central to normalization theory.

Functional Dependency

A functional dependency is a special kind of relationship between two attributes, irrespective of the relations into which the attributes might be placed. In Small Bank's Customers relation, the attribute *Cust. Name* is *functionally dependent* on the attribute *Customer #*. That means that for any given value of *Customer #*, there will be one and only one value of *Cust. Name* associated with it. In other words, the value that *Cust. Name* takes depends upon the value of *Customer #*. In terms of the meaning of these attributes, that makes sense—there will be only one customer name for any given customer number. That does not mean that the customer name associated with a particular customer number will never change; it only means that at any given time, there is only one customer name for each customer number.

The functional dependency is written:

Customer # → Cust. Name

and is read as either "*Customer #* determines *Cust. Name*" or "*Cust. Name* is functionally dependent on *Customer #*." In the relationship, *Customer #* is called the *determinant*, since its value determines the value of another attribute.

The determinant does not have to be a single attribute. For example, in the Federated Taxi Company's relation Shift Driven,

Shift Name + WkDate + Cab # → Starting Odom.

This means that for any given cab on any given day during any given shift, there will be only one starting odometer reading. In other words, each time a cab is taken out on the road at the beginning of a shift, the value on its odometer is entered into the database.

It is important to realize that functional dependence is a one-way relationship. While it is true, for example, that the customer name is determined by the customer number, the reverse is not true—the customer number is not determined by the customer name. Since it is possible that two or more customers can have exactly the same name, we cannot guarantee that there will be only one customer number associated with any one customer name at any given time. For example, if there are two Jon Doughs who have accounts at Small Bank, each will have a different customer number. In that case, one name is associated with two different customer numbers, which violates the rule for a functional dependence.

The definition of 2NF includes the term *fully functionally dependent*. If an attribute is fully functionally dependent on another attribute or combination of attributes, then the determinant is made up of the smallest number of attributes possible to retain the functional dependence. For example, it is true that

Customer # + Cust. Name → Cust. Address, Cust. Phone, SSN

For each customer number and customer name pair there is indeed only one address, phone number, and social security number that will be associated with it at any given time. However, it is also true that

Customer # → Cust. Address, Cust. Phone, SSN

While the address, phone number and social security number are functionally dependent on the concatenated determinant, they are not fully functionally dependent on it, since it is possible to remove part of the determinant (Cust. Name) and still preserve the functional dependence. A full functional dependence exists when the determinant consists of the smallest number of attributes needed to maintain the functional dependence. Generally, when database people speak of functional dependence, they mean full functional dependence.

Bubble diagrams, such as those in Figure 5.6 for Small Bank's attributes, are often used to represent the functional dependencies within a database environment. Each attribute is placed in a bubble. Determinants are connected by an arrow to the attributes they determine. The direction of the arrowhead indicates the direction of the dependency. Concatenated determinants are indicated either by a brace or by a large bubble surrounding them (as in Figure 5.6). Typically, each determinant and the attributes it determines are placed in a separate diagram. When drawn in this way, each bubble diagram contains the attributes that describe a single entity, including inherited attributes.

Incidentally, functional dependencies provide another explanation for the insertion and deletion anomalies found in first normal form relations. As you will remember, the primary key of the first normal form relation in Figure 5.2 is *Transaction #*. However, the functional dependencies between those

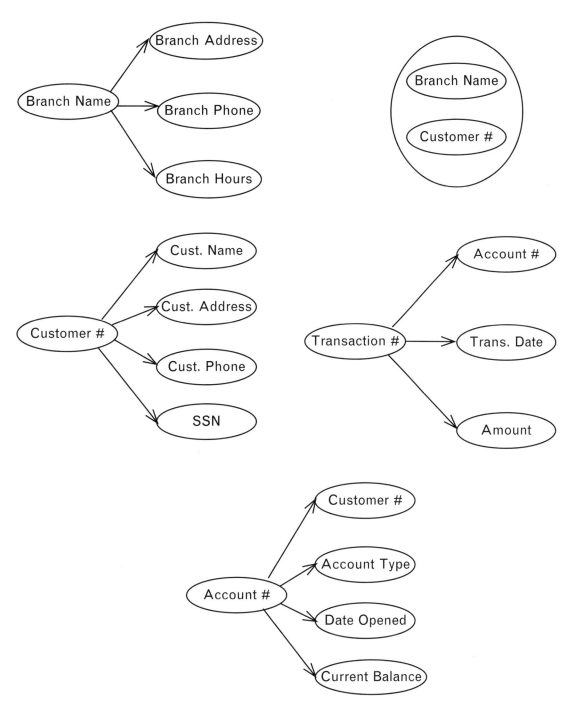

Figure 5.6   Functional dependencies between Small Bank's attributes

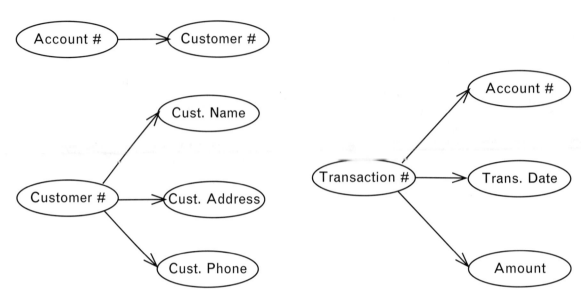

Figure 5.7   Functional dependencies in the relation in Figure 5.2

attributes are as in Figure 5.7. Notice that there are two determinants (*Customer #* and *Account #*) that aren't the primary key. This is the underlying theoretical cause of the anomalies.

Reaching Second Normal Form

Relations are transformed from 1NF to 2NF by *decomposing* them into a set of smaller relations. The easiest way to do so is to create a new relation for each determinant in the 1NF relation. The determinants become the primary keys in the new relations; the non-key attributes are all attributes which are fully functionally dependent upon them.

This is one way to create Figure 5.3 from Figure 5.2. As you saw in Figure 5.7, there are three determinants in Figure 5.2 (*Customer #*, *Account #*, and *Transaction #*). Each becomes the primary key of its own table; the attributes it determines are the table's non-key attributes.

In this case, the transformation to second normal form removes the insertion, deletion, and modification anomalies found in first normal form. Customer data can be inserted by adding a row to the Customers table, without needing to know a transaction number; account data can be inserted by adding a row to the Account table, without needing to know a transaction number.

The insertion anomalies have therefore been removed. By the same token, all the data in the Transaction table can be deleted without affecting either the customer data in the Customers table or the account data in the Account table. The deletion anomalies have therefore also been removed. Because customer data is only stored once for each customer (in the Customer table), the unnecessary duplicated data that could cause modification anomalies are gone as well.

Understanding Third Normal Form

3NF relations meet the following criteria:

- They are expressed in tabular form with a unique primary key and without any repeating groups (this qualifies them as 1NF)
- All non-key attributes are fully functionally dependent on the primary key (this qualifies them as second normal form, 2NF)
- All transitive dependencies have been eliminated (this qualifies them as 3NF)

This definition includes a special type of dependency, a *transitive dependency*.

Transitive Dependencies

Unfortunately, placing relations in 2NF, where all non-key attributes are fully functionally dependent on the primary key, does not necessarily remove all insertion, deletion, and update anomalies. Some may remain if *transitive dependencies* are present in the relation. For this reason, 2NF is rarely a design objective, but rather a stepping-stone to 3NF.

To understand the nature of a transitive dependency, consider the relation Account Access:

Account Access (<u>Account #</u>, Branch Name, Branch Hours)

The functional dependencies in this relation can be diagrammed as in Figure 5.8. As you know, each account is carried at only one branch. Therefore, Account # → Branch Name. It is also true that each branch has only one set of hours that it is open, so Branch Name → Branch Hours. Because each

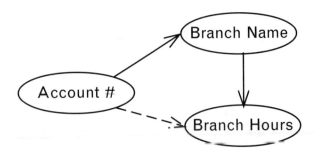

Figure 5.8   A transitive dependency

account is carried at only one branch and each branch has only one set of business hours, it is also true that a customer can enter the bank to talk with a teller or bank officer about the account during only one set of hours. As a result, Account → Branch Hours (the dependency shown with a dashed line in Figure 5.8).

This round-robin type of dependency is a transitive dependency. It can be written:

Account # → Branch Name→ Branch Hours

In other words, the only reason that Account # → Branch Hours is because Account # → Branch Name and Branch Name → Branch Hours.

In general, a transitive dependency exists in a relation if AttributeA → AttributeB → AttributeC *and* if AttributeB isn't a candidate key for the relation. For example, if we assume that social security number is never null, then it is true that:

Customer # → SSN → Customer Name

In other words, there is only one social security number and one customer name associated with each customer number, and only one customer name associated with each social security number. However, if social security number is never null, it becomes a candidate key for the relation. Therefore, a transitive dependency does not exist. (Note that if social security number can be null, the dependency SSN → Customer Name no longer holds.)

Transitive dependencies can be the source of anomalies, even for relations that are in second normal form. For example, the Account Access relation, whose functional dependencies are diagrammed in Figure 5.8, is in 2NF—both Branch Name and Branch Hours are functionally dependent on Account #. Nonetheless, there are insertion, deletion, and update anomalies in Account Access. For example, a new branch cannot be added until at least one account has been opened at that branch. By the same token, if the last account at a branch is closed and its row deleted from the relation, information about the branch's operating hours are lost. Since the branch's hours are duplicated for every account located at that branch, a change in branch hours must be made in as many rows as there are accounts at that branch.

Reaching Third Normal Form

Anomalies in 2NF relations can be eliminated by decomposing them into 3NF relations which have no transitive dependencies. As with the decomposition from 1NF to 2NF, each determinant becomes the primary key in a new relation along with those attributes which are dependent upon it. For example, Account Access could be decomposed into:

Account Locations (<u>Account #</u>, Branch Name)
Branch Hours (<u>Branch Name</u>, Branch Hours)

Using the two 3NF relations above, it is possible to record data about a branch's operating hours before any accounts are opened at that branch. It is also possible to delete all accounts located at a branch without losing the operating hours data. In addition, a change in branch hours needs to be made in only a single row in the Branch Hours relation. In other words, the transformation to 3NF has removed the anomalies present in 2NF.

Do the set of relations for Small Bank that you saw on pages 115–117 actually represent a database in 3NF? To make a statement to that effect, each relation in the database must meet all three 3NF criteria. Let's examine the relations to see if they really are in third normal form.

To meet the first criterion, the relations must be in tabular form (1NF). Any relational database will meet this criterion, even if it is a single-relation database, since it cannot be relational unless the data are expressed in tables.

The second criterion requires that all non-key attributes be fully functionally dependent upon the primary key. To make a judgment as to whether a relation meets this rule, you must first identify the primary key and all of the functional dependencies. You saw the functional dependencies for each of the Small Bank attributes in Figure 5.6. Notice that each diagram corresponds to one of the relations on pages 115–117. All of the non-key attributes are fully functionally dependent on the primary key, qualifying these relations as second normal form. (Branch Patronage, which has no non-key attributes, qualifies by default.)

To meet the final criterion for third normal form, the relations must each be free of transitive dependencies. The easiest way to determine this is to look at the bubble diagrams in Figure 5.6. Notice that there are no determinants that aren't primary keys, indicating that no transitive dependencies are present. The Small Bank relations therefore meet all the theoretical criteria for third normal form.

Boyce-Codd Normal Form

Boyce-Codd normal form was designed to handle the special situation in which there are multiple, overlapping candidate keys in a relation. For example, consider the following relation from the FTC database:

Shift Driven (Shift Name, WkDate, Cab #, Driver #, WkFlag,
    Starting Odom., Ending Odom.)

There are two candidate keys in this relation: Shift Name + WkDate + Cab # and Shift Name + WkDate + Driver #. These keys overlap because they have attributes in common (Shift Name and WkDate).

The definition of Boyce-Codd normal form states that:

- The relation must be in third normal form.
- Every determinant must be a candidate key.

In the Shift Driven relation, the only determinants are the two candidate keys. Therefore, the relation is in Boyce-Codd normal form.

However, consider what might happen if FTC adds a relation to its database to store data about the training courses its maintenance personnel have taken and the certifications they received from those courses:

Training (Worker, Certification, Course)

A worker can hold many types of certification; a worker can also take many courses. However, he earns each type of certification only once. At the same time, a course offers only one type of certification but a given type of certification can come from many different courses.

Because the worker can take many courses and earn many certifications, the worker's name won't do as the primary key; neither will the name of the course (many workers can take the same course) nor the type of certification (many workers can earn the same type of certification). The primary key must therefore be either Worker + Course or Worker + Certification.

In either case, the remaining attributes are functionally dependent on the entire primary key. If you choose Worker + Course for the primary key, then the Certification attribute indicates which certification the worker earned after taking the course. If the key is Worker + Certification, then the Course attribute indicates which course was taken to earn the certification. In other words, regardless of which of the overlapping candidate keys you choose as the primary key, the relation is in third normal form.

However, this relation has anomalies. Because Worker is part of both candidate keys, you can't store data about a course and the certification it offers until at least one worker has taken a course and earned a certification from it (an insertion anomaly). By the same token, if the only worker who earned a certification from a given course leaves FTC, deleting the row from the table causes the loss of data describing the course (a deletion anomaly).

The Training relation is therefore in third normal form but not Boyce-Codd normal form. As you can see in Figure 5.9, there is a determinant—Course—that isn't a candidate key. This not only violates the rules for Boyce-Codd normal form, but is the source of the anomalies in this relation.

To solve the problem, FTC needs to decompose the relation as follows:

Certifications Earned (<u>Worker</u>, <u>Course</u>)
Certifications Offered (<u>Course</u>, Certification)

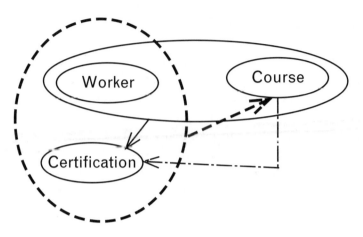

Figure 5.9   The functional dependencies in the Training relation

The Certifications Offered relation now stores data about which courses offer which certifications, independent of workers actually taking the courses. The Certifications Earned relation takes care of which workers actually enrolled in each course. Notice that the Course attribute in Certifications Earned is a foreign key, referencing the primary key of Certifications Offered.

The Importance of "Meaning"

There is an important issue raised by the whole idea of functional and transitive dependence. The ability to identify the functional dependencies in a relation depends a great deal on the meaning of the database environment. What happens, for example, if we change the rules by which Small Bank assigns transaction numbers? We have assumed that transaction numbers are unique throughout the bank—they are never repeated. In this situation,

Account # + Transaction # → Amount

does not constitute a full functional dependence. Because the transaction numbers are unique, each transaction number will have one and only one set of details associated with it. The full functional dependence is therefore

Transaction # → Amount

However, if transaction numbers are unique only within the account (in other words, they repeat within the bank for different accounts), then the concatenated determinant represents the full functional dependence.

Because the definition of functional dependencies relies so heavily on a database designer's interpretation of the environment, there are rarely any absolutes in terms of what constitutes a functional dependency. Whenever you specify functional dependencies, you must therefore also indicate the assumptions you are making about the way the database environment works.

Third Normal Form and the Federated Taxi Company

Let's take another look at the set of relations that represent the data for the Federated Taxi Company and see if they meet the theoretical criteria for third normal form. The easiest way to do so is to identify all the functional dependencies. The bubble diagrams showing those dependencies can be found in Figure 5.10. There is one bubble diagram for each relation in the database (beginning on page 117).

In the relation Cab, the only determinant is *Cab #*. For each vehicle that is identified by a cab number, there will be only one make/model, model year, license plate number, condition, status, and current odometer reading. As the only determinant, *Cab #* becomes the primary key. Since the primary key is a single attribute, these functional dependencies also constitute full functional dependencies. The relation Cab does at least meet the criteria for 2NF. Because there are no transitive dependencies, the Cab table is also in 3NF.

The relation Driver is also in 3NF. For any given driver number, there will only be one name, address, phone number, and status (while it is true that there be more than one phone number at which a driver could conceivably be reached, a driver must designate one as his or her single contact point). It is also true that there are no transitive dependencies.

What about Shift? The relation is all-key (no non-key attributes). Any relation that is all-key can't have any functional or transitive dependencies. It is therefore, by default, in 3NF. By the same token, the Maintenance activity relation, which has only one attribute, is also in 3NF.

As you will remember from the discussion of Boyce-Codd normal form, Shift Driven has two candidate keys. If you look at Figure 5.10, you can see that these are the only determinants: *Shift Name + WkDate + Cab #*

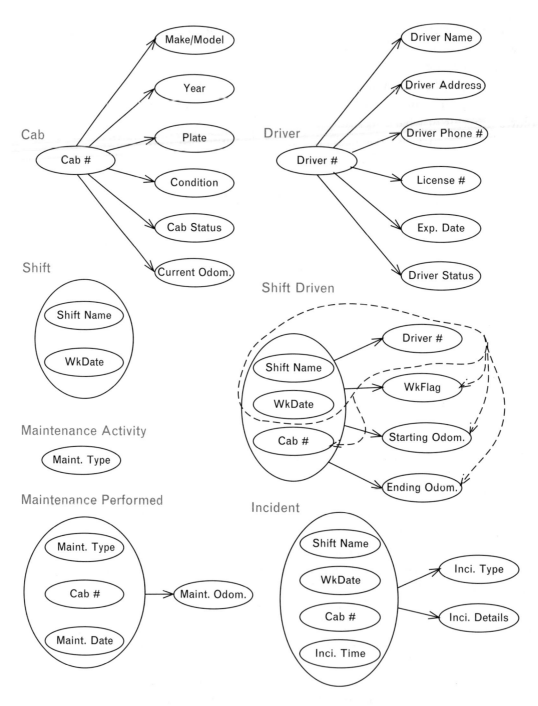

Figure 5.10 The functional dependencies in the Federated Taxi Company database

(encircled by a solid line) and *Shift Name + WkDate + Driver #* (encircled by a dashed line). All of the attributes that aren't part of a given determinant depend entirely on that determinant. Therefore, regardless of which one we pick as the primary key, the relation will be in second normal form. Does the presence of two determinants mean that there is a transitive dependency in this relation? Not in this case. Remember that a transitive dependency exists only when there is a functional dependency such that AttributeA → AttributeB → AttributeC, a situation that does not appear in this relation. Shift Driven is therefore in third normal form.

Incident has two nonkey attributes—the type of incident and the details of the incident. The contents of both of these fields do depend on when the incident occurred (the day, shift, and time) and which cab was involved. There are also no transitive dependencies because the concatenated primary key is the only determinant. Incident is therefore in 3NF.

Maintenance Performed, too, is in 3NF. It has only one nonkey attribute, *Maint. Odom*, which stores the cab's odometer reading at the time the maintenance was performed. Its value does depend on the full primary key—*Cab #*, *Maint. Date*, and *Maint. Type*, even if more than one type of maintenance is performed on a single day, there is no way to ensure that the cab isn't driven between trips to the service bays. Since there is only one non-key attribute, there is no need to consider transitive dependencies (it takes at least two non-key attributes to define a transitive dependency). The relation therefore meets the criteria for 3NF by default.

Because all the relations in the Federated Taxi Company's database are in 3NF, the entire database is in 3NF. However, when the database is expanded to include more of FTC's operations, each new relation added to the system must also be in third normal form to ensure that the entire database remains in 3NF.

Summary

Normalization theory deals with the way in which a given pool of attributes are grouped into relations. Normal forms, the ways in which the attributes can be arranged, provide an increasingly stringent set of rules that relations must meet.

While database theorists recognize seven normal forms, many database designers consider only the first three to be of use for practical database design. Third normal form is considered a practical design objective. Third normal form tables can be created directly from well-constructed ER diagrams or can be created by looking for functional dependencies between attributes and following the theoretical definitions.

To be in first normal form, data must simply be stored in a two-dimensional table which has no repeating groups. First normal form relations, which contain a great deal of data redundancy, have three major classes of problems:

- Insertion anomalies—data are not available to provide a complete primary key (i.e., some parts of the primary key are null), preventing the insertion of data into the relation
- Deletion anomalies—deletion of all or part of a primary key forces the deletion of data that should be retained
- Update problems—redundant data storage leads to data disintegrity

Second normal form relations must be in first normal form and have all non-key attributes fully functionally dependent on the primary key. Functional dependence is a special relationship between two attributes or groups of attributes such that one (the determinant) has one and only one value of a second associated with it at any given time. The second is functionally dependent on the first. Second normal form is rarely used as a design objective (second normal form relations can still contain insertion and deletion anomalies); it is more commonly viewed as a mid-point between first and third normal form.

Third normal form relations must be in second normal form. All transitive dependencies must also be removed. A transitive dependency exists if AttributeA → AttributeB → AttributeC, where AttributeA is the primary key in the relation and AttributeB isn't a candidate key for the relation. Third normal form relations are generally free of anomalies and, because they contain much less redundant data than first or second normal form relations, are less prone to update problems.

Boyce-Codd normal form handles the situation where a relation has multiple overlapping primary keys. To be in Boyce-Codd normal form, all determinants must be candidate keys.

References

Bass, Paul. 1985. "Six Steps to Design a Normalized Relational Database." *Small Systems World.* 13(7):14–17.

Codd, E. F. 1972. "Further normalization of the data base relational model." In *Data Base Systems*, edited by R. Rustin. Englewood Cliffs, N.J.:Prentice-Hall. pp. 33-64.

Curtice, Robert M. 1985. "Normalization Facilitates Data Design Process." *Computerworld.* 19(25):14–15.

Finkelstein, Richard. 1990. "Database Design: Normalizing Your Database Can Save Resources and Make Maintenance Easier." *DBMS.* 3(12):16–18.

Kemm, Tom. 1989. "A Practical Guide to Normalization." *DBMS.* 2(3):46–52.

Kent, W. 1983. "A Simple Guide to Five Normal Forms in Relational Database Theory." *Communications of the ACM.* 26:120–125.

McClanahan, David. 1991. "Database Design: Relational Rules." *DBMS.* 4(12):54–58.

Sandifer, Alice, and Barbara Von Halle. 1991. "Designing by the Rules." *DBMS.* 4(1):11–14.

Sandifer, Alice, and Barbara Von Halle. 1991. "Linking Rules to Models." *Database Programming and Design.* 4(3):13–16.

Exercises

1. In the first normal form relations below (all are drawn from either the office of Margaret Holmes, D.M.D. or East Coast Aquarium), indicate the following:

    - All functional dependencies that make sense to you in terms of the database environment as described in the interviews in Appendixes A and B.
    - The insertion anomalies
    - The deletion anomalies

Then transform each 1NF relation into a set of 3NF relations. Verify that each meets the criteria for 3NF by indicating the following:

- How the relations meet the criteria for second normal form (in other words, justify the claim that all non-key attributes are fully functionally dependent on the primary key)
- How the relations meet the criteria for third normal form (in other words, justify the claim that all transitive dependencies have been removed)

A. From the office of Margaret Holmes, D.M.D.

Payments (<u>Vendor</u>, <u>Payment Date</u>, Check #, Amount Paid, Amount Owed)

Attributes:

Vendor	Vendor from whom supplies or drugs are ordered
Payment Date	Date a payment is made
Check #	Number of check used to make payment
Amount Paid	Amount of check
Amount Owed	Amount left unpaid with this vendor

B. From East Coast Aquarium

Feeding (<u>Species Code</u>, <u>Type of Food</u>, English Name, Latin Name, Feeding Interval)

Attributes:

Species Code	Unique number assigned to each species
Type of Food	A type of food a species can eat
English Name	English name of a species
Latin Name	Latin name of a species
Feeding Interval	How often species is fed a type of food

C. From the East Coast Aquarium

Volunteers (<u>Volunteer #</u>, <u>Work Date</u>, <u>Starting Time</u>, Vol. Name,
    Vol. Address, Vol. Phone, Skill, Job)

Attributes:

Volunteer #	Unique number assigned to each volunteer
Work Date	A date on which a volunteer will work
Starting Time	The time at which the volunteer will begin work
Vol. Name	The volunteer's name
Vol. Address	The volunteer's address
Vol. Phone	The volunteer's phone number
Skill	Something the volunteer has been trained to do, such as "feed dolphins" or "lead a tour"
Job	The job a volunteer will perform when he/she comes in to work on a given day

2. Using the ER diagram you created for the exercises at the end of Chapter 3, create set of a third normal form relations for the Office of Margaret Holmes, D.M.D. Once you have finished, verify that your design meets the theoretical criteria for third normal form.

3. Using the ER diagram you created for the exercises at the end of Chapter 3, create a set of third normal form relations for the East Coast Aquarium. Once you have finished, verify that your design meets the theoretical criteria for third normal form.

Relational Algebra

As well as the definition of a relation, mathematical set theory brings a group of operations that manipulate relations to a relational database. Known as the *relational algebra,* these operations are used by a DBMS to process queries submitted by users.

Users typically do not work directly with relational algebra, but instead use query languages built on the *relational calculus.* Each relational algebra operation performs one action on one or two relations; each relational calculus command can ask for many relational algebra operations. Even though you will probably be using a non-procedural query language built on the relational calculus, you will be better equipped to understand how that query language works and to formulate more efficient queries if you are aware of exactly what relational algebra you are asking the DBMS to perform.

This chapter looks at nine relational algebra operations that underlie most of the queries you will issue to a DBMS and how they work together to retrieve data.

To be considered *relationally complete*, a DBMS must support at least five operations from the relational algebra: project, join, select, union, and difference. *Project* is used to take a subset of the columns of a relation. *Join* is used to paste two relations together by matching values against a condition. *Select* is used to retrieve rows from a relation. *Union* combines all rows from two relations, and *difference* produces all rows from one relation that are not contained in another.

DBMSs also occasionally make use of four other relational operations: product, intersect, divide, and outer join. *Product* (the Cartesian product of two sets) combines two relations by creating new rows for all possible combinations of rows. *Intersecting* two relations produces a result consisting of all rows that appear in both relations. *Divide*, which works on a relation with one column (a unary relation) and another with two columns (a binary relation), extracts values from the binary relation in a manner that will be discussed later in this chapter. The *outer join* is a variation of the join operation that produces a result which is not a legal relation; it is, however, very useful for data retrieval.

It is important to keep in mind that while full-featured DBMSs use five or more of the relational algebra operations to implement data retrieval, it is not necessarily true that the DBMS's query language contains individual commands that perform those operations. As you will see in Chapter 8, many SQL commands perform more than one relational algebra operation. (SQL, like most relational query languages, is based on the relational calculus.)

The result of all relational algebra operations is a virtual table that is retained in main memory while an application needs it; none of the relational operations modify a base table.

There is no official syntax for expressing relational algebra operations. The syntax used in this chapter is therefore arbitrary. Each relational algebra operation will be represented in the following general format:

OPERATION parameters FROM source_table_name GIVING
    result_table_name

The "parameters" are optional and vary depending on the specific operation. They may specify a second table which is part of the operation, or they may specify attributes which are to be included in the result.

Project

A projection of a relation is a new relation created by copying one or more of the columns from the original relation into a new table. As an example, consider Figure 6.1. The relation Trans is a projection of the relation Bank with the attributes *Customer #*, *Account #*, *Transaction #*, and *Amount*.

> **By the way:** Don't forget that the terms "relation," "attribute," and "tuple" are equivalent to "table," "column," and "row."

In the relational algebra, the projection in Figure 6.1 is written:

PROJECT Customer #, Account #, Transaction #, Amount FROM Bank
    GIVING Trans

The order of the columns in the result table is based on the order in which the column names appear in the PROJECT statement; the order in which they are defined in the source table has no affect on the result.

Projection, like all relational algebra operations, removes duplicate rows from the result table. That means that projections may have fewer rows than the relation from which they were taken. The middle table in Figure 6.2 contains the intermediate result from the following projection:

PROJECT Customer #, Account # FROM Trans GIVING Account Owners

Note that this relation contains duplicate pairs of customer number and account number. The final result (the bottom table in Figure 6.2), however, contains no duplicate rows.

While it is theoretically possible to create projections from any combination of the columns in a relation, not all projections may be meaningful. In other words, some projections may produce resultant relations that contain misleading or meaningless information. Consider the projection in Figure 6.3:

PROJECT Customer Address, Transaction # FROM Bank GIVING Place

Bank

Customer #	Cust. Name	Cust. Address	Cust. Phone	Transaction #	Account #	Trans. Date	Amount
10010	Jones, Samuel	105 W. 99th, Newtown 02899	555-0105	3333333001	000-001	02/01/93	+100.00
10010	Jones, Samuel	105 W. 99th, Newtown 02899	555-0105	3333333002	000-002	02/01/93	-25.00
10010	Jones, Samuel	105 W. 99th, Newtown 02899	555-0105	3333333003	000-002	02/01/93	-52.50
10010	Jones, Samuel	105 W. 99th, Newtown 02899	555-0105	3333333004	000-002	02/02/93	+1500.00
10010	Jones, Samuel	105 W. 99th, Newtown 02899	555-0105	3333333005	000-002	02/02/93	+100.00
10020	Abrams, Max	2204 Nox Hill, Newtown 02845	555-2204	3333333006	000-009	02/02/93	+2599.99
10020	Abrams, Max	2204 Nox Hill, Newtown 02845	555-2204	3333333007	000-009	02/02/93	-25.00
10020	Abrams, Max	2204 Nox Hill, Newtown 02845	555-2204	3333333008	000-009	02/03/93	-10.00
10030	Cohen, Esther	39 Summer, Newtown 02845	555-0039	3333333009	000-006	02/03/93	+525.00
10040	Khan, Satya	1001 N. 54th, Newtown 02898	555-1001	3333333010	000-010	02/03/93	-824.00
10040	Khan, Satya	1001 N. 54th, Newtown 02898	555-1001	3333333011	000-010	02/03/93	-115.00
10010	Jones, Samuel	105 W. 99th, Newtown 02899	555-0105	3333333012	000-004	02/03/93	+190.25
10050	Brown, Judith	RR1 Box 99C, Rural City 02811	555-9900	3333333013	000-018	02/03/93	-190.25
10050	Brown, Judith	RR1 Box 99C, Rural City 02811	555-9900	3333333014	000-018	02/03/93	-165.99
10050	Brown, Judith	RR1 Box 99C, Rural City 02811	555-9900	3333333015	000-005	02/04/93	-25.00
10060	Wales, Miranda	33 Summer, Apt. #18, Newtown 02945	555-0033	3333333016	000-012	02/04/93	-40.99
10070	Smith, Samuel	RR6 Box 125, Rural City 02811	555-1250	3333333017	000-017	02/04/93	-886.00
10070	Smith, Samuel	RR6 Box 125, Rural City 02811	555-1250	3333333018	000-017	02/04/93	+1920.23

PROJECT Customer #, Account #, Transaction #,
Amount FROM Bank GIVING Trans

Trans

Customer #	Account #	Transaction #	Amount
10010	000-001	3333333001	+100.00
10010	000-002	3333333002	-25.00
10010	000-002	3333333003	-52.50
10010	000-002	3333333004	+1500.00
10010	000-002	3333333005	+100.00
10020	000-009	3333333006	+2599.99
10020	000-009	3333333007	-25.00
10020	000-009	3333333008	-10.00
10030	000-006	3333333009	+525.00
10040	000-010	3333333010	-824.00
10040	000-010	3333333011	-115.00
10010	000-004	3333333012	+190.25
10050	000-018	3333333013	-190.25
10050	000-018	3333333014	-165.99
10050	000-005	3333333015	+25.00
10060	000-012	3333333016	-40.99
10070	000-017	3333333017	-886.00
10070	000-017	3333333018	+1920.23

Figure 6.1   Taking a projection

Trans

Customer #	Account #	Transaction #	Amount
10010	000-001	3333333001	+100.00
10010	000-002	3333333002	-25.00
10010	000-002	3333333003	-52.50
10010	000-002	3333333004	+1500.00
10010	000-002	3333333005	+100.00
10020	000-009	3333333006	+2599.99
10020	000-009	3333333007	-25.00
10020	000-009	3333333008	-10.00
10030	000-006	3333333009	+525.00
10040	000-010	3333333010	-824.00
10040	000-010	3333333011	-115.00
10010	000-004	3333333012	+190.25
10050	000-018	3333333013	-190.25
10050	000-018	3333333014	-165.99
10050	000-005	3333333015	+25.00
10060	000-012	3333333016	-40.99
10070	000-017	3333333017	-886.00
10070	000-017	3333333018	+1920.23

PROJECT Customer #, Account # FROM Trans
GIVING Account Owners

Customer #	Account #
10010	000-001
10010	000-002
10010	000-002
10010	000-002
10010	000-002
10020	000-009
10020	000-009
10020	000-009
10030	000-006
10040	000-010
10040	000-010
10010	000-004
10050	000-018
10050	000-018
10050	000-005
10060	000-012
10070	000-017
10070	000-017

Intermediate result
containing duplicate rows

Account Owners

Customer #	Account #
10010	000-001
10010	000-002
10020	000-009
10030	000-006
10040	000-010
10010	000-004
10050	000-018
10050	000-005
10060	000-012
10070	000-017

Figure 6.2   The steps in taking a projection

Bank

Customer #	Customer	Cust. Address	Cust. Phone	Transaction #	Account #	Trans. Date	Amount
10010	Jones, Samuel	105 W. 99th, Newtown 02899	555-0105	3333333001	000-001	02/01/93	+100.00
10010	Jones, Samuel	105 W. 99th, Newtown 02899	555-0105	3333333002	000-002	02/01/93	-25.00
10010	Jones, Samuel	105 W. 99th, Newtown 02899	555-0105	3333333003	000-002	02/01/93	-52.50
10010	Jones, Samuel	105 W. 99th, Newtown 02899	555-0105	3333333004	000-002	02/02/93	+1500.00
10010	Jones, Samuel	105 W. 99th, Newtown 02899	555-0105	3333333005	000-002	02/02/93	+100.00
10020	Abrams, Max	2204 Nox Hill, Newtown 02845	555-2204	3333333006	000-009	02/02/93	+2599.99
10020	Abrams, Max	2204 Nox Hill, Newtown 02845	555-2204	3333333007	000-009	02/02/93	-25.00
10020	Abrams, Max	2204 Nox Hill, Newtown 02845	555-2204	3333333008	000-009	02/03/93	-10.00
10030	Cohen, Esther	39 Summer, Newtown 02845	555-0039	3333333009	000-006	02/03/93	+25.00
10040	Khan, Satya	1001 N. 54th, Newtown 02898	555-1001	3333333010	000-010	02/03/93	-24.00
10040	Khan, Satya	1001 N. 54th, Newtown 02898	555-1001	3333333011	000-010	02/03/93	-115.00
10010	Jones, Samuel	105 W. 99th, Newtown 02899	555-0105	3333333012	000-004	02/03/93	+190.25
10050	Brown, Judith	RR1 Box 99C, Rural City 02811	555-9900	3333333013	000-018	02/03/93	-190.25
10050	Brown, Judith	RR1 Box 99C, Rural City 02811	555-9900	3333333014	000-018	02/03/93	-165.99
10050	Brown, Judith	RR1 Box 99C, Rural City 02811	555-9900	3333333015	000-005	02/04/93	+25.00
10060	Wales, Miranda	33 Summer, Apt. #18, Newtown 02945	555-0033	3333333016	000-012	02/04/93	-40.99
10070	Smith, Samuel	RR6 Box 125, Rural City 02811	555-1250	3333333017	000-017	02/04/93	-886.00
10070	Smith, Samuel	RR6 Box 125, Rural City 02811	555-1250	3333333018	000-017	02/04/93	+1520.23

PROJECT Cust. Address, Transaction # FROM
Bank GIVING Place

Place

Cust. Address	Transaction #
105 W. 99th, Newtown 02899	3333333001
105 W. 99th, Newtown 02899	3333333002
105 W. 99th, Newtown 02899	3333333003
105 W. 99th, Newtown 02899	3333333004
105 W. 99th, Newtown 02899	3333333005
2204 Nox Hill, Newtown 02845	3333333006
2204 Nox Hill, Newtown 02845	3333333007
2204 Nox Hill, Newtown 02845	3333333008
39 Summer, Newtown 02845	3333333009
1001 N. 54th, Newtown 02898	3333333010
1001 N. 54th, Newtown 02898	3333333011
105 W. 99th, Newtown 02899	3333333012
RR1 Box 99C, Rural City 02811	3333333013
RR1 Box 99C, Rural City 02811	3333333014
RR1 Box 99C, Rural City 02811	3333333015
33 Summer, Apt. #18, Newtown 02945	3333333016
RR6 Box 125, Rural City 02811	3333333017
RR6 Box 125, Rural City 02811	3333333018

Figure 6.3   A meaningless projection

The relation Place is meaningless. It implies that there is some relationship between a transaction and a physical address. In terms of the meaning of this database environment, an address is related to a customer and a transaction number to an account, but when the customer number and account number are missing from a relation, the associations are lost.

There is no set of rules as to what constitutes a meaningful projection. As with determining functional dependencies, judgments as to the usefulness of projections depends a great deal on the meaning of the data the database is attempting to capture.

Join

The join operation creates one result table from two source tables. It is used primarily to implement retrieval operations in which data are stored in two or more relations. The general form of the join operation is:

JOIN table_1 TO table_2 OVER attributes_used_for_matching GIVING
    result_table

Remember that Small Bank's customer and account data are stored as follows:

Customers (<u>Customer #</u>, Cust. Name, Cust. Address, Cust. Phone,
    SSN)
Account (<u>Account #</u>, Customer #, Branch Name, Account Type,
    Current Balance, Date Opened)

If the DBMS receives a request to print out the name, address, and account numbers for each of Small Bank's customers, not only must it consult the Account table to discover which customer number is associated with which account number, but it must have some way to associate names and addresses with the account numbers.

Rows in Customers and Account are related by the value of *Customer #*, the foreign key in Account that references the primary key of Customers. Therefore, rows with matching values for *Customer #* can be joined together, side by side, and included in a new relation that is the result of the join. Using the relational algebra, the operation is written:

JOIN Customer TO Account OVER Customer # GIVING List

A join includes all columns in both source relations. In a *natural join*, the column or columns used to perform the join are duplicated in the result. In an *equi-join*, the matching column or columns are not duplicated. The joins used in this book are all equi-joins. Like project, join also excludes duplicate rows.

The result of this join appears in Figure 6.4. Notice that two customers, numbers 10015 and 10055, have no accounts. (In other words, there are no rows for their customer numbers in Account.) Since no matching customer number could be found for these two people, neither appears in the result table.

While it is theoretically possible to join any two relations, the result of a join is not always valid. A meaningless projection is useless but harmless; however, an invalid join actually contains facts that aren't true. As an example, consider what happens if someone were to look at the Small Bank database and decide that the *Customer #* column wasn't needed in the Account table. Instead, to find out who owns which account, the Branch Patronage table could be joined to the Account table over Branch Name, the column that the two tables have in common:

JOIN Branch Patronage TO Account OVER Branch Name GIVING Branch
    Owners

The result of this join appears in Figure 6.5. Something is clearly wrong; this relation indicates that each account belongs to every customer at the account's branch, a conclusion that is clearly in error. How did this happen? Remember how a join works: the DBMS takes the branch name associated with each account number in Account and looks for a match in Branch Patronage. Whenever a match is found, a new row is created for Account Owners. In this case, the join wasn't between a primary key and a foreign key, but between two foreign keys that reference the primary key of the Branch table. Therein lies the problem. In general, joins between a primary key and a foreign key are valid; joins between two primary keys are also valid (should your database have two tables with the same primary key). However, other joins (such as the example you have just seen) are usually invalid.

The joins that you have seen to this point are based on matching values of an attribute held in common by the two relations being joined. It is also possible to join relations based on other criteria, such as an inequality of values in the shared attribute.

Customers

Customer #	Cust. Name	Cust. Address	Cust. Phone	SSN
10010	Jones, Samuel	105 W. 99th, Newtown 02899	555-0105	123-45-6789
10015	Jones, Patricia	85 Humbolt, Newtown 02899	555-0085	151-51-5151
10020	Abrams, Max	2204 Nox Hill, Newtown 02845	555-2204	234-56-7890
10030	Cohen, Esther	39 Summer, Newtown 02845	555-0039	345-67-8901
10040	Khan, Satya	1001 N. 54th, Newtown 02898	555-1001	456-78-9012
10050	Brown, Judith	RR1 Box 99C, Rural City 02811	555-9900	567-89-0123
10055	Fredricks, Louis	909 Summer, Newtown 02845	555-9090	555-55-5555
10060	Wales, Miranda	33 Summer, Apt. # 18, Newtown 02945	555-0033	678-90-1234
10070	Smith, Samuel	RR6 Box 125, Rural City 02811	555-1250	789-09-2345

JOIN Customers TO Account OVER Customer #
GIVING Account Owners

Account

Account #	Customer #	Branch	Account Type	Date Opened	Current Balance
000-001	10010	Central	NOW	10/10/82	2568.12
000-002	10010	Central	CD	02/02/92	10520.00
000-003	10010	Central	Safe Deposit	05/15/56	NULL
000-009	10020	Eastside	NOW	10/21/89	512.89
000-006	10030	Central	NOW	06/30/91	3888.00
000-010	10040	Central	Savings	01/05/51	25.00
000-004	10010	Westlake	Loan	11/25/92	15085.85
000-018	10050	Westlake	NOW	10/31/87	2500.12
000-005	10050	Westlake	CD	04/18/92	5012.89
000-012	10060	Eastside	NOW	10/10/90	386.00
000-017	10070	Eastside	NOW	07/16/92	259.00

Account Owners

Account #	Customer #	Branch	Account Type	Date Opened	Current Balance	Cust. Name	Cust. Address	Current Balance	Cust. Phone	SSN
000-001	10010	Central	NOW	10/10/82	2568.12	Jones, Samuel	105 W. 99th, Newtown 02899	2568.12	555-0105	123-45-6789
000-002	10010	Central	CD	02/02/92	10520.00	Jones, Samuel	105 W. 99th, Newtown 02899	10520.00	555-0105	123-45-6789
000-003	10010	Central	Safe Deposit	05/15/56	NULL	Jones, Samuel	105 W. 99th, Newtown 02899	NULL	555-0105	123-45-6789
000-009	10020	Eastside	NOW	10/21/89	512.89	Abrams, Max	2204 Nox Hill, Newtown 02845	512.89	555-2204	234-56-7890
000-006	10030	Central	NOW	06/30/91	3888.00	Cohen, Esther	39 Summer, Newtown 02845	3888.00	555-0039	345-67-8901
000-010	10040	Central	Savings	01/05/51	25.00	Khan, Satya	1001 N. 54th, Newtown 02898	25.00	555-1001	456-78-9012
000-004	10010	Westlake	Loan	11/25/92	15085.85	Jones, Samuel	105 W. 99th, Newtown 02899	15085.85	555-0105	123-45-6789
000-018	10050	Westlake	NOW	10/31/87	2500.12	Brown, Judith	RR1 Box 99C, Rural City 02811	2500.12	555-9900	567-89-0123
000-005	10050	Westlake	CD	04/18/92	5012.89	Brown, Judith	RR1 Box 99C, Rural City 02811	5012.89	555-9900	567-89-0123
000-012	10060	Eastside	NOW	10/10/90	386.00	Wales, Miranda	33 Summer, Apt. # 18, Newtown 02945	386.00	555-0033	678-90-1234
000-017	10070	Eastside	NOW	07/16/92	259.00	Smith, Samuel	RR6 Box 125, Rural City 02811	259.00	555-1250	789-09-2345

Figure 6.4   Performing a join

Account

Account #	Branch Name	Account Type	Date Opened	Current Balance
000-001	Central	NOW	10/10/82	2568.12
000-002	Central	CD	02/02/92	10520.00
000-003	Central	Safe Deposit	05/15/56	NULL
000-009	Eastside	NOW	10/21/89	512.89
000-006	Central	NOW	06/30/91	3888.00
000-010	Central	Savings	01/05/51	25.00
000-004	Westlake	Loan	11/25/92	15085.85
000-018	Westlake	NOW	10/31/87	2500.12
000-005	Westlake	CD	04/18/92	5012.89
000-012	Eastside	NOW	10/10/90	386.00
000-017	Eastside	NOW	07/16/92	259.00

JOIN Branch Patronage TO Account OVER Branch Name GIVING Account Owners

Branch Patronage

Branch Name	Customer #
Central	10010
Eastside	10020
Central	10030
Central	10040
Westlake	10010
Westlake	10050
Eastside	10060
Eastside	10070

Account Owners

Account #	Branch Name	Account Type	Date Opened	Current Balance	Customer #
000-001	Central	NOW	10/10/82	2568.12	10010
000-001	Central	NOW	10/10/82	2568.12	10030
000-001	Central	NOW	10/10/82	2568.12	10040
000-002	Central	CD	02/02/92	10520.00	10010
000-002	Central	CD	02/02/92	10520.00	10030
000-002	Central	CD	02/02/92	10520.00	10040
000-003	Central	Safe Deposit	05/15/56	NULL	10010
000-003	Central	Safe Deposit	05/15/56	NULL	10030
000-003	Central	Safe Deposit	05/15/56	NULL	10040
000-009	Eastside	NOW	10/21/89	512.89	10020
000-009	Eastside	NOW	10/21/89	512.89	10060
000-009	Eastside	NOW	10/21/89	512.89	10070
000-006	Central	NOW	06/30/91	3888.00	10010
000-006	Central	NOW	06/30/91	3888.00	10030
000-006	Central	NOW	06/30/91	3888.00	10040
000-010	Central	Savings	01/05/51	25.00	10010
000-010	Central	Savings	01/05/51	25.00	10030
000-010	Central	Savings	01/05/51	25.00	10040
000-004	Westlake	Loan	11/25/92	15085.85	10010
000-004	Westlake	Loan	11/25/92	15085.85	10050
000-018	Westlake	NOW	10/31/87	2500.12	10010
000-018	Westlake	NOW	10/31/87	2500.12	10050
000-005	Westlake	CD	04/18/92	5012.89	10010
000-005	Westlake	CD	04/18/92	5012.89	10050
000-012	Eastside	NOW	10/10/90	386.00	10020
000-012	Eastside	NOW	10/10/90	386.00	10060
000-012	Eastside	NOW	10/10/90	386.00	10070
000-017	Eastside	NOW	07/16/92	259.00	10020
000-017	Eastside	NOW	07/16/92	259.00	10060
000-017	Eastside	NOW	07/16/92	259.00	10070

Figure 6.5   An invalid join

Select

The select operation is often misunderstood, primarily because it is used as a retrieval operator by SQL. As defined in the relational algebra, select creates a new table by copying rows from a relation that meet a specified criteria. Select copies all attributes in the relation; it has no way to specify which attributes should be included in the resulting table.

Select identifies which rows are to be included in the result table with a logical criteria. The operation therefore takes the general form:

SELECT FROM source_table_name WHERE logical_selection_criteria
    GIVING result_table

For example, suppose we want to retrieve the customer numbers of those customers who have accounts at Small Bank's Central branch. The operation might be expressed as:

SELECT FROM Account WHERE Branch Name = "Central" GIVING One
    Branch

The result appears in Figure 6.6. This select does retrieve the numbers of all customers at Central branch; however, since select cannot choose which attributes to include, all of the other columns in the Account table are also included in the result table, One Branch.

Union

Union combines all rows from two relations into a single, resultant relation. For union to work, however, the two relations being combined must be *union-compatible.* That means that their structure must be identical; they must contain the same columns. The columns do not necessarily have to have the same names, but they must have the same logical domains.

For example, assume that Small Bank merges with Smaller Bank. Smaller Bank is also using a database system. Some of the relations in its database are:

Clients (<u>Client#</u>, CName CAdd, CPhone, CSSN)
Accounts (<u>Client#</u>, <u>Acct#</u>)
Transactions (<u>TCode</u>, Acct#, TDate, TAmt)

Account

Account #	Customer #	Branch Name	Account Type	Date Opened	Current Balance
000-001	10010	Central	NOW	10/10/82	2568.12
000-002	10010	Central	CD	02/02/92	10520.00
000-003	10010	Central	Safe Deposit	05/15/56	NULL
000-009	10020	Eastside	NOW	10/21/89	512.89
000-006	10030	Central	NOW	06/30/91	3888.00
000-010	10040	Central	Savings	01/05/51	25.00
000-004	10010	Westlake	Loan	11/25/92	15085.85
000-018	10050	Westlake	NOW	10/31/87	2500.12
000-005	10050	Westlake	CD	04/18/92	5012.89
000-012	10060	Eastside	NOW	10/10/90	386.00
000-017	10070	Eastside	NOW	07/16/92	259.00

SELECT FROM Account WHERE Branch name = "Central" GIVING One Branch

One Branch

Account #	Customer #	Branch Name	Account Type	Date Opened	Current Balance
000-001	10010	Central	NOW	10/10/82	2568.12
000-002	10010	Central	CD	02/02/92	10520.00
000-003	10010	Central	Safe Deposit	05/15/56	NULL
000-006	10030	Central	NOW	06/30/91	3888.00
000-010	10040	Central	Savings	01/05/51	25.00

Figure 6.6   Selecting rows from a relation

While none of these relations have the same column names as Small Bank's Customers, Account, and Transaction relations, some union-compatibility does exist. Clients is union-compatible with Customers, since each attribute in Clients corresponds exactly to an attribute in Customers. The same is not true for Small Bank's Account table; it contains many more columns than Smaller Bank's Account table. Small Bank's Transaction table also isn't union-compatible with Smaller Bank's Transaction table.

Because Clients and Customers are union-compatible, Small Bank can use the union operation to compile a single list of customers. Figure 6.7 shows the result of a union operation on Small Bank's Customers relation and Smaller Bank's Clients relation. Notice that the two banks actually have one customer in common (Samuel Jones). However, because Mr. Jones has different customer numbers at each bank, the union operation does not recognize that his row in Customers actually represents the same person as his row in Clients. Union does remove duplicate rows, but only when the entire rows are the same. In this case, the rows are the same *except* for the customer number.

Difference

The difference operation produces a result that consists of all rows in the first relation that are not present in the second (in other words, it subtracts the second relation in the command from the first). Rows that appear in the second relation but not the first are ignored. Difference can only be performed on union-compatible relations.

Difference is a very handy retrieval tool. It is used primarily to answers questions involving a negative. For example, if Small Bank removes the customer number columns from Customers and Clients, it can be used to identify all Small Bank customers who are not Smaller Bank customers. That operation

Temp Customers MINUS Temp Clients GIVING Small Bank Only

is summarized in Figure 6.8.

Difference is the only relational algebra operation in which the order or the tables in the operation changes the result. Consider the result of the operation

Temp Clients MINUS Temp Customers GIVING Smaller Bank Only

As you can see from Figure 6.9, reversing the order of the relations reverses the meaning of the operation. This difference operation states in effect, "Show me all the people who are customers of Smaller Bank but not Small Bank." The result table contains all customers from Temp Clients who don't appear in Temp Customers. In this case, only Samuel Smith has accounts at both banks and therefore doesn't appear in the result.

Customers

Customer #	Cust. Name	Cust. Address	Cust. Phone	SSN
10010	Jones, Samuel	105 W. 99th, Newtown 02899	555-0105	123-45-6789
10020	Abrams, Max	2204 Nox Hill, Newtown 02845	555-2204	234-56-7890
10030	Cohen, Esther	39 Summer, Newtown 02845	555-0039	345-67-8901
10040	Khan, Sarya	1001 N. 54th, Newtown 02898	555-1001	456-78-9012
10050	Brown, Judith	RR1 Box 99C, Rural City 02811	555-9900	567-89-0123
10060	Wales, Miranda	33 Summer, Apt. # 18, Newtown 02945	555-0033	678-90-1234
10070	Smith, Samuel	RR6 Box 125, Rural City 02811	555-1250	789-09-2345

Clients

Client #	CName	CAdd	CPhone	CSSN
44411	Lamb, Jackson	25 W. 6th Ave., Newtown 02899	555-0025	222-22-2222
44433	Morrow, Woodrow	12 Summer, Newtown 02845	555-1200	777-77-7777
44400	Smith, Jane	33 Summer, Apt. #25, Newtown 02945	555-0303	252-52-5252
44466	Smith, Samuel	RR6 Box 125, Rural City 02811	555-1250	789-09-2345

Customers UNION Clients GIVING Both Banks

Both Banks

Customer #	Cust. Name	Cust. Address	Cust. Phone	SSN
10010	Jones, Samuel	105 W. 99th, Newtown 02899	555-0105	123-45-6789
10020	Abrams, Max	2204 Nox Hill, Newtown 02845	555-2204	234-56-7890
10030	Cohen, Esther	39 Summer, Newtown 02845	555-0039	345-67-8901
10040	Khan, Sarya	1001 N. 54th, Newtown 02898	555-1001	456-78-9012
10050	Brown, Judith	RR1 Box 99C, Rural City 02811	555-9900	567-89-0123
10060	Wales, Miranda	33 Summer, Apt. # 18, Newtown 02945	555-0033	678-90-1234
10070	Smith, Samuel	RR6 Box 125, Rural City 02811	555-1250	789-09-2345
44411	Lamb, Jackson	25 W. 6th Ave., Newtown 02899	555-0025	222-22-2222
44433	Morrow, Woodrow	12 Summer, Newtown 02845	555-1200	777-77-7777
44400	Smith, Jane	33 Summer, Apt. #25, Newtown 02945	555-0303	252-52-5252
44466	Smith, Samuel	RR6 Box 125, Rural City 02811	555-1250	789-09-2345

Figure 6.7   The union of two relations

Temp Customers

Cust. Name	Cust. Address	Cust. Phone	SSN
Jones, Samuel	105 W. 99th, Newtown 02899	555-0105	123-45-6789
Abrams, Max	2204 Nox Hill, Newtown 02845	555-2204	234-56-7890
Cohen, Esther	39 Summer, Newtown 02845	555-0039	345-67-8901
Khan, Satya	1001 N. 54th, Newtown 02898	555-1001	456-78-9012
Brown, Judith	RR1 Box 99C, Rural City 02811	555-9900	567-89-0123
Wales, Miranda	33 Summer, Apt. # 18, Newtown 02945	555-0033	678-90-1234
Smith, Samuel	RR6 Box 125, Rural City 02811	555-1250	789-09-2345

Temp Customers MINUS Temp Clients GIVING Small Bank Only

Temp Clients

CName	CAdd	CPhone	CSSN
Lamb, Jackson	25 W. 6th Ave., Newtown 02899	555-0025	222-22-2222
Morrow, Woodrow	12 Summer, Newtown 02845	555-1200	777-77-7777
Smith, Jane	33 Summer, Apt. #25, Newtown 02945	555-0303	252-52-5252
Smith, Samuel	RR6 Box 125, Rural City 02811	555-1250	789-09-2345

Small Bank Only

Cust. Name	Cust. Address	Cust. Phone	SSN
Jones, Samuel	105 W. 99th, Newtown 02899	555-0105	123-45-6789
Abrams, Max	2204 Nox Hill, Newtown 02845	555-2204	234-56-7890
Cohen, Esther	39 Summer, Newtown 02845	555-0039	345-67-8901
Khan, Satya	1001 N. 54th, Newtown 02898	555-1001	456-78-9012
Brown, Judith	RR1 Box 99C, Rural City 02811	555-9900	567-89-0123
Wales, Miranda	33 Summer, Apt. # 18, Newtown 02945	555-0033	678-90-1234

Figure 6.8   The difference of two relations

Temp Clients

CName	CAdd	CPhone	CSSN
Lamb, Jackson	25 W. 6th Ave., Newtown 02899	555-0025	222-22-2222
Morrow, Woodrow	12 Summer, Newtown 02845	555-1200	777-77-7777
Smith, Jane	33 Summer, Apt. #25, Newtown 02945	555-0303	252-52-5252
Smith, Samuel	RR6 Box 125, Rural City 02811	555-1250	789-09-2345

Temp Clients MINUS Temp Customers GIVING Smaller Bank Only

Temp Customers

Cust. Name	Cust. Address	Cust. Phone	SSN
Jones, Samuel	105 W. 99th, Newtown 02899	555-0105	123-45-6789
Abrams, Max	2204 Nox Hill, Newtown 02845	555-2204	234-56-7890
Cohen, Esther	39 Summer, Newtown 02845	555-0039	345-67-8901
Khan, Satya	1001 N. 54th, Newtown 02898	555-1001	456-78-9012
Brown, Judith	RR1 Box 99C, Rural City 02811	555-9900	567-89-0123
Wales, Miranda	33 Summer, Apt. # 18, Newtown 02945	555-0033	678-90-1234
Smith, Samuel	RR6 Box 125, Rural City 02811	555-1250	789-09-2345

Smaller Bank Only

CName	CAdd	CPhone	CSSN
Lamb, Jackson	25 W. 6th Ave., Newtown 02899	555-0025	222-22-2222
Morrow, Woodrow	12 Summer, Newtown 02845	555-1200	777-77-7777
Smith, Jane	33 Summer, Apt. #25, Newtown 02945	555-0303	252-52-5252

Figure 6.9   The effect of the position of relations in a difference operation

Intersect

The intersect operation is the opposite of union. While union produces a result containing all rows that appear in either relation, intersection produces a result containing all rows that appear in both relations. Intersection can therefore only be performed on two union-compatible relations.

Intersection is useful for identifying entities that have some characteristic in common. For example, if Small Bank wished to know which of its customers also had accounts at Smaller Bank, it could intersect Temp Customers and Temp Clients. The result, seen in Figure 6.10, contains only rows for only those individuals who have matching rows in both Temp Customers and Temp Clients.

Be aware that there is a potential problem with an intersection. For a row to be included in the result, it must exist in exactly the same way in the two relations being intersected. In the example we have just seen, if a customer's address is stored as "105 W. 99th" in Temp Customers but as "105 W. 99th Place" in Temp Clients, the intersection will not recognize the two rows as being equivalent.

Product

The product operation (the Cartesian product) creates new rows by concatenating every row from one relation onto every row in another. In other words, it creates all possible pairs of rows. If one of the relations in the operation has 15 rows and the other 20 rows, the virtual table created by taking their product will contain 300 rows. Columns that appear in both tables participating in the operation are duplicated in the result table.

Product is generally not used directly to produce the result of a query. Instead, a DBMS may perform a product followed by a select operation to implement a join. To see how this works, consider a query that asks for the customer numbers of all people who have accounts at each of Small Bank's branches. This query requires a join between the Branch and Branch Patronage tables over the Branch Name column. However, rather than doing the join directly, a DBMS might perform a product on Branch and Branch Patronage:

Branch TIMES Branch Patronage GIVING Intermediate Product

Temp Customers

Cust. Name	Cust. Address	Cust. Phone	SSN
Jones, Samuel	105 W. 99th, Newtown 02899	555-0105	123-45-6789
Abrams, Max	2204 Nox Hill, Newtown 02845	555-2204	234-56-7890
Cohen, Esther	39 Summer, Newtown 02845	555-0039	345-67-8901
Khan, Sarya	1001 N. 54th, Newtown 02898	555-1001	456-78-9012
Brown, Judith	RR1 Box 99C, Rural City 02811	555-9900	567-89-0123
Wales, Miranda	33 Summer, Apt. # 18, Newtown 02945	555-0033	678-90-1234
Smith, Samuel	RR6 Box 125, Rural City 02811	555-1250	789-09-2345

Temp Clients INTERSECT Temp Customers GIVING Smaller Bank Only

Temp Clients

CName	CAdd	CPhone	CSSN
Lamb, Jackson	25 W. 6th Ave., Newtown 02899	555-0025	222-22-2222
Morrow, Woodrow	12 Summer, Newtown 02845	555-1200	777-77-7777
Smith, Jane	33 Summer, Apt. #25, Newtown 02945	555-0303	252-52-5252
Smith, Samuel	RR6 Box 125, Rural City 02811	555-1250	789-09-2345

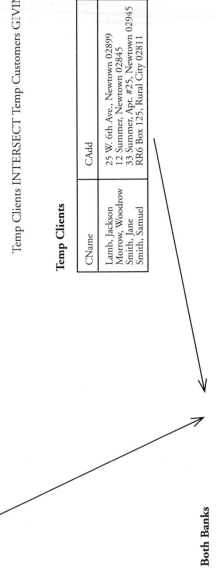

Both Banks

Cust. Name	Cust. Address	Cust. Phone	SSN
Smith, Samuel	RR6 Box 125, Rural City 02811	555-1250	789-09-2345

Figure 6.10 The intersection of two relations

The result table, which appears in Figure 6.11 as Intermediate Product, contains 24 rows (the three rows in Branch multiplied by the eight rows in Branch Patronage). The join, however, needs only those rows where the branch name in both tables is the same. Therefore, the select that completes the implementation of the join is written:

SELECT FROM Intermediate Product WHERE Branch Name (from
    Branch) = Branch Name (from Branch Patronage) GIVING Result of
    Join

As you will see in Chapter 8, this two-step procedure for implementing a join is very similar to the syntax used to request a join in a SQL query.

Divide

The divide operation is perhaps the least intuitive of all the operations in the relational algebra. As most commonly performed, division uses two relations: a unary relation (one with only a single column) and a binary relation (one with two columns).

To see how it works, assume that we have a new relation for Small Bank, Branch Names (Branch Name). In Figure 6.12, Branch Names contains only two rows, one for the Central branch and one for the Westlake branch. If we divide Branch Patronage (the dividend) by Branch Names (the divisor), we get a unary relation (Two Branch Customers) as the result. Its single column is *Customer #*, the column that Branch Patronage and Branch Names do not have in common. If you look at the data in Two Branch Customers, you will see that it contains the customer numbers of all people who have an account at both the Central branch and the Westlake branch.

Division retrieves values from the column of the dividend relation that it does not share with the divisor relation. However, values are selected by looking for matches between the overlapping column (for example, *Branch Name*). To be included in the result, a value in the non-overlapping column (*Customer #*) must be associated, in the dividend relation, with every value in the divisor relation. In our example, a given customer number may occur at least twice in Branch Patronage; one row might have a value of Central for *Branch Name*, the other a value of Westlake for *Branch Name*. If those two rows do appear, then

Branch

Branch Name	Branch Address	Branch Phone	Branch Hours
Eastside	4232 E. 44th, Newtown 02311	555-4232	0900-1200 M-S
Westlake	109 Lake Street, Newtown 02315	555-0109	0830-1630 M-F
Central	100 Central Square, Newtown 02311	555-0100	0830-1800 M-S

Branch Patronage

Branch Name	Customer #
Central	10010
Eastside	10020
Central	10030
Central	10040
Westlake	10010
Westlake	10050
Eastside	10060
Eastside	10070

Branch TIMES Branch Patronage
GIVING Intermediate Product

Intermediate Product

Branch Name (from Branch)	Branch Address	Branch Phone	Branch Hours	Branch Name (from Branch Patronage)	Customer #
Eastside	4232 E. 44th, Newtown 02311	555-4232	0900-1200 M-S	Central	10010
Westlake	109 Lake Street, Newtown 02315	555-0109	0830-1630 M-F	Eastside	10020
Central	100 Central Square, Newtown 02311	555-0100	0830-1800 M-S	Central	10030
Eastside	4232 E. 44th, Newtown 02311	555-4232	0900-1200 M-S	Central	10040
Westlake	109 Lake Street, Newtown 02315	555-0109	0830-1630 M-F	Westlake	10010
Central	100 Central Square, Newtown 02311	555-0100	0830-1800 M-S	Westlake	10050
Eastside	4232 E. 44th, Newtown 02311	555-4232	0900-1200 M-S	Eastside	10060
Westlake	109 Lake Street, Newtown 02315	555-0109	0830-1630 M-F	Eastside	10070
Central	100 Central Square, Newtown 02311	555-0100	0830-1800 M-S	Central	10010
Eastside	4232 E. 44th, Newtown 02311	555-4232	0900-1200 M-S	Eastside	10020
Westlake	109 Lake Street, Newtown 02315	555-0109	0830-1630 M-F	Central	10030
Central	100 Central Square, Newtown 02311	555-0100	0830-1800 M-S	Central	10040
Eastside	4232 E. 44th, Newtown 02311	555-4232	0900-1200 M-S	Westlake	10010
Westlake	109 Lake Street, Newtown 02315	555-0109	0830-1630 M-F	Westlake	10050
Central	100 Central Square, Newtown 02311	555-0100	0830-1800 M-S	Eastside	10060
Eastside	4232 E. 44th, Newtown 02311	555-4232	0900-1200 M-S	Eastside	10070
Westlake	109 Lake Street, Newtown 02315	555-0109	0830-1630 M-F	Central	10010
Central	100 Central Square, Newtown 02311	555-0100	0830-1800 M-S	Eastside	10020
Eastside	4232 E. 44th, Newtown 02311	555-4232	0900-1200 M-S	Central	10030
Westlake	109 Lake Street, Newtown 02315	555-0109	0830-1630 M-F	Central	10040
Central	100 Central Square, Newtown 02311	555-0100	0830-1800 M-S	Westlake	10010
Eastside	4232 E. 44th, Newtown 02311	555-4232	0900-1200 M-S	Westlake	10050
Westlake	109 Lake Street, Newtown 02315	555-0109	0830-1630 M-F	Eastside	10060
Central	100 Central Square, Newtown 02311	555-0100	0830-1800 M-S	Eastside	10070

SELECT FROM Intermediate Product WHERE Branch Name
(from Branch) = Branch Name (from Branch Patronage)
GIVING Result of Join

Result of Join

Branch Name	Branch Address	Branch Phone	Branch Hours	Customer #
Central	100 Central Square, Newtown 02311	555-0100	0830-1800 M-S	10010
Eastside	4232 E. 44th, Newtown 02311	555-4232	0900-1200 M-S	10020
Central	100 Central Square, Newtown 02311	555-0100	0830-1800 M-S	10030
Central	100 Central Square, Newtown 02311	555-0100	0830-1800 M-S	10040
Westlake	109 Lake Street, Newtown 02315	555-0109	0830-1630 M-F	10010
Westlake	109 Lake Street, Newtown 02315	555-0109	0830-1630 M-F	10050
Eastside	4232 E. 44th, Newtown 02311	555-4232	0900-1200 M-S	10060
Eastside	4232 E. 44th, Newtown 02311	555-4232	0900-1200 M-S	10070

Figure 6.11 Using the product to implement a join

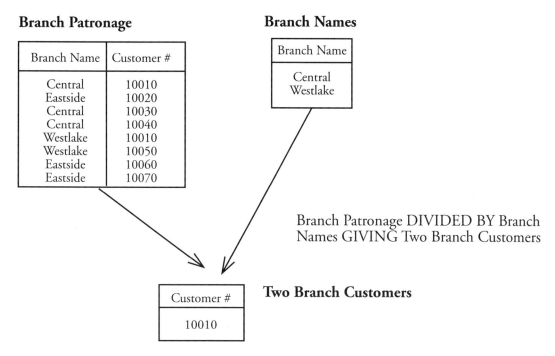

Figure 6.12   Dividing one relation by another

the customer number will be placed in the result. In general, divide retrieves entities that have multiple rows in a table (in this example, customers who have accounts at two specific branches).

The result of a divide can also be obtained by performing one select for each value in the unary relation and then joining the results of the selects. (If there are *n* rows in the unary relation, you will need *n-1* joins.) As you can see in Figure 6.13, each select retrieves rows for one of the values in the unary relation. The join is then performed over customer number, placing a row for each customer who has rows in *both* of the selects' result tables into the join's result table.

Outer Join

The outer join is generally not considered one of the eight basic relational algebra operations. It has, however, been implemented in a number of query languages (including some SQL implementations) because it is so very useful for data retrieval.

Branch Patronage

Branch Name	Customer #
Central	10010
Eastside	10020
Central	10030
Central	10040
Westlake	10010
Westlake	10050
Eastside	10060
Eastside	10070

SELECT FROM Branch Patronage
WHERE Branch Name = "Central"

Central Branch Customers

Branch Name	Customer #
Central	10010
Central	10030
Central	10040

Branch Patronage

Branch Name	Customer #
Central	10010
Eastside	10020
Central	10030
Central	10040
Westlake	10010
Westlake	10050
Eastside	10060
Eastside	10070

SELECT FROM Branch Patronage
WHERE Branch Name = "Westlake"

Westlake Branch Customers

Branch Name	Customer #
Westlake	10010
Westlake	10050

JOIN Central Branch Customers TO Westlake Branch Customers
OVER Customer # GIVING Two Branch Customers

Two Branch Customers

Branch Name	Branch Name	Customer #
Central	Westlake	10010

Figure 6.13   Implementing a divide with two selects and a join

As you will remember from earlier in this chapter, a join excludes rows
from the result table when it can find no matching values in the column or columns over which the join is performed. The outer join, however, includes all
rows from both source tables. When it cannot find a matching value in the column or columns over which the join is performed, it fills the remainder of the

row with null values. As a result, the result table of an outer join may have no primary key and therefore may not be a legal relation. However, because the result table is a virtual table (not stored in the database), the fact that it might not be a legal relation presents no problem.

As an example, take a look at Figure 6.14, which contains an outer join of Small Bank's Customer and Account relations. (Remember that two customers, numbers 10015 and 10055, have no accounts.) The intent of the outer join is not only to find out the names to which account numbers belong, but to identify people who currently have no accounts. (Small Bank may wish to delete those former customers from Customers.) It is written:

OUTER JOIN Customers TO Account OVER Customer # GIVING
    Account Owners

The result is somewhat different from that produced by the equi-join in Figure 6.4. The outer join result table includes rows for customers 10015 and 10055. The value "null" has been placed in all attributes from the Account relation except *Customer #*, since no row for those customers appears in Account. Small Bank then knows that any row with null for an account number represents a customer who no longer has an active account.

It is important to realize that the table in Figure 6.14 is not a legal relation. Its primary key should be *Customer # + Account #*. However, the two customers with no accounts have null for their account number. The table therefore violates both entity integrity and the requirement for a unique primary key. Though outer joins often produce relations with primary key problems of this nature, they are nonetheless extremely useful for data retrieval.

Retrieval with Operations from the Relational Algebra

DBMSs use sequences of relational algebra operations to satisfy the queries presented by users. A part of the DBMS known as a *query optimizer* makes decisions as to the order in which the operations will be performed. In instances where there is a choice of the order of operations to produce a given result, the query optimizer picks the order that manipulates the smallest amount of data.

Customers

Customer #	Cust. Name	Cust. Address	Cust. Phone	SSN
10010	Jones, Samuel	105 W. 99th, Newtown 02899	555-0105	123-45-6789
10015	Jones, Patricia	85 Humbolt, Newtown 02899	555-0085	151-51-5151
10020	Abrams, Max	2204 Nox Hill, Newtown 02845	555-2204	234-56-7890
10030	Cohen, Esther	39 Summer, Newtown 02845	555-0039	345-67-8901
10040	Khan, Satya	1001 N. 54th, Newtown 02898	555-1001	456-78-9012
10050	Brown, Judith	RR1 Box 99C, Rural City 02811	555-9900	567-89-0123
10055	Fredricks, Louis	909 Summer, Newtown 02845	555-9090	555-55-5555
10060	Wales, Miranda	33 Summer, Apt # 18, Newtown 02945	555-0033	678-90-1234
10070	Smith, Samuel	RR6 Box 125, Rural City 02811	555-1250	789-09-2345

OUTER JOIN Customers TO Account OVER
Customer # GIVING Account Owners

Account

Account #	Customer #	Branch	Account Type	Date Opened	Current Balance
000-001	10010	Central	NOW	10/10/82	2568.12
000-002	10010	Central	CD	02/02/92	10520.00
000-003	10010	Central	Safe Deposit	05/15/56	NULL
000-009	10020	Eastside	NOW	10/21/89	512.89
000-006	10030	Central	NOW	06/30/91	3888.00
000-010	10040	Central	Savings	01/05/51	25.00
000-004	10010	Westlake	NOW	11/25/92	15085.85
000-018	10050	Westlake	Loan	10/31/87	2500.12
000-005	10050	Westlake	CD	04/18/92	5012.89
000-012	10060	Eastside	NOW	10/10/90	386.00
000-017	10070	Eastside	NOW	07/16/92	259.00

Account Owners

Account #	Customer #	Branch	Account Type	Date Opened	Current Balance	Cust. Name	Cust. Address	Cust. Phone	SSN
000-001	10010	Central	NOW	10/10/82	2568.12	Jones, Samuel	105 W. 99th, Newtown 02899	555-0105	123-45-6789
000-002	10010	Central	CD	02/02/92	10520.00	Jones, Samuel	105 W. 99th, Newtown 02899	555-0105	123-45-6789
000-003	10010	Central	Safe Deposit	05/15/56	NULL	Jones, Samuel	105 W. 99th, Newtown 02899	555-0105	123-45-6789
NULL	10015	NULL	NULL	NULL	NULL	Jones, Patricia	85 Humbolt, Newtown 02899	555-0085	151-51-5151
000-009	10020	Eastside	NOW	10/21/89	512.89	Abrams, Max	2204 Nox Hill, Newtown 02845	555-2204	234-56-7890
000-006	10030	Central	NOW	06/30/91	3888.00	Cohen, Esther	39 Summer, Newtown 02845	555-0039	345-67-8901
000-010	10040	Central	Savings	01/05/51	25.00	Khan, Satya	1001 N. 54th, Newtown 02898	555-1001	456-78-9012
000-004	10010	Westlake	NOW	11/25/92	15085.85	Jones, Samuel	105 W. 99th, Newtown 02899	555-0105	123-45-6789
000-018	10050	Westlake	Loan	10/31/87	2500.12	Brown, Judith	RR1 Box 99C, Rural City 02811	555-9900	567-89-0123
000-005	10050	Westlake	CD	04/18/92	5012.89	Brown, Judith	RR1 Box 99C, Rural City 02811	555-9900	567-89-0123
NULL	10055	NULL	NULL	NULL	NULL	Fredricks, Louis	909 Summer, Newtown 02845	555-9090	555-55-5555
000-012	10060	Eastside	NOW	10/10/90	386.00	Wales, Miranda	33 Summer, Apt # 18, Newtown 02945	555-0033	678-90-1234
000-017	10070	Eastside	NOW	07/16/92	259.00	Smith, Samuel	RR6 Box 125, Rural City 02811	555-1250	789-09-2345

Figure 6.14 Performing an outer join

To help you understand how a DBMS processes queries, this section contains several examples of how a DBMS might execute queries on both the Small Bank and Federated Taxi Company databases. It uses the relational algebra syntax you have seen through the first portion of this chapter.

As a simple example, consider completing the query presented earlier: Retrieve the numbers of all customers served by Small Bank's Central branch. It's really a two-step operation:

1. SELECT FROM Account WHERE Branch Name = "Central" GIVING One Branch
2. PROJECT Customer # FROM One Branch GIVING Customer Number Only

In this case, the DBMS has no choice in the order of operations. If the project was performed first, the DBMS would lose the column used in the select and be unable to select rows.

Realistically, simply retrieving customer numbers doesn't provide a great deal of useful information. This would be a more useful query: Retrieve the names of all the customers who have accounts at Small Bank's Central branch. This retrieval requires three steps:

1. SELECT FROM Account WHERE Branch Name = "Central" GIVING One Branch
2. JOIN Customer Number Only TO Customers OVER Customer # GIVING All Info
3. PROJECT Customer name FROM All Info GIVING Central Branch Customers

In this example, the DBMS could have performed the join in step 2 before executing the select in step 1. However, the select cuts down on the amount of data that is included in the join. A query optimizer is therefore likely to choose to perform the select first.

If a customer telephoned Small Bank's main office, asking for the operating hours of each branch at which he or she had an account, the bank's DBMS could retrieve the information with the following sequence of operations:

1. SELECT FROM Customers WHERE Cust. Name = "Dough, Jon" GIVING One Customer
2. JOIN One Customer TO Branch Patronage OVER Customer # GIVING Customer and Branches
3. JOIN Customer and Branches TO Branch OVER Branch Name GIVING With Branch Info
4. PROJECT Branch Name, Branch Hours FROM With Branch Info GIVING Times

This query could also have been performed by joining Customers to Account in step 2, since the branch data is also part of the Account table. However, any given customer may have more than one account at any given branch, whereas Branch Patronage contains only one row for each branch at which a customer has any number of accounts. Therefore, using Branch Patronage in step 2 reduces the amount of data handled by the join.

One of the typical queries issued by the Federated Taxi Company is a request for all cabs not reserved for a given shift. As you will remember, queries asked in the negative typically require a difference operation:

1. SELECT FROM Shift Driven WHERE Shift Name = "ngt" and WkDate = *today* GIVING On Reserve (This returns all the cabs that *are* reserved.)

> **By the way:** The preceding assumes that the DBMS has a function that inserts the current system date wherever *today* appears

2. PROJECT Cab # FROM On Reserve GIVING Reserved Cabs
3. PROJECT Cab # FROM Cab GIVING All Cabs (Remember that difference requires union-compatible tables.)
4. All Cabs MINUS Reserved Cabs GIVING Available Cabs

Every week, the Federated Taxi Company needs to see a list of the cabs that need to have tune-ups. In this case, a user is actually asking the DBMS to make a decision about which cabs need maintenance. To make that sort of decision, the DBMS must be given a rule by which it should select cabs. For example, if FTC's chief mechanic has determined that cabs should be given complete tune-ups at least every three months, then the DBMS should be instructed to select all cabs whose date of last tune-up is more than 90 days prior to the current date.

Because the maintenance chief also wants to see all of the maintenance performed on cabs needing tune-ups, executing this query takes a number of steps. The process might be as follows:

1. SELECT FROM Maintenance Performed WHERE Maint. Type = "tune-up" and Maint. Date > *today* - 90 GIVING Have Been Tuned (This produces all the cabs that *have* been tuned up in the past three months.)
2. PROJECT Cab # FROM Have Been Tuned GIVING Tuned Up Cabs
3. PROJECT Cab # FROM Cabs GIVING All Cabs
4. All Cabs MINUS Tuned Up Cabs GIVING Needing Tune-ups
5. JOIN Needing Tune-ups TO Maintenance Performed GIVING All Maintenance Done (This creates a relation containing the maintenance records of only those cabs needing tune-ups.)

Summary

A relationally complete DBMS supports five operations from the relational algebra: select, project, join, union, and difference. The result of each of these operations is a virtual table; none modify base tables. Data retrieval from a relational database can be performed by combining sequences of these five operations.

Select extracts rows from a table based on some logical criteria. The result of select is a virtual table that contains all attributes from the original table but only those rows that meet the logical criteria contained in the command; select cannot restrict which columns will be included in the result. Select is the most easily confused of the relational algebra operations, since many DBMSs use SELECT as a retrieval command. The retrieval command is more powerful than the relational algebra operation, since it can perform multiple relational algebra operations to implement a query.

Project extracts columns from a table. The result of a project is a virtual table that contains all rows from the original table but only those columns specified in the project command. Project cannot restrict which rows are included in the result. Project is the major tool used to create 3NF relations from 1NF relations. 3NF databases are sets of projections taken from a 1NF database.

Join combines two tables into one. The most common forms, the natural join and equi-joins, create new rows in a virtual table by searching for matching values in the columns that the two tables have in common. Other, less frequently used types of joins create new rows based on relationships other than equality between attributes in the two tables.

Union and *difference* are applicable only to tables with the same columns. (Though the columns do not necessarily require the same names, they must have the same logical domains.) Union combines two tables into a single result, including all rows from both the source tables. The result of a difference operation is a virtual table containing all rows from one relation that are not in the second.

The relational algebra also provides three less frequently used operations: intersect, product, and divide. *Intersect*, which is applicable only to union-compatible relations, produces a resultant relation that contains rows found in both the relations being intersected. *Product* produces every possible pair of concatenated rows from two relations. *Divide* retrieves values from the dividend relation that match all the values from the divisor relation in a column shared by both relations.

In addition, the *outer join* operation is often included for retrieval purposes. An outer join performs a join which does not exclude rows for which matching values in overlapping columns cannot be found. Instead, NULL is used for those attributes for which values cannot be determined. Outer joins therefore often produce result tables which are not legal relations.

References

Aho, A. V. et al. 1979. "The theory of joins in relational databases." *ACM Transactions on Database Systems.* 4(3):297-314.

Codd, E. F. 1972. "Relational completeness of data base sublanguages." In *Data Base Systems. Courant Computer Science Symposia Series,* Vol. 6. Englewood Cliffs, N.J.: Prentice-Hall.

Hall, P. A. V., P. Hitchcock, and S. J. P. Todd. 1975. "An algebra of relations for machine computation." Conference Record of the Second ACM Symposium on Principles of Programming Languages.

Hall, P. A. V. 1984. "Relational algebras, logic, and functional programming." *Proceedings of the 1984 AMC SIGMOD International Conference on Management of Data.* June.

Things to Think About

1. One of the things that often surprises people when they begin to query a database is how slow a join of two tables can be. This is because many DBMSs use a combination of the product and select operations to implement a join.

   a. What would be the effect of joining two tables with 1,000 rows?
   b. How could you design a database to avoid the problem? What new problems does this type of design change introduce?

2. As you read in this chapter, it is possible to synthesize some relational algebra operations from others. For example, the divide operation can be implemented as a series of selects and joins. Try to find a way to synthesize the difference operation from other relational algebra operations. Based on the results of your experience, how important is it that a DBMS support difference directly? What effect does the lack of a difference operation have on the query capabilities of a DBMS?

Exercises

1. Given the instances of relations in Figure 6.15 (from the office of Margaret Holmes, D.M.D.), perform the relational operations indicated. Express your result as the instance of a new relation.

   1. PROJECT Patient #, Patient Name, Phone FROM Patient Master GIVING Patient List
   2. PROJECT Who Pays, Employer, Payer Phone, Work Phone FROM Payers GIVING Payer List

Patient Master

Patient #	Patient Name	Address	Phone	SSN	Who Pays	Relation to Who Pays	Payment Source
001	Fields, Thomas	23 Oak, 18106	555-0009	543-21-0000	Fields, Joan	husband	insurance
002	Jackson, Louise	23 Oak, 18106	555-0009	123-12-1234	Fields, Joan	foster-child	insurance
003	Barsky, Harvard	45 Lincoln, 18224	555-1212	098-76-5432	Barsky, Wilson	daughter	cash
004	Waterman, Lyn	1004 S. 9th, 18106	555-0987	987-65-4321	Waterman, Lyn	self	insurance
005	Fields, Linda	23 Oak, 18106	555-0009	876-54-3210	Fields, Joan	daughter	insurance
006	Waterman, Marty	1004 S. 9th, 18106	555-0987	765-43-2109	Waterman, Lyn	son	insurance
007	Waterman, Erik	1004 S. 9th, 18106	555-0987	654-32-1098	Waterman, Lyn	son	insurance
008	Barsky, Yale	45 Lincoln, 18224	555-1212	543-21-0987	Barsky, Wilson	son	cash
009	Barsky, Wilson	45 Lincoln, 18224	555-1212	432-10-9876	Barsky, Wilson	self	cash

Payers

Who Pays	Payer Address	Payer Phone	Employer	Work Phone	Insurance Carrier
Barsky, Wilson	45 Lincoln, 18224	555-1212	U. Archaeological Museum	555-0676	none
Fields, Joan	23 Oak, 18106	555-0009	Small Bank	555-9988	Connecticut General
Waterman, Lyn	1004 S. 9th, 18106	555-0987	Federated Taxi Co.	555-3214	Blue Cross

Costs

Procedure	Price
Cleaning	45.00
Extraction, bicuspid	75.00
Extraction, eye tooth	75.00
Extraction, incisor	75.00
Extraction, molar	100.00
Extraction, wisdom tooth	150.00
Filling, bicuspid	50.00
Filling, eye tooth	50.00
Filling, incisor	50.00
Filling, molar	50.00
Filling, wisdom tooth	75.00
X-ray, bite-wing	30.00
X-ray, whole mouth	50.00

Visits

Patient #	Date	Procedure	Comments
003	10-12-93	Cleaning	
003	10-12-93	X-ray, bite-wing	
004	10-12-93	Cleaning	4 fillings need replacement
005	10-12-93	Cleaning	
005	10-12-93	X-ray, whole mouth	Overbite is getting worse
001	10-13-93	Cleaning	
006	10-13-93	Extraction, wisdom tooth	Impacted lower-left
009	10-13-93	Cleaning	Heavy smoker; much tartar
009	10-13-93	X-ray, whole mouth	
009	10-13-93	Filling, bicuspid	Upper-right

Figure 6.15   Relations for exercises

3. JOIN Patient Master TO Visits OVER Patient # GIVING Patient Temp
   - PROJECT Patient #, Patient Name, Date, Procedure FROM Patient Temp GIVING Patient History
4. JOIN Visits TO Costs OVER Procedure GIVING Charges Temp
   - PROJECT Patient #, Procedure, Date, Price FROM Charges Temp GIVING Costs by Patient
   - JOIN Costs by Patient TO Patient Master OVER Patient # GIVING Payer Temp
   - PROJECT Who Pays, Name, Procedure, Date, Price FROM Payer Temp GIVING Costs by Payer
5. SELECT FROM Visits WHERE Procedure = "Cleaning" GIVING Patients Cleaned
   - JOIN Patients Cleaned TO Patient Master GIVING Cleaned Temp
   - PROJECT Patient #, Name FROM Cleaned Temp GIVING Who Cleaned
6. SELECT FROM Payers WHERE Insurance Carrier = "none" GIVING No Insurance
   - JOIN No Insurance TO Patient Master GIVING Cash Temp
   - PROJECT Patient #, Name FROM Cash Temp GIVING Cash Patients

2. Given the following set of relations from the East Coast Aquarium database, list the sequence of relational algebra operations needed to implement the queries below.

   Species (Species Code, Latin Name, English Name)
   Location (Location Code, Place in Building, Size, Head Keeper)
   Population (Species Code, Location Code, Number of Animals)
   Food (Type of Food)
   Feeding (Species Code, Type of Food, Amount of Food, Feeding Interval)
   Habitats (Habitat Type)
   Can Live (Species Code, Habitat Type)
   Where Found (Location Code, Habitat Type)

Source (<u>Source Code</u>, Source Name, Source Address, Source Phone, Contact Person)
Can Supply (<u>Source Code</u>, <u>Species Code</u>)
Shipment (<u>P.O. #</u>, Source Code, Order Date, Order Total $)
Shipment Items (<u>P.O. #</u>, <u>Species Code</u>, Number of Animals, Each $, Line $)

1. List the types of food eaten by species code 155.
2. List the place in the building of all locations that are more than 50 gallons in size.
3. List the types of food eaten by Bottlenose Dolphins.
4. List the English name and species code of each species that live in location code 222.
5. List the English name of all species that can live in a coral reef habitat.
6. List the names of all head keepers who are responsible for Hammerhead Sharks.
7. List the Latin name of all species that eat meal worms.
8. List the Latin name of all species that do not eat mealworms.
9. List the Latin name of all species that do not live in location 1 (the main tank).
10. List the contact person and phone number at each source that can supply harbor seals.
11. List the name of each source from which an animal costing more than $5,000 was ordered.
12. List the English name of all species that were ordered on purchase order # 85093.
13. List the name of all sources that can supply Yellow Tangs, Niger Triggers, *and* Blue Damselfish.
14. List the names of all sources from which the Aquarium *has not* ordered in the past two years.

7

Manipulating Data: QBE

QBE (query by example) is a graphic query language available with some DBMSs. Many end users prefer it over a command-line query language such as SQL because it lets them query and modify data without needing to type commands. It has therefore become an important alternative to SQL. This chapter introduces basic QBE operations as performed on a microcomputer platform. Its intent is to show you the way in which one type of query language interacts with data stored in a database.

QBE was developed by IBM for use with DB2 and *SQL/DS* (its relational DBMSs for mainframes). Several microcomputer DBMSs have also implemented QBE. Paradox has the most complete implementation and is therefore used for the examples in this chapter. (*dBASE IV* and *R:BASE* use QBE as an alternative to their command-line query languages for data retrieval only.)

QBE is a complete query language. It can be used to retrieve data, add data, modify data, and delete data. However, unlike SQL, it cannot be used to modify the structure of a database. In other words, it cannot be used to create or delete base tables or view definitions.

QBE operations are performed by making entries in tables that appear on the screen. Such tables may be called "skeletons" or "images," depending on the DBMS. (Because there is no national standard for QBE as there is for SQL, QBE implementations tend to differ more than SQL implementations.)

Sample Tables

The examples in this chapter use data from the Federated Taxi Company database. The tables on which the queries are based appear in Figure 7.1.

Cab

Cab #	Make/Model	Year	Plate	Cab Status	Condition	Current Odom.
002	Checker sedan	83	345 YAO	road safe	New engine - runs great	0
006	Checker sedan	82	997 IUF	not road safe	Needs new brake pads	485001
045	Ford LTD	92	867 POP	road safe	Excellent; under warranty	45999
104	Checker sedan	73	356 QLT	road safe	Needs new seat covers	204998
105	Checker sedan	73	111 ABC	road safe	Excellent	286003
108	Ford LTD	90	760 PLP	road safe	Excellent; warranty expired	56667
144	Ford LTD	88	290 AAQ	not road safe	Needs major body work	103245
215	Lincoln Towncar	93	776 IKL	road safe	Excellent; under warranty	23000
238	Lincoln Towncar	92	980 JAM	road safe	Excellent	256256
378	Checker sedan	78	771 TOW	road safe	Should be repainted	388990
404	Ford LTD	91	206 TTL	road safe	Excellent	321409

Incident

Inci. Date	Inci. Time	Cab #	Driver #	Inci. Type	Inci. Details
11/15/94	10:17 A.M.	104	06	ticket	Stopped in front of a fire hydrant to pick up a fare
11/15/94	7:20 P.M.	144	12	accident	Front of cab crashed into Jersey barrier on I-128. Driver was speeding.
11/15/94	1:05 A.M.	215	08	ticket	Speeding

Figure 7.1   Sample tables used for the Federated Taxi Company Database

Driver

Driver #	Driver Name	Driver Address	Driver Phone	License #	Exp. Date	Driver Status
01	Bailey, Max	1 North 1 St., Anytown, 10001	555-0001	US0101	12/15/95	pay before
02	Baker, Mary Ann	2 South 2 St., Anytown, 10002	555-0002	US0202	7/30/95	pay after
03	Lewis, John	3 North 3 St., Anytown 10003	555-0003	US0303	12/10/94	pay after
04	Santiago, Jorge	4 W. 4 Blvd., Anytown 10004	555-0004	US0404	3/18/95	pay after
05	Miller, Pat	1 W. 5th, Apt. 5, Anytown 10005	555-0005	US0505	12/1/96	do not reserve
06	Miller, Phyllis	2 N. 6th, Apt. 6B, Anytown 10006	555-0006	US0606	2/2/95	pay before
07	Phong, Quen	7 S.W. 7 Ave., Anytown 10007	555-0007	US0707	3/12/95	pay after
08	Wong, David	8 N. 8th, Anytown 10008	555-0008	US0808	5/15/96	pay after
09	Young, Leslie	9 W. East St., Anytown 10009	555-0009	US0909	3/12/96	pay before
10	Zilog, Charlie	10 W. 10th, Anytown 10010	555-0010	US1010	5/15/96	pay after
11	Erlich, Martin	11th & South, Anytown 10011	555-0011	US1111	3/15/95	pay before
12	Eastman, Rich	1200 N. 12th, Anytown 10012	555-0012	US1212	2/6/96	pay after
13	Kowalski, Pete	13th & Clay, Anytown 10013	555-0013	US1313	12/5/94	pay before
14	Mariott, Emily	14 W. 14 St., Anytown 10014	555-0014	US1414	12/23/94	do not reserve
15	French, Janice	1500 15th S., Anytown 10015	555-0015	US1515	12/16/95	pay after
16	Thieu, Lin Van	16 W. 16 Ave., Anytown 10016	555-0016	US1616	4/3/96	pay after
17	Jackson, Rafael	1700 Market, Anytown 10017	555-0017	US1717	3/2/95	pay before
18	Wilson, Carter	18 Town Ctr., Anytown 10018	555-0018	US1818	4/3/96	do not reserve
19	Kolson, Jan	19 N.E. 19th, Anytown 10019	555-0019	US1919	5/21/96	pay before
20	Abelman, John	20 E. 20th, Anytown 10020	555-0020	US2020	11/24/96	pay before

Maintenance activity

Maint. Type
body work
brake pads
inspect damage
new engine
new shocks
new upholstery
new windshield
oil change
replace tires
rotate tires
tune-up
wheel bearings

Figure 7.1 Sample tables used in the Federated Taxi Company database

Shift

Shift Name	WkDate
day	11/15/94
eve	11/15/94
ngt	11/15/94
day	11/16/94
eve	11/16/94
ngt	11/16/94
day	11/17/94
eve	11/17/94
ngt	11/17/94
day	11/18/94
eve	11/18/94
ngt	11/18/94
day	11/19/94
eve	11/19/94
ngt	11/19/94
day	11/20/94
eve	11/20/94
ngt	11/20/94

Maintenance performed

Maint. Type	Maint. Date	Cab #	Maint. Odom.
new engine	9/18/94	002	0
tune-up	9/18/94	002	0
tune-up	9/28/94	238	244809
wheel bearings	9/28/94	378	375122
new upholstery	10/12/94	404	313991
new windshield	10/12/94	404	313991
tune-up	10/12/94	104	197883
tune-up	10/12/94	215	15089
tune-up	10/12/94	404	313991
tune-up	10/15/94	006	485000
tune-up	11/2/94	108	55305
tune-up	11/14/94	045	40100
tune-up	11/15/94	104	286001
tune-up	11/15/94	378	388888
inspect damage	11/16/94	144	350190

Figure 7.1 Sample tables used in the Federated Taxi Company Database

Shift Driven

Shift Name	WkDate	Cab #	Driver #	WkFlag	Starting Odom.	Ending Odom.
day	11/15/94	104	06	T	202622	202771
day	11/15/94	238	10	T	210965	211104
day	11/15/94	404	20	T	319333	319487
eve	11/15/94	045	11	F		
eve	11/15/94	104	01	T	202771	202905
eve	11/15/94	144	12	T	350002	350190
ngt	11/15/94	045	16	T	48830	49190
ngt	11/15/94	108	01	T	53885	53900
ngt	11/15/94	215	08	T	20107	20255
day	11/16/94	238	10	F		
eve	11/19/94	238	03	F		
eve	11/20/94	238	03	F		
day	11/16/94	404	20	F		
eve	11/16/94	002	04	F		
eve	11/18/94	002	04	F		
eve	11/16/94	104	01	F		
eve	11/19/94	104	01	F		
eve	11/20/94	104	01	F		
ngt	11/16/94	002	07	F		
day	11/17/94	104	06	F		
day	11/18/94	104	06	F		
day	11/19/94	104	06	F		
day	11/17/94	238	10	F		
day	11/17/94	404	20	F		
ngt	11/17/94	108	02	F		
ngt	11/18/94	108	02	F		
day	11/18/94	238	10	F		
eve	11/18/94	045	11	F		
ngt	11/18/94	045	16	F		
ngt	11/18/94	215	08	F		

Figure 7.1 Sample tables used in the Federated Taxi Company Database

Simple QBE Retrieval

A QBE query begins by instructing the DBMS to draw the image of a table on the screen. The columns that should appear in the result and criteria by which rows are to be selected are entered into the image. Additional images can be added to the screen when a query requires more than one table.

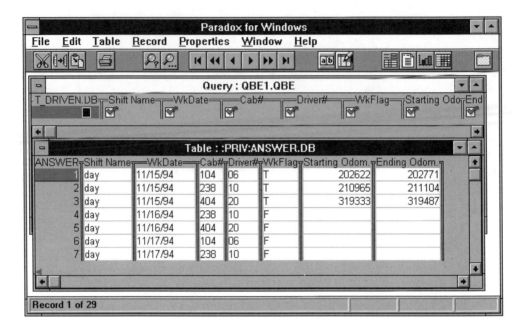

Figure 7.2   Retrieving contents of an entire table

Retrieving Every Row

The simplest QBE retrieval operation presents all of the data stored in one table. At the top of the screen is an image representing the table being queried. A check mark is placed in each column that is to be included in the result table (the table named ANSWER at the bottom of the screen in Figure 7.2).

> **By the way:** How you indicate which columns appear in the result table is one area in which QBE implementations differ. *Paradox* uses the check mark; *R:BASE* asks you to construct a result table image by selecting the columns that should appear; *DB2* and *SQL/DS* use "P." ("P" followed by a period).

In Figure 7.2, the entire image can be seen. However, for large tables that may not always be the case; the horizontal scroll bars can therefore be used to bring unseen parts of tables into view. As you can see, every column in the T_DRIVEN image contains a check mark. The result table therefore contains all of the columns. Because no selection criteria are part of the query, every row is also included. (Only seven rows appear in the screen; the remaining 22 rows appear when the ANSWER table's window is scrolled down with its vertical scroll bars.)

By the way: Like many DBMSs, *Paradox* places a limit on the length of table names. Therefore, some of the table names in the FTC database have been shortened. "T_DRIVEN" is the Shift Driven table.

Paradox automatically sorts the contents of the ANSWER table by every column in the table, beginning with the leftmost column. Although this ordering can be changed, keep in mind that automatic sorting is a feature of *Paradox* and not a general characteristic of QBE.

To restrict the columns that appear in the result table, check only those columns from which data should be retrieved. For example, the query in Figure 7.3 displays only the shift name and work date columns.

Unlike SQL queries, QBE automatically removes duplicate rows. The result table therefore contains only 13 rows, even though Shift Driven contains 29. However, you can request that QBE retain duplicate rows. As you can see

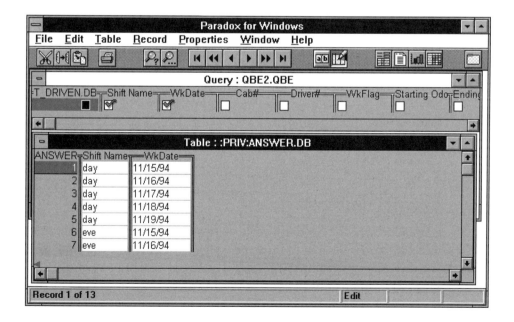

Figure 7.3   Retrieving selected columns

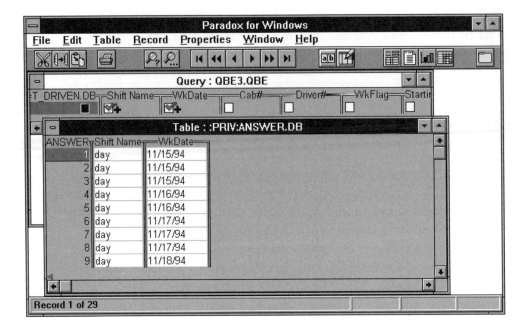

Figure 7.4   Including duplicate rows in a result table

in Figure 7.4, the Shift Name and WkDate columns in the image contain a check mark and a plus, producing the ANSWER table that contains duplicate rows.

By default, the rows in the result table are sorted in ascending order. The sort order on any given column can be changed by using a check mark followed by an arrowhead that points down. As you can see from Figure 7.5, the column marked with the check and the arrow (the date) is sorted in descending order, while the column that contains a plain check mark (the shift name) remains sorted in ascending order.

Restricting Rows

Logical criteria for restricting which rows are to be included in a QBE result table are entered directly into the image. When the condition to be met is equality, then the value that is to be matched can be entered directly into the image. The query in Figure 7.6 looks for rows that match a specific driver number. Notice that the driver number column in the image contains simply the value 10. The result table therefore includes the date and shift from those rows that have a matching driver number.

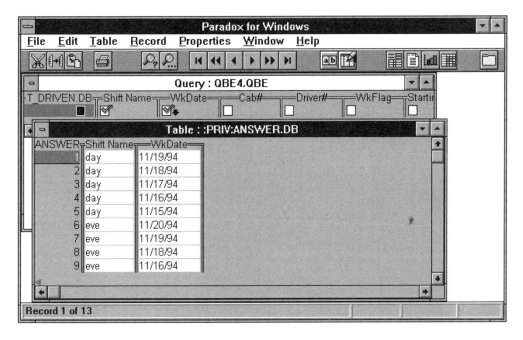

Figure 7.5   Sorting output in descending order

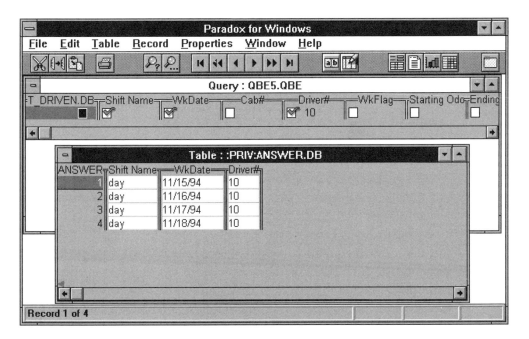

Figure 7.6   Restricting rows with a single equality condition

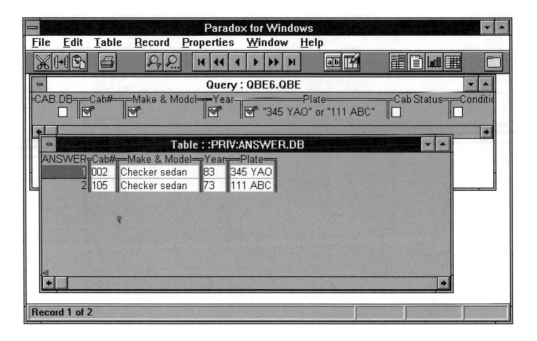

Figure 7.7   A query with multiple conditions linked with OR

> **By the way:** It isn't necessary to include the column or columns containing row restriction criteria in the ANSWER table. However, column(s) containing row selection criteria have been included in the examples in this chapter to make it easier for you to verify the results of the queries.

When the condition being tested is something other than equality, the entire logical expression is written in the column to which it applies. For example, the query in Figure 7.7 retrieves data that meet either portion of two simple conditions joined by OR.

Inequality is expressed with the keyword "not." The query in Figure 7.8 includes three inequalities, separated by commas. QBE interprets inequalities separated by commas as if they were joined by AND. (Equalities and other conditions (for example, greater than and less than) separated by commas are linked by OR.) Therefore, all three conditions must be true before a row will be included in the result table.

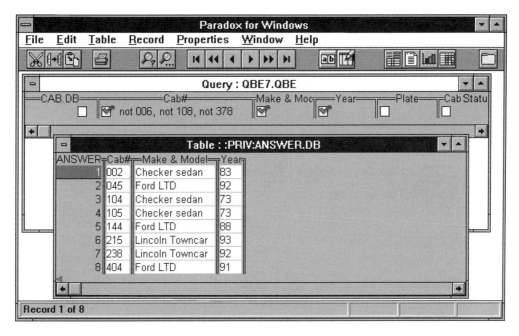

Figure 7.8   A query with multiple negative conditions

When multiple conditions are placed on the same line in the image, QBE automatically links the conditions with AND. For example, in Figure 7.9, QBE retrieves rows that meet the condition "Make/Model = Checker sedan AND Year > 80." However, when conditions are placed on different lines in the image, as in Figure 7.10, QBE links the conditions with OR. Figure 7.10 evaluates the condition "Make/Model = check sedan OR Year > 80."

Retrieval from Multiple Tables

QBE gets its name from the technique used to instruct the DBMS to perform a join to retrieve data from multiple tables. The query in Figure 7.11 retrieves the shifts scheduled for the driver named Charlie Zilog without knowing his driver number.

The data needed to process the query are stored in two tables, Shift Driven and Driver. Images for both tables must first be placed on the screen. Then, an *example* is used to show the DBMS where values are to be matched to make the join. In Figure 7.11, the example is the characters "abcd." It makes no difference what the example is (although *Paradox* restricts examples to letters and numbers); the trick is to make sure the same example appears in the driver

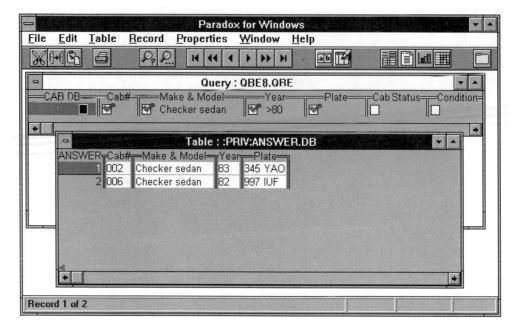

Figure 7.9   Linking multiple conditions with **AND**

number column in both images. The query in Figure 7.11 instructs the DBMS to match values on the driver number and to include only those rows where the driver name is "Zilog, Charlie."

The Outer Join

Paradox is one of the DBMSs that supports the outer join operation. The query in Figure 7.12 retrieves the name, phone number, and cab number of every driver scheduled to drive the day shift on 11/15/94. However, as you can see from the result table in Figure 7.13, the names of those not scheduled to drive also appear; for those drivers, the cab number column is blank (null).

To obtain a QBE outer join, an exclamation point (!) is placed directly after the example in the image whose rows are to be included in the result table even if a matching value can't be found in the table to which it is being joined. In all other respects the query is performed just as any other QBE query.

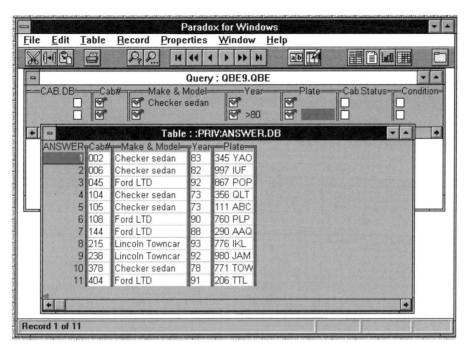

Figure 7.10   Linking multiple conditions with OR

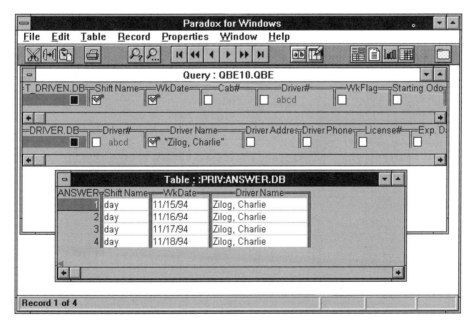

Figure 7.11   Using an example to join tables

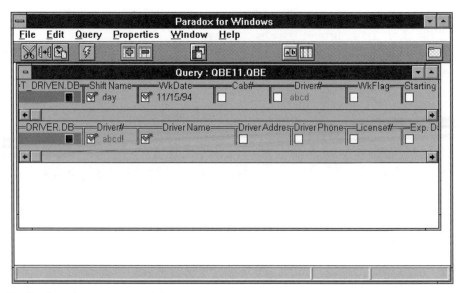

Figure 7.12   Performing an outer join

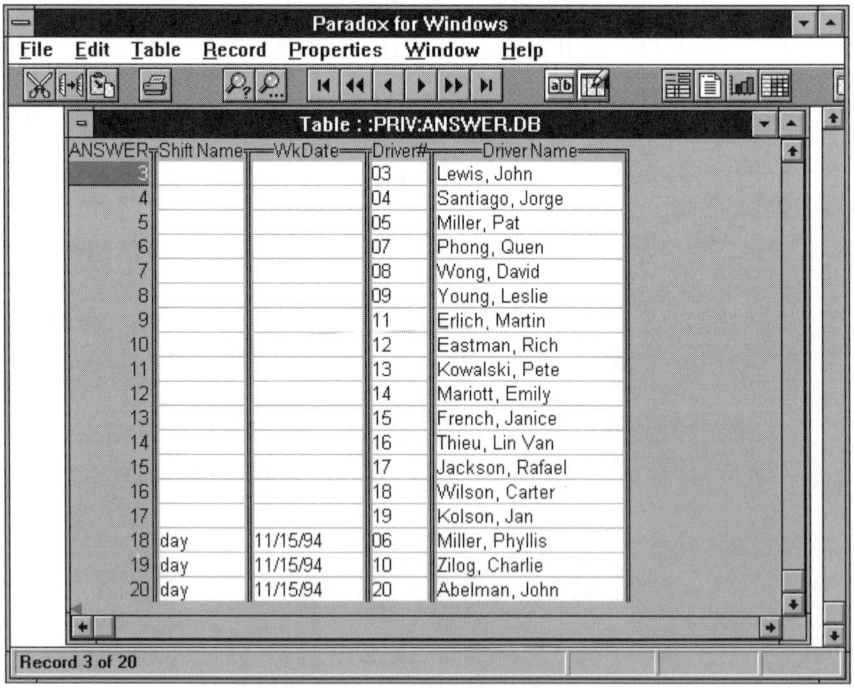

Figure 7.13   The result of an outer join

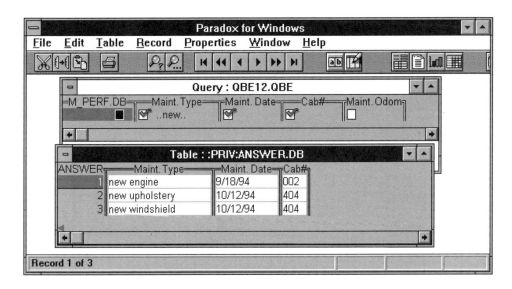

Figure 7.14 Retrieving rows that match a pattern

Pattern Matching

QBE supports wildcards in query conditions to provide pattern matching. If the @ symbol is placed in an image it matches any one character; two periods (..) match any number of characters. (The @ and .. work just like MS-DOS file name wildcards, where a ? matches one character and * matches any number of characters.) In Figure 7.14 you will find a QBE query using the double period pattern matching operator. Because the characters "new" are surrounded by double periods, QBE retrieves any row that *contains* those characters, regardless of where they appear in the column. If the expression had been written "new..", QBE would retrieve only those rows that begin with the search characters. To retrieve those rows that don't match a pattern, QBE required "not" in front of the search criteria (Figure 7.15).

Retrieving Nulls

QBE does not recognize null values as such. Instead, the intersection of a column and a row that has no value is considered to be blank. Like null, blank can be used as part of a query. In Figure 7.16, you can see a query that retrieves every row in the Shift Driven table for which there is no starting odometer

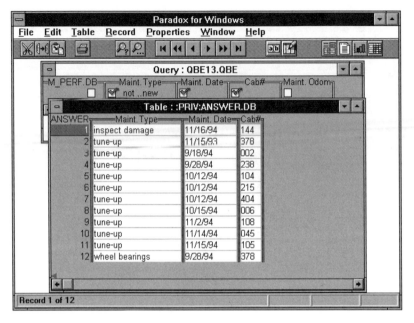

Figure 7.15 Retrieving rows that don't match a pattern

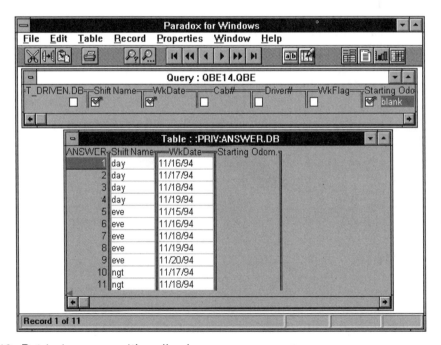

Figure 7.16 Retrieving rows with null values

value. (These will be all shifts that have not been driven.) By the same token, rows for which a value is not null can be retrieved with the operator "not blank."

Set Queries

QBE queries that require a relational algebra difference operation need special handling. Consider the query: "List the names of all drivers not scheduled to drive today." The strategy for processing the query is to take the difference between all drivers and those who are scheduled to drive. The problem is that the query is actually two queries, one to retrieve all drivers who *are* scheduled from Shift Driven and another to perform the difference on the result of the first query and the contents of the Driver table. Using QBE, the trick is to define the query on Shift Driven as a *set*. QBE then creates the set and performs the rest of the query on the contents of the set.

In Figure 7.17 you will see a query that retrieves the names of all drivers that are not scheduled to drive on 11/15/94. The set is defined as part of the Shift Driven table by placing the keyword *set* in the far left column of the Shift Driven image. An example is then placed in the driver number column in both the Shift Driven and Driver images to instruct QBE to join the two tables. Because this query wants those drivers who are not driving, the keyword *no* is placed in front of the example in the Driver image, indicating that only those rows that are not part of the set are to be retrieved.

In addition to the *no* operator, the following comparisons can be made with members of a set:

- only: retrieve only those rows that are part of the set (the opposite of the *no* operator).
- every: retrieve only those rows that include every member of the set.
- exactly: retrieve only those rows that exactly match every member of the set (a combination of only and every).

Calculations and Summary Values

Like many query languages, QBE can be used to perform computations on data. Although such computations generally aren't as powerful or flexible as what can be achieved with a report produced by an application program, they can provide useful ad hoc summaries of data. Each calculation appears as a new column in the result table.

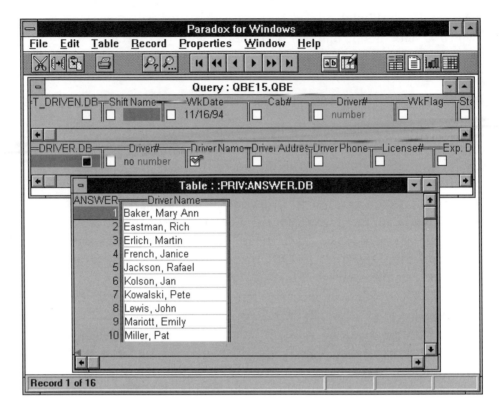

Figure 7.17   A QBE set query that performs a difference operation

Simple Calculations

Figure 7.18 contains a query that calculates the miles driven each time a cab was taken on the road. To perform this calculation, each column whose value will be used in the computation is filled with an example. The calculation itself can be placed in any column and uses the examples rather than the column names. The formula is prefaced by the keyword *calc* and followed by *as* and the name that the new column is to be given in the result table (e.g., Driven).

In general, calculations use standard arithmetic operators. They can contain both constants and arithmetic operators (+, -, *, /). The string concatenation operator (+) and date arithmetic are also supported. Parentheses may be used for grouping and to override the default precedence of operations (multiplication and division have higher precedence than addition and subtraction). A single calculation can contain examples from multiple tables so long as the

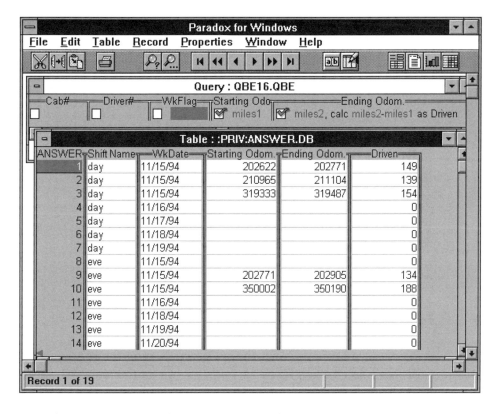

Figure 7.18   Calculating values for a new column from stored data

images for all tables involved are displayed. Keep in mind that a join condition must also be included in a query before a calculation involving multiple tables will make sense.

Summary Calculations

QBE also supports a number of operators that summarize the values in one or more columns:

- average: compute the average of the values in a column
- count: count the values in a column
- max: find the maximum value in a field
- min: find the minimum value in a column
- sum: sum the values in a column

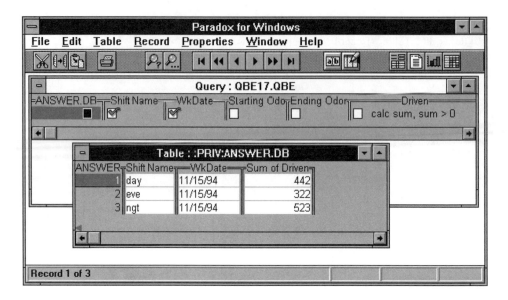

Figure 7.19   A query that uses a previously generated result table

If no check marks appear in the image containing the summary calculation, QBE performs its computations on every row in the table. However, if check marks appear in one or more columns, QBE forms groups of data based on matching values in the checked columns, performing the computation separately on each group.

When FTC needs to sum the miles driven during any given date and shift, the sum operation can be performed on the result table seen in Figure 7.18. To do so, the user removes the images in Figure 7.18 from the screen. The result table, ANSWER, however, is still retained in main memory. (It remains until another query is processed and a new ANSWER table is generated.) The user then instructs the DBMS to display the ANSWER image. As you can see from Figure 7.19, the image appears without the result data it held in Figure 7.18.

The request for the sum appears in the Driven column (the keyword *sum*). In addition, a condition has been added to restrict the sum to those rows where the sum is greater than zero. This makes sure that reservations for future shifts do not clutter the result. The date and shift columns have been checked. QBE displays them as well as uses them to form groups. Notice that the result table contains one row for each unique pair of shift name and date where the sum of the miles driven is greater than zero.

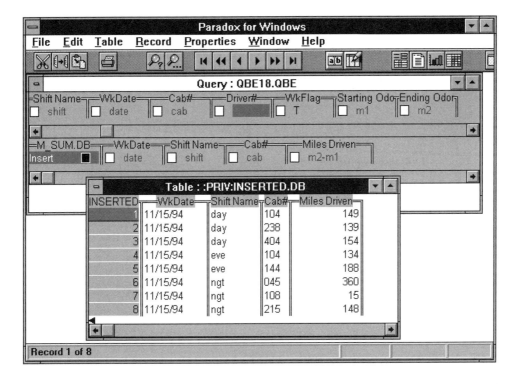

Figure 7.20   Copying data from one table into another

Data Maintenance

QBE provides a very natural metaphor for data maintenance: Data modification specifications can be entered directly into an image. In addition, QBE makes it possible to add, update, and delete more than one row in a table at a time. (As you may remember, the ability to modify an entire table is one of Codd's 12 rules for a fully relational DBMS.)

Inserting Data

The QBE insert operation is used to copy data from one table to another. The data copied are usually the result of a query issued against one or more tables other than the table into which data are being inserted. The query in Figure 7.20, for example, makes a permanent record of the mileage driven each time a car is taken on the road by storing the data in a table named MilesSum.

The insert operation requires the following steps:

1. Display images for the table from which data are to be copied (the source table) and the table into which data are to be inserted (the target table).
2. Place an example in each column in the source data whose values are to be copied into the target table. If the data are to be restricted in some way, enter the logical condition into the appropriate column in the source table. In this case, the *WkFlag* column contains the value "T," indicating that only rows for reservations that were actually driven should be included.
3. Enter the keyword *insert* into the far left column of the target table.
4. Enter examples into the target table to identify which data are to be inserted into which column.

Notice in Figure 7.20 that the examples for the starting and ending odometer readings are used in a calculation whose result is to be stored in the target table. The result table shows all rows that were inserted into the target table.

Modifying Data

Changes to data can also be performed with a QBE query. The query in Figure 7.21, for example, changes the address for one of FTC's drivers. The procedure for changing data using a query is:

1. Display an image for the table in which data are to be changed.
2. Enter conditions that will select the rows that are to be changed; if no row selection criteria are present, then every row in the table will be affected. In Figure 7.21, the value *06* has been placed in the driver number column so that the row with that driver number will be the only row changed.
3. For each column that is to receive a new value, enter the keywords *change to* followed by the new value for the column. (If the column has a data type of text, the new value must be surrounded by quotes.)

The result table shows the existing contents of all rows that were modified. It shows the rows *before* the change rather than the result of the change.

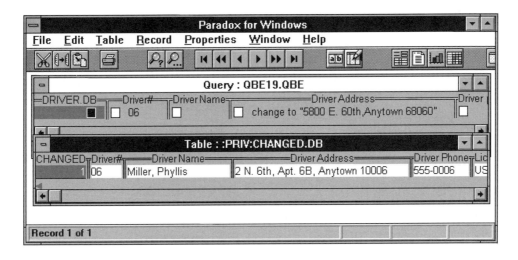

Figure 7.21   Changing data with a QBE query

Deleting Rows

The QBE delete operation affects one or more rows of a table. For example, the delete operation in Figure 7.22 removes all rows from Shift Driven for the evening shift on 11/20/94. In this particular case, the delete affects only one row because only one row meets the query's criteria. However, *all* rows that satisfy the query are deleted.

The procedure for performing a delete operation is:

1. Display an image for the table from which rows are to be deleted.
2. Enter logical conditions that identify the rows that are to be deleted; if no logical condition is entered, then all rows will be deleted.

The result table displays the rows that were deleted (*not* the rows that remain in the table).

Summary

QBE (Query by Example) is a graphic query language for the retrieval and maintenance of data in a relational database. Unlike SQL, it cannot be used to define the structure of a database. The major microcomputer implementation

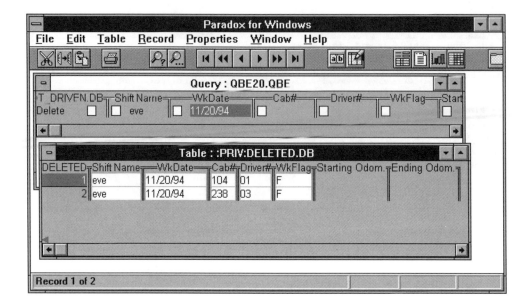

Figure 7.22   Deleting multiple rows with a QBE query

is *Paradox*, although other DBMSs such as *dBASE IV* and *R:BASE* do use a QBE interface to define views. QBE is also available with *DB2* and *SQL/DS*, IBM's mainframe DBMSs.

QBE retrieval criteria are entered into *images*, or *skeletons*, of tables directly on the screen. The result is also displayed as a table. Although only one result table is retained in main memory at any given time, the current result table may be queried in the same fashion as a base table.

QBE gets its name from the technique it uses to indicate how columns in two tables are to be matched (in other words, for performing a join). The same arbitrary string of characters (an *example*) is placed in the columns that are to be used to join tables. QBE recognizes that matching examples mean that data are to be matched. The names given to the examples have no further meaning. QBE provides the following features:

- Retrieval from a single table based on logical criteria
- Retrieval from multiple tables using "examples" (placeholders for matching data) to specify join conditions
- Support for the outer join operation
- Summary operations such as average, count, sum, min, max

- Calculation features to create new columns in answer tables based on arithmetic and string transformations of existing data.
- Set operations for evaluating data against the members of a previously defined set of data
- Insert operations to copy data from one table to another
- Change operations that affect one or more rows
- Delete operations that affect one or more rows

References

Borland International, Inc. 1992. *Paradox for Windows Users Guide.*

IBM Corp. 1980. *Query-by-Example: Terminal Users Guide.* Form SH2-2078-1. IBM Corp.

Thomas, J. C. and J. D. Gould. 1975. "A Psychological Study of Query by Example." *Proceedings of National Computer Conference.* AFIPS Press.

Zloof, M. M. 1977. "Query-by-Example: A Data Base Language." *IBM Systems Journal.* 16(4):324–343.

Exercises

1. Consider what it means to a user to be faced with a graphic (as opposed to text) interface for querying a database.

   a. List the characteristics of the type of user who might benefit from a graphic query language.
   b. List the characteristics of the type of user who might prefer a text-based query language.
   c. List the benefits that using a graphic query language can bring. Are these benefits also drawbacks to a text-based query language?
   d. List the drawbacks to a graphic query language. Are these drawbacks also benefits of a text-based query language?

2. Using the following tables for the Office of Margaret Holmes, D.M.D., draw the QBE images necessary to complete the queries below.

Patient (Patient #, Patient Name, Patient Address, Patient Phone,
    Bill Payer, Birth Date, Relationship to Bill Payer)
Appointment (Patient #, Visit Date, Visit Time)
Treatment (Treatment Type, Cost)
Treatment performed (Patient #, Visit Date, Treatment Type)
Payer (Bill Payer Name, Payer Address, Payer Home Phone,
    Payer Work Phone, Insurance Company, Employer, $ Owed)
Bill (Statement #, Bill Payer Name, Statement Date, Statement $)
Payment (Bill Payer Name, Payment Source, Check #, Check $,
    Payment Date)

a. List the names of all patients under 18 years of age.
b. List all patients seen by Dr. Holmes along with the names and work phone numbers of who pays their bills.
c. List the types of treatments and their costs for Jason Jackson for the month of April, 1994.
d. List the names and phone numbers of patients who have appointments on May 15, 1994.
e. Display the names and birthdates of all patients for whom Patrick Swan pays bills.
f. List the source, payment date, and check number for all payments made by Emily Jones during 1993.
g. For each patient whose bills are paid by Samantha Thule, display the patient name, treatment type, and treatment cost for all appointments during August 1994. (This query gathers part of the data for a bill.)
h. Display the total cost of all treatments received by Fred Kagan on August 1, 1994.
i. List the names and phone numbers of all patients who have not had their teeth cleaned in the past year. (Hint: this is a set query.)
j. List the names of all patients who have had both extractions and root canals in the past five years. (Hint: this is a set query.)

3. Using the following tables for the East Coast Aquarium, draw the QBE images necessary to complete the queries below:

Species (Species Code, Latin Name, English Name)
Location (Location Code, Place in Building, Size, Head Keeper)
Population (Species Code, Location Code, Number of Animals)

Food (<u>Type of Food</u>)
Feeding (<u>Species Code</u>, <u>Type of Food</u>, Amount of Food,
    Feeding Interval)
Habitats (<u>Habitat Type</u>)
Can Live (<u>Species Code</u>, <u>Habitat Type</u>)
Where Found (<u>Location Code</u>, <u>Habitat Type</u>)

Source (<u>Source Code</u>, Source Name, Source Address, Source Phone,
    Contact Person)
Can Supply (<u>Source Code</u>, <u>Species Code</u>)

a. List the English name and the Latin name for each species housed in
the aquarium.
b. For location number 101, list the place in the building where the
location can be found, its size, and its head keeper.
c. List all the habitats provided by the aquarium.
d. List the English and Latin names of species number 256.
e. List the habitats available in location number 95.
f. List the places in the building where a coral reef habitat can be found.
g. Display the English name of all species living in location number 109.
h. List the English name of all species that eat mealworms.
i. Display the Latin name of all species that do not eat mealworms.
j. List English and Latin name of all species supplied by Westcoast
Animal Supply.
k. List the names of all sources that can supply Yellow Tangs.

8

SQL Retrieval

Early in 1986, SQL (Structured Query Language) was accepted by ANSI (the American National Standards Institute) as the national standard query language for relational databases. Since that time, a number of microcomputer implementations have become available. Some of these DBMSs (for example, *Oracle, Informix, Ingres*) are microcomputer versions of software that originally ran on minicomputers. Other DBMSs, including *dBASE IV* and *R:BASE*, have SQL implementations that were written directly for a microcomputer.

This chapter looks at using SQL to retrieve data from an existing set of tables. Although it may seem backwards to talk about retrieval before learning to create tables and insert data, some of the data modification commands use a variation of the retrieval command. It is therefore easier to learn retrieval before data modification.

DBMSs that support SQL refer to relations as *tables*. Attributes are called *columns*; tuples are *rows*. SQL views are implemented as virtual tables (in other words, only view definitions are stored on disk; view tables are created only when referenced). The catalog in which table and view definitions are stored is on-line and dynamic; it is called a *data dictionary*.

SQL supports a very powerful command, SELECT, which is used to locate and retrieve data. The SQL SELECT is not the same as the select operation from the relational algebra. While the relational select retrieves data from all columns of one or more rows from a single table, the SQL SELECT command can retrieve from multiple tables (using a join), can project specific columns from the result, and can perform some computations. In fact, in many SQL implementations, SELECT can perform all nine of the relational algebra operations described in Chapter 6.

The ability to perform more than one relational algebra operation with a single command means that SELECT is based on the *relational calculus*, not the relational algebra. It is a *non-procedural* command in that you specify *what* you want the SQL command processor to do but not exactly *how* it should perform the query. In other words, you don't give SQL step-by-step instructions, as you might if you were using relational algebra or writing a program in a language such as Pascal or COBOL, but instead specify what operations you want performed and then let SQL figure out on its own the order in which it should perform those operations.

Every DBMS that supports SQL has program code that functions as a *SQL command processor*. Its job is to take a query presented by an end user or an application program and perform the relational algebra operations needed to obtain the result of the query.

The part of a SQL command processor that determines the most efficient way to perform relational algebra operations is known as a *query optimizer*. Although there are many strategies for optimizing queries, in general a SQL command processor always tries to perform relational algebra operations in such a way that it manipulates the smallest amount of data.

By the way: There is a major trade-off where query optimization is concerned. A DBMS doesn't want its query optimizer to spend so much time figuring out the best way to perform a query that the total time involved is as long as performing the query in an inefficient manner, without any query optimization at all!

Introducing the **SQL SELECT**

As you read earlier, the SQL SELECT command is a powerful retrieval tool that can trigger many relational algebra operations with a single command. In addition, all or part of the SELECT syntax is used in a number of other SQL commands, including those to insert, modify, and delete data and to create views.

The general form of the SELECT command has a number of options:

```
SELECT [DISTINCT] column_name1 [,column_name2]...
FROM table_name [,table_name2]...
[WHERE predicate][ORDER BY column_name1 [,column_name2]...]
[GROUP BY column_name1 [,column_name2]...]
[HAVING predicate]
```

The notation used above places brackets ([]) around any part of the command that is optional. An ellipsis (...) indicates that a portion of the command may be repeated. Most SQL command processors let you split a command onto several lines for clarity. To make multiple lines possible, each SQL implementation has some way of letting you indicate that a command is ready to be processed. For example, *Oracle* requires a semicolon at the end of a command. *R:BASE* requires a continuation character (the plus sign) at the end of each line of a command; a line without a plus sign at the end is interpreted as the end of the command. This is one of the few areas in which SQL implementations differ significantly; check your DBMS's documentation to find out exactly what it expects when you want to split a command onto more than one line.

The examples in this chapter are based on the same sample tables for the Federated Taxi Company used for the QBE query examples in Chapter 7 (Figure 7.1).

Simple **SQL Retrieval**

In its simplest form, SELECT must specify which columns should be included in the output and the table from which they should come. The list of columns to be included in the result can specify all columns in the table by using an asterisk (*) or can contain the names of the columns.

For example,

SELECT * FROM Shift_Driven

Figure 8.1 produces output identical to the Shift Driven table stored in the database. (The column names have been truncated to the width of the column.) All columns and all rows have been selected; the * indicates all columns while the absence of WHERE, GROUP BY, and/or HAVING clauses allows all rows to be included.

By the way: This type of query is asking for a relational algebra project operation.

The use of the wildcard * can be dangerous. If the number of columns in a table is increased or decreased, output with * will change. Although use of the * operator is convenient for quickly seeing the contents of a table, it provides a potential violation of Codd's Logical Independence rule. For that reason, SELECT * should only be used interactively; it should be avoided when SQL is embedded in an application program.

Instead of displaying every column in a table with *, specify exactly which columns you want to see by including the column names immediately after SELECT. For example, to see only the days and shifts for which cabs have been reserved, use a query like Figure 8.1:

SELECT Shift_Name, WkDate FROM Shift_Driven

The output contains every row from the base table but only those columns whose names appear following the keyword SELECT. The output in Figure 8.1 contains duplicate rows, since the attributes *WkDate* and *Shift Name* don't constitute an entire primary key.

SELECT can be instructed to return only unique rows by adding the keyword DISTINCT to the query Figure 8.1:

SELECT DISTINCT Shift_Name, WkDate FROM Shift_Driven

```
SELECT * FROM Shift_Driven
```

Shi	WkDate	Cab	Dr	W	Start_	End_Od
day	11/15/94	104	06	T	202622	202771
day	11/15/94	238	10	T	210965	211104
day	11/15/94	404	20	T	319333	319487
eve	11/15/94	045	11	F		
eve	11/15/94	104	01	T	202771	202905
eve	11/15/94	144	12	T	350002	350190
ngt	11/15/94	045	16	T	48830	49190
ngt	11/15/94	108	16	T	53885	53900
ngt	11/15/94	215	08	T	20107	20255
day	11/16/94	238	10	F		
eve	11/19/94	238	03	F		
eve	11/20/94	238	03	F		
day	11/16/94	404	20	F		
eve	11/16/94	002	04	F		
eve	11/18/94	002	04	F		
eve	11/16/94	104	01	F		
eve	11/19/94	104	01	F		
eve	11/20/94	104	01	F		
ngt	11/16/94	002	07	F		
day	11/17/94	104	06	F		
day	11/18/94	104	06	F		
day	11/19/94	104	06	F		
day	11/17/94	238	10	F		
day	11/17/94	404	20	F		
ngt	11/17/94	108	02	F		
ngt	11/18/94	108	02	F		
day	11/18/94	238	10	F		
eve	11/18/94	045	11	F		
ngt	11/18/94	045	16	F		
ngt	11/18/94	215	08	F		

Figure 8.1   SQL SELECT command—example 1

The result of this query can be found in Figure 8.1. Note that the rows have been sorted by shift and date. This is because the SQL command processor must sort the table before it can identify duplicate rows. In other words, whenever you include a DISTINCT clause, the SQL command processor sorts the result table by every column in the table. After sorting, it begins at the top of the table and scans it row by row, looking for adjacent, identical rows.

```
SELECT Shift_Name, WkDate FROM Shift_Driven
```

<u>Shi</u>	<u>WkDate</u>
day	11/15/94
day	11/15/94
day	11/15/94
eve	11/15/94
eve	11/15/94
eve	11/15/94
ngt	11/15/94
ngt	11/15/94
ngt	11/15/94
day	11/16/94
eve	11/19/94
eve	11/20/94
day	11/16/94
eve	11/16/94
eve	11/18/94
eve	11/16/94
eve	11/19/94
eve	11/20/94
ngt	11/16/94
day	11/17/94
day	11/18/94
day	11/19/94
day	11/17/94
day	11/17/94
ngt	11/17/94
ngt	11/18/94
day	11/18/94
eve	11/18/94
ngt	11/18/94
ngt	11/18/94

Figure 8.2   SQL SELECT command—example 2

By the way: As you might suspect, adding a DISTINCT clause to a query can have a major impact on the performance of a query, especially if the result table has many columns and many rows.

```
SELECT DISTINCT Shift_Name, WkDate FROM Shift_Driven
```

Shi	WkDate
day	11/15/94
day	11/16/94
day	11/17/94
day	11/18/94
day	11/19/94
eve	11/15/94
eve	11/16/94
eve	11/18/94
eve	11/19/94
eve	11/20/94
ngt	11/15/94
ngt	11/16/94
ngt	11/17/94
ngt	11/18/94

Figure 8.3   SQL SELECT command—example 3

Unless you specify otherwise, the rows in a SQL result table generated by a query without a DISTINCT clause appear in the order in which the rows were entered into the table; DISTINCT clause result tables are sorted in the order in which the columns were listed after the SELECT keyword in the query.

However, the order of rows in the virtual table produced by a SELECT can be changed before the result table is displayed on the screen by using the ORDER BY clause. For example, in Figure 8.1 the rows appear in the order in which they were entered into the table. If, however, FTC's office clerk wishes to see the output by shift and then date, the SELECT command must be issued as:

SELECT DISTINCT Shift_Name, WkDate
FROM Shift_Driven
ORDER BY WkDate, Shift_Name

This query produces the result in Figure 8.4. Since the shift names are stored as text, they are ordered alphabetically in ascending order. The dates, stored using a SQL data type of date, are ordered chronologically in ascending order.

```
SELECT DISTINCT Shift_Name, WkDate
FROM Shift_Driven
ORDER BY WkDate, Shift_Name
```

Shi	WkDate
day	11/15/94
eve	11/15/94
ngt	11/15/94
day	11/16/94
eve	11/16/94
ngt	11/16/94
day	11/17/94
ngt	11/17/94
day	11/18/94
eve	11/18/94
ngt	11/18/94
day	11/19/94
eve	11/19/94
eve	11/20/94

Figure 8.4   SQL Select command—example 4

Output can also be sorted in descending order by using the keyword DESC after any attribute that is to be sorted in that manner. For example, to produce Figure 8.1 in descending order by date the query might be written:

SELECT DISTINCT Shift_Name, WkDate
FROM Shift_Driven
ORDER by WkDate DESC, Shift_Name

This query produces the table in Figure 8.4.

Restricting Rows with WHERE

Criteria for retrieving specific rows from one or more tables can be included in a SELECT command by using a WHERE clause. The keyword WHERE is followed by an expression that identifies which rows should be retrieved. The expression is known as a *predicate*. Predicates ask a SQL command processor to perform the relational algebra select, join, and difference operations.

```
SELECT DISTINCT Shift_Name, WkDate
FROM Shift_Driven
ORDER BY WkDate DESC, Shift_Name
```

Shi	WkDate
eve	11/20/94
day	11/19/94
eve	11/19/94
day	11/18/94
eve	11/18/94
ngt	11/18/94
day	11/17/94
ngt	11/17/94
day	11/16/94
eve	11/16/94
ngt	11/16/94
day	11/15/94
eve	11/15/94
ngt	11/15/94

Figure 8.5   SQL Select command—example 5

Simple WHERE Clauses

The simplest form of the WHERE clause asks a SQL command processor to perform a relational algebra select; it contains a logical expression against which rows are evaluated. For example, to see all the shifts reserved for driver number 10:

> SELECT Shift_Name, WkDate
> FROM Shift_Driven
> WHERE Driver# = 10

In this case, the predicate is a logical expression that contains a constant value against which the value of an attribute must be matched. Predicates can contain any of the standard logical operators ($<$, $<=$, $=$, $>=$, $>$). Multiple expressions may be included by linking single expressions with AND or OR; any expression or operator may also be inverted with NOT. Parentheses can be used to control the order in which logical comparisons are performed. The result of this query appears in Figure 8.6.

```
SELECT Shift_Name, WkDate
FROM Shift_Driven
WHERE Driver# = 10
```

Shi	WkDate
day	11/15/94
day	11/16/94
day	11/17/94
day	11/18/94

Figure 8.6   SQL SELECT command—example 6

Joining Tables

The WHERE clause is used to request a join. Suppose, for example, that an office worker doesn't remember a driver number, but only has the driver's name? The query must then begin in the Driver relation and follow the primary key-foreign key relationship between Driver and Shift Driven. In other words, SQL must be told to join the Driver and Shift Driven tables over the driver number. The query might be issued as:

```
SELECT Shift_Name, WkDate
FROM Driver, Shift_Driven
WHERE Driver_Name = 'Zilog, Charlie'
        AND Driver.Driver# = Shift_Driven.Driver #
```

The FROM clause lists all relations that must be used in the query. In the predicate, the names of attributes that appear in more than one relation are prefaced by the name of the relation and a period. For example, Driver. Driver#, means the *Driver #* attribute from the Driver relation. A row is created in the result table (which is exactly the same as the table in Figure 8.6) whenever two things are true: A row in Driver has a value of "Zilog, Charlie" for Driver Name and a row in Shift Driven has the same driver number as the driver number from the "Zilog, Charlie" row in Driver. The "Driver.Driver# = Shift_Driven.Driver#" portion of the WHERE clause is known as a *join condition*. A join condition must be present whenever a join is required in a query.

> **By the way:** If you think back to Chapter 6, you will remember that one way to implement a join is to take the product of the tables being joined and then apply row selection criteria to choose only those rows where the primary key column value matches the foreign key column value. This is exactly what a join condition in a WHERE clause is asking SQL to do. Because the result table of a product operation can be very big, a join of even two moderate-sized tables can cause serious performance problems.

As well as joining two different tables, a WHERE clause can be used to join a table to itself. This technique might be used, for example, to find the names of all drivers that have driven or are scheduled to drive two specific cabs. The SQL is written:

```
SELECT DISTINCT Driver_Name
FROM Driver, Shift_Driven T1, Shift_Driven T2
WHERE Driver.Driver# = T1.Driver#
        AND T1.Driver# = T2.Driver#
        AND T1.Cab# = '104'
        AND T2.Cab# = '108'
```

Notice that the Shift_Driven table appears twice after FROM. The first time it is followed by T1, the second by T2. T1 and T2 are *aliases* for the table. They instruct the SQL command processor to act as if there were two copies of the table, named T1 and T2. Once an alias has been defined, it can be used throughout the rest of the query in place of the table's name.

> **By the way:** The use of aliases isn't restricted to joining a table to itself. They can be used at any time and in any query. They are particularly useful when tables have long names.

This query, the result of which can be seen in Figure 8.7, requires two joins. The first joins one of the copies of Shift Driven to Driver so that the driver's name is available for the result. The second joins the two copies of Shift Driven. The WHERE clause also contains selection criteria that choose rows containing numbers 104 or 108, one cab number from each copy of Shift Driven.

```
SELECT DISTINCT Driver_Name
FROM Driver, Shift_Driven T1, Shift_Driven T2
WHERE Driver.Driver# = T1.Driver#
    AND T1.Driver# = T2.Driver#
    AND T1.Cab# = '104'
    AND T2.Cab# = '108'
```

Driver_Name
Bailey, Max

Figure 8.7   SQL SELECT command—example 7

By the way: The query in Figure 8.7 actually requests a divide operation. As you will remember from Chapter 6, a divide can be implemented as two selects (T1.Cab# = '104' and T2.Cab# = '108') and a join (T1.Driver# = T2.Driver#).

Special WHERE Clause Operators

As well as the standard logical operators mentioned earlier, predicates in a WHERE clause may contain additional operators: IN and NOT IN (used to specify a set of values), LIKE and NOT LIKE (used for pattern matching), BETWEEN and NOT BETWEEN (used to specify a range), and IS NULL and IS NOT NULL.

For example, to retrieve data about the two cabs with license plates '345 YAO' and '111 ABC,' the SQL query could be written:

    SELECT Cab#, Make_Model, Year, Curr_Odom
    FROM Cab
    WHERE Plate IN ('345 YAO', '111 ABC')

This query produces the output seen in Figure 8.8. The IN operator is followed by a list of those values against which some attribute should be matched. The list is surrounded by parentheses; items in the list are separated by commas. IN is really a shorthand for multiple OR expressions dealing with the same attribute. In other words, this same predicate could have been written as:

```
SELECT Cab#, Make_Model, Year, Curr_Odom
FROM Cab
WHERE Plate IN ('345 YAO','111 ABC')
```

Cab	Make_Model	Ye	Curr_O
002	Checker sedan	83	0
105	Checker sedan	73	286003

Figure 8.8   SQL SELECT command—example 8

Plate = '345 YAO' OR Plate = '111 ABC'

NOT IN is a shorthand for a series of negative AND expressions concerning the same attribute. Suppose, for example, that FTC's chief mechanic needs to see data on all cabs except cabs numbered 006, 108, and 378. That data can be retrieved with:

SELECT Cab#, Make_Model, Plate, Curr_Odom
FROM Cab
WHERE Cab# NOT IN ('006', '108', '378')

The result of this query appears in Figure 8.9. Only those rows from Cab that have a cab number not equal to any of the cab numbers in the list are included in the result. Just as the IN predicate could be written as a series of OR expressions, the NOT IN could be rewritten as a series of ANDs:

Cab# != '006' AND Cab# != '108' AND Cab# != '378'

In the preceding statement, the characters != mean "not equal to." This is the notation for "not equal to" most commonly used by SQL implementations. However, you should check your DBMS's documentation to find out exactly how this operator should be specified.

It is also possible to write this same predicate as a single negated OR:

NOT (Cab# = '006' OR Cab# = '108' OR Cab# = '378')

It is important to recognize that there is often more than one way to write a SQL query to obtain a desired result.

```
SELECT Cab#, Make_Model, Plate, Curr_Odom
FROM Cab
WHERE Cab# NOT IN ('006','108','378')
```

Cab	Make_Model	Plate	Curr_O
002	Checker sedan	345 YAO	0
045	Ford LTD	867 POP	45999
104	Checker sedan	356 QLT	204998
105	Checker sedan	111 ABC	286003
144	Ford LTD	190 AAQ	103245
215	Lincoln Towncar	776 IKL	23000
238	Lincoln Towncar	980 JAM	256256
404	321409	206 TTL	321409

Figure 8.9   SQL SELECT command—example 9

BETWEEN and NOT BETWEEN can also be used as shorthand for combinations of standard logical operators. To retrieve the names of all drivers who are scheduled to drive the day shift over a three-day period, a SQL query might be written:

> SELECT Driver_Name
> FROM Driver, Shift_Driven
> WHERE Driver.Driver# = Shift_Driven.#
>   AND Shift_Name = 'day"
>   AND WkDate BETWEEN 11/15/94 AND 11/17/94

The result, seen in Figure 8.10, contains only driver names. As discussed earlier, the names are retrieved by matching the driver number of all rows from Shift Driven that meet the other criteria (day shift and an appropriate date) with the driver number in Driver. The predicate can also be written as two logical inequalities linked with AND:

> WkDate >= 11/15/94 AND WkDate <= 11/17/94

In a similar manner, a list of all drivers *not* scheduled to drive during that three-day period can be obtained by simply negating the BETWEEN operator:

```
SELECT DISTINCT Driver_Name
FROM Driver, Shift_Driven
WHERE Driver.Driver# = Shift_Driven.Driver#
    AND Shift_Name = 'day'
    AND WkDate BETWEEN 11/15/94 AND 11/17/94
```

Driver_Name
Abelman, John
Bailey, Max
Baker, Mary Ann
Eastman, Rich
Erlich, Martin
Miller, Phyllis
Phong, Quen
Santiago, Jorge
Thieu, Lin Van
Wong, David
Zilog, Charlie

Figure 8.10 **SQL SELECT** command—example 10

SELECT Driver_Name
FROM Driver, Shift_Driven
WHERE Driver.Driver# = Shift_Driven.Driver#
        AND Shift_Name = 'day'
        AND WkDate NOT BETWEEN 11/15/94 AND 11/17/94

The result of this query can be seen in Figure 8.11. The predicate, like the predicate using BETWEEN, can be rewritten to obtain the same results as either:

WkDate < 11/15/94 OR WkDate > 11/17/94

or:

NOT (WkDate < 11/15/94 AND WkDate < 11/17/94)

```
SELECT DISTINCT Driver_Name
FROM Driver, Shift_Driven
WHERE Driver.Driver# = Shift_Driven.#
   AND Shift_Name = 'day'
   AND WkDate NOT BETWEEN 11/15/94 AND 11/17/94
```

Driver_Name
Bailey, Max
Baker, Mary Ann
Erlich, Martin
Lewis, John
Miller, Phyllis
Santiago, Jorge
Thieu, Lin Vin
Wong, David
Zilog, Charlie

Figure 8.11 SQL SELECT command—example 11

The operators LIKE and NOT LIKE allow wild-cards to be used as part of character constants in logical expressions. SQL supports two wild-card characters. When used in a quoted string, % (the percent sign) means that any characters may be substituted. For example, 'Sm%' matches Smith, Smythe, Smithson, Smithers, etc. In other words, it matches anything that starts with "Sm." (Don't forget that upper and lower case are significant between quotes.) The second wild-card, _ (the underscore), holds the place of a single character. 'Sm_th', for example, matches Smith or Smyth, but not Smooth. The wild-card characters can appear anywhere within the quoted string. If FTC's chief mechanic wants to see information about all cabs that have received new parts, he might use the SQL query:

SELECT Cab#, Maint_Type, Maint_Date
FROM Maint_Perf
WHERE Maint_Type LIKE 'new%'

The query returns the rows seen in Figure 8.12.

On the other hand, to retrieve information about all cabs whose maintenance involved something other than new equipment, the query would be written:

```
SELECT Cab#, Maint_Type, Maint_Date
FROM Maint_Perf
WHERE Maint_Type LIKE 'new%'
```

Cab	Maint_Type	Maint_Da
002	new engine	9/18/94
404	new upholstery	10/12/94
404	new windshield	10/12/94

Figure 8.12 SQL SELECT command—example 12

```
SELECT Cab#, Maint_Type, Maint_Date
FROM Maint_Perf
WHERE Maint_Type NOT LIKE 'new%'
```

Cab	Maint_Type	Maint_Da
002	tune-up	9/18/94
238	tune-up	9/28/94
378	wheel bearings	9/28/94
104	tune-up	10/12/94
215	tune-up	10/12/94
404	tune-up	10/12/94
006	tune-up	10/15/94
108	tune-up	11/2/94
045	tune-up	11/14/94
105	tune-up	11/15/94
378	tune-up	11/15/94
144	inspect damage	11/15/94

Figure 8.13 SQL SELECT command—example 13

SELECT Cab#, Maint_Type, Maint_Date
FROM Maint_Perf
WHERE Maint_Type NOT LIKE 'new%'

The above version of the query produces the result in Figure 8.13.

The IS NULL and IS NOT NULL operators are fairly straightforward. For example, if FTC's office clerk needs to see the names of all drivers for whom there is no phone number, the query might be written:

SELECT Driver_Name
FROM Driver
WHERE Driver_phone IS NULL

The IS NULL and IS NOT NULL operators provide a way to retrieve rows with or without null values regardless of what is actually being stored in the base tables for null values. In other words, some DBMSs store blanks or zeros for null; others store the characters NULL; some give the user control over what is stored.

Grouping Queries

SELECT can perform a number of summary functions on data, returning grouped information. For example, a table reporting the total number of miles driven in each day and shift contained in Shift Driven, can be obtained by using:

SELECT WkDate, Shift_Name, SUM(End_Odom - Start_Odom)
FROM Shift_Driven
GROUP BY WkDate, Shift_Name

This query produces the result seen in Figure 8.14. SUM is a function. It performs the computation indicated in parentheses and then sums the values for each distinct pair of WkDate and Shift_Name, the attributes by which the data should be grouped.

Most SQL implementations provide several useful functions:

- AVG (computes the average value of each group)
- MAX (returns the maximum value in each group)
- MIN (returns the minimum value in each group)
- COUNT (returns the number of members in the group)

```
SELECT WkDate, Shift_Name, SUM(End_Odom - Start_Odom)
FROM Shift_Driven
GROUP BY WkDate, Shift_Name
```

WkDate	Shi	SUM(End_Odom - Start_Odom)
11/15/94	day	444
11/15/94	eve	324
11/15/94	ngt	509
11/16/94	day	0
11/16/94	eve	0
11/16/94	ngt	0
11/17/94	eve	0
11/17/94	ngt	0
11/18/94	day	0
11/18/94	ngt	0
11/19/94	day	0
11/19/94	eve	0
11/19/94	eve	0

Figure 8.14   SQL SELECT command—example 14

The table in Figure 8.14 contains some undesirable data, those zeros that correspond to rows for future reservations. To make the result more meaningful, we might wish to exclude all shifts that haven't been driven:

    SELECT WkDate, Shift_Name, SUM(End_Odom - Start_Odom)
    FROM Shift_Driven
    WHERE WkFlag = 'T'
    GROUP BY WkDate, Shift_Name

The addition of the WHERE clause restricts the rows to those with a WkFlag of 'T,' producing the more meaningful table that appears in Figure 8.15.

The HAVING clause can be used to restrict which groups are included in the final table. For example, to report the average mileage for only the day and evening shifts:

    SELECT WkDate, Shift_Name, AVG(End_Odom - Start_Odom)
    FROM Shift_Driven
    GROUP BY WkDate, Shift_Name
            HAVING Shift_Name != 'ngt'

```
SELECT WkDate, Shift_Name, SUM(End_Odom - Start_Odom)
FROM Shift_Driven
GROUP BY WkDate, Shift_Name
```

WkDate	Shi	SUM(End_Odom - Start_Odom)
11/15/94	day	444
11/15/94	eve	324
11/15/94	ngt	509

Figure 8.15 **SQL SELECT** command—example 15

```
SELECT WkDate, Shift_Name, AVG(End_Odom - Start_Odom)
FROM Shift_Driven
GROUP BY WkDate, Shift_Name
HAVING Shift_Name != 'ngt'
```

WkDate	Shi	SUM(End_Odom - Start_Odom)
11/15/94	day	148.3
11/15/94	eve	108.3
11/16/94	day	0
11/16/94	eve	0
11/17/94	eve	0
11/18/94	day	0
11/19/94	day	0
11/19/94	eve	0
11/19/94	eve	0

Figure 8.16 **SQL SELECT** command—example 16

Since no WHERE clause is present, data on all day and evening shifts currently in the database are included in the result (Figure 8.16). To exclude shifts that have not been driven, a WHERE clause can be used in conjunction with GROUP BY and HAVING:

> SELECT WkDate, Shift_Name, AVG(End_Odom - Start_Odom)
> FROM Shift_Driven
> WHERE WkFlag = 'T'
> GROUP BY WkDate, Shift_Name
>   HAVING Shift_Name != 'ngt'

The preceding query produces the two-line result in Figure 8.17.

```
SELECT WkDate, Shift_Name, AVG(End_Odom - Start_Odom)
FROM Shift_Driven
WHERE WkFlag = 'T'
GROUP BY WkDate, Shift_Name
HAVING Shift_Name != 'ngt'
```

WkDate	Shi	SUM(End_Odom - Start_Odom)
11/15/94	day	148.3
11/15/94	eve	108.3

Figure 8.17 SQL SELECT command—example 17

Subqueries

A *subquery* is a complete SELECT command used as part of a WHERE clause predicate. In some cases, it can be used to produce a more efficient query; in other cases, it provides the only way to obtain a particular type of result. There are two major types of subqueries: *uncorrelated* and *correlated*. This section first looks at uncorrelated subqueries, which are typically used to increase the efficiency of queries that could be expressed in another way. Correlated subqueries, on the other hand, are often required to obtain output that can't be obtained any other way.

Uncorrelated Subqueries

An uncorrelated subquery is evaluated completely before the SQL command processor proceeds to the remainder of the query. For example, a query to retrieve the cab and license plate numbers of all cabs made before 1980 could be written:

```
SELECT Cab#, Plate
FROM Cab
WHERE Year = ANY (SELECT Year
                  FROM Cab
                  WHERE Year < '80')
```

```
SELECT Cab#, Plate
FROM Cab
WHERE Year = ANY (SELECT Year
                         FROM Cab
                         WHERE Year < '80')


Cab   Plate
104   356 QLT
105   111 ABC
378   771 TOW
```

Figure 8.18   SQL SELECT command—example 18

The subquery is the SELECT command that appears in parentheses. The result of the subquery is a table containing the year of manufacture of each cab that was made before 1980. The subquery table is a temporary table and is not displayed or stored in main memory for the user.

The contents of that subquery table are used to evaluate the year = ANY portion of the WHERE clause predicate. ANY is a special operator used only with subqueries; it can be paired with any of the standard logical operators. = ANY, used in the above example, is equivalent to IN; this is true as long as only one attribute is being compared. If more than one attribute is involved, the operator must be IN. Rows will be included in the final result (Figure 8.18) only if their year of manufacture is equal to any of the entries in the table returned by the subquery.

A subquery isn't limited to the same table as the outer query. When a subquery is based on a different table than the outer query, it can take the place of a join. For example, to see the names of all drivers who were scheduled to drive on November 15, 1994, a query could be written as:

```
SELECT Driver_Name
FROM Driver
WHERE Driver# IN   (SELECT Driver#
                    FROM Shift_Driven
                    WHERE WkDate = 11/15/94)
```

```
SELECT Driver_Name
FROM Driver
WHERE Driver# IN (SELECT Driver#
        FROM Shift_Driven
        WHERE WkDate = 11/15/94)
```

Driver_Name
Miller, Phyllis
Zilog, Charlie
Abelman, John
Erlich, Martin
Bailey, Max
Eastman, Rich
Thieu, Lin Van
Bailey, Max
Wong, David

Figure 8.19 SQL SELECT command—example 19

The subquery produces a temporary table that contains the Driver# for each driver scheduled to drive on November 15, 1994. The SQL command processor then compares each row in the Driver against the result of the subquery. Whenever it finds a match between Driver and the subquery result table, it places the driver's name in the final result table (Figure 8.19). Note that Max Bailey appears twice because he drove a double shift (evening and night) on that day.

This query could just as easily have been written:

SELECT Driver_Name
FROM Driver, Shift_Driven
WHERE Driver.Driver# = Shift_Driven.Driver#
AND WkDate = 11/15/94

Should you use a subquery or join? If your source tables are very large, a subquery can significantly speed up performance. It prevents the SQL command processor from performing a product of the source tables but instead lets it handle one table at a time.

```
SELECT Driver_Name, Driver_Phone
FROM Driver
WHERE Driver# IN (SELECT Driver#
                  FROM Shift_Driven
                  WHERE WkDate = 11/15/94
                  AND Cab# IN (SELECT Cab#
                               FROM Maint_Perf
                               WHERE Maint_Type = 'tune-up'
                               AND Maint_Date = 11/15/94))


Driver_Name        Driver_p
Miller, Phyllis    555-0006
Bailey, Max        555-0001
```

Figure 8.20 **SQL SELECT** command—example 20

Subqueries can also be nested, one within the other. For example, a nested subquery can be used to retrieve the name and phone number of everyone who drove a cab on November 15, 1994 that received a tune-up that day:

SELECT Driver_Name, Driver_Phone
FROM Driver
WHERE Driver# IN (SELECT Driver#
      FROM Shift_Driven
      WHERE WkDate = 11/15/94
      AND Cab# IN (SELECT Cab#
            FROM Maint_Perf
            WHERE Maint_Type = 'tune-up'
            AND Maint_Date = 11/15/94))

Like nesting loops within a programming language, nested subqueries must be completely contained within one another. The innermost subquery is evaluated first. In the example above, the result of which appears in Figure 8.20, the innermost subquery returns the number of each cab in Maintenance Performed that received a tune up on 11/15/94. The outer subquery retrieves the Driver# from rows in the Shift Driven table that have a date of 11/15/94 and

```
SELECT DISTINCT Cab#
FROM Cab
WHERE Cab# NOT IN (SELECT Cab#
                   FROM Shift_Driven
                   WHERE WkDate = 11/15/94)
```

Cab
002
006
105
378

Figure 8.21   SQL SELECT command—example 21

whose Cab# is in the table returned by the inner subquery. Finally, the outer query looks in the Driver table and returns the name and phone number for those rows that have their Driver# in the outer subquery table.

A subquery is the only way to use SQL to perform a relational algebra difference operation. The NOT IN and != ANY operators can be used to answer questions phrased in the negative. For example, the SQL query to list all the cabs not reserved for a given day might be written:

> SELECT DISTINCT Cab#
> FROM Cab
> WHERE Cab# NOT IN (SELECT Cab#
>   FROM Shift_Driven
>   WHERE WkDate = 11/15/94)

The subquery retrieves the cab number of cabs that are reserved on the desired date. The NOT IN operator indicates that cab numbers should be included in the final result (Figure 8.21) only if a cab number from Cab is not contained in the subquery table. To process this query, the SQL command processor first creates a subquery table that contains cab numbers for all cabs that are scheduled to be driven on 11/15/94 (nine cabs). It then takes a row from Cab and compares its cab number to each row in the subquery table. If the cab number from Cab isn't equal to every row in the subquery table, then it should be included in the final result table. As a matter of fact, each cab number from Cab that isn't in the subquery table appears nine times in the initial result table, once for every row in the subquery table (once for each cab number to which it isn't equal). The DISTINCT keyword in the query prevents all the duplicates from appearing in the final result.

Correlated Subqueries

A correlated subquery is a subquery that cannot be evaluated completely before proceeding to the outer query. Instead, the SQL command processor works back and forth between the subquery and the outer query, processing the subquery once for every row in the outer query.

For example, the Kellys might want to see the names of all drivers who drove more than the average number of miles during their shifts. Such a query might be written:

```
SELECT Driver_Name, WkDate, (End_Odom - Start_Odom)
FROM Driver, Shift_Driven
WHERE Driver.Driver# = Shift_Driven.Driver#
AND End_Odom - Start_Odom >
        (SELECT AVG(End_Odom - Start_Odom)
        FROM Shift_Driven
        WHERE WkFlag = 'T')
```

To process this query, the result of which appears in Figure 8.22, the DBMS computes the miles driven (Ending odometer reading - Starting odometer reading) for a row in Shift Driven. It then computes the average miles driven for all rows in Shift Driven that have a WkFlag value of "T" and compares that value to the miles driven for the single row being considered in the outer query. If the value computed for the row in the outer query is greater than the average, it is added to the result table. This process is repeated for every row in Shift Driven. In other words, the average miles driven is recomputed each time the SQL command processor looks at a row in Shift Driven.

Using Union

UNION is a keyword available with many SQL implementations that lets you perform a relational algebra UNION on the result tables of two or more SQL SELECTs. The tables on which the UNION operates must be union compatible. However, SQL's rules for union compatibility are stricter than those

```
SELECT Driver_Name, WkDate, (End_Odom - Start_Odom)
FROM Driver, Shift_Driven
WHERE Driver.Driver# = Shift_Driven.Driver#
AND End_Odom - Start_Odom >
    (SELECT AVG(End_Odom - Start_Odom)
    FROM Shift_Driven
    WHERE WkFlag = 'T')
```

Driver_Name	Shift_da	End_Odom - Start_Odom
Eastman, Rich	11/15/94	188
Thieu, Lin Van	11/15/94	360

Figure 8.22 SQL SELECT command—example 22

imposed by relational algebra. Not only must the tables have the same columns, but the columns must be in the same order, must have the same data type, and must be of the same length.

Assume, for example, that the Kellys want to see a list of the names of all drivers to whose status is "do not reserve" as well as those drivers who have been involved in an accident. The query can be written:

```
SELECT Driver_Name, Driver_Status
FROM Driver
WHERE Driver_Status = 'do not reserve'
UNION
SELECT Driver_Name, Driver_Status
FROM Driver, Incident
WHERE Driver.Driver# = Incident.Driver#
        AND Inci_Type = 'accident'
```

The result of this query appears in Figure 8.23. Note that the UNION is applied to the result of the individual selects. That means that the second SELECT can perform the necessary join to retrieve the driver name and status from Driver.

```
SELECT Driver_Name,Driver_Status
FROM Driver
WHERE Driver_Status = 'do not reserve'
UNION
SELECT Driver_Name, Driver_Status
FROM Driver, Incident
WHERE Driver.Driver# = Incident.Driver#
    AND Inci_Type = 'accident'
```

Driver Name	Driver Status
Miller, Pat	do not reserve
Mariott, Emily	do not reserve
Wilson, Carter	do not reserve
Eastman, Rich	pay after

Figure 8.23 SQL SELECT command—example 23

The Outer Join

The outer join is not part of the SQL standard. However, it is a handy retrieval operation and is available as part of some SQL implementations.

Assume, for example, that the FTC scheduling clerk wishes to see the names and phone numbers of all drivers who have been driving regularly, along with the cabs that they have driven. In addition, the clerk wants to see the names and phone numbers of all drivers who haven't reserved a shift in a long time. The query to see those who have been scheduled to drive might be written:

SELECT DISTINCT Driver_Name, Driver_Phone, Cab#
FROM Driver, Shift_Driven
WHERE Driver_Driver# = Shift_Driven.Driver#
ORDER BY Driver_Name

The drivers that do not have rows in the Shift Driven table do not appear in the output. A very subtle modification to the syntax, however, instructs SQL to include rows for those drivers that don't match:

SELECT DISTINCT Driver_Name, Driver_Phone, Cab#
FROM Driver, Shift_Driven
WHERE Driver_Driver# = Shift_Driven.Driver# (+)
ORDER BY Driver_Name

```
SELECT DISTINCT Driver_Name, Driver_Phone, Cab#
FROM Driver, Shift_Driven
WHERE Driver_Driver# = Shift_Driven.Driver# (+)
```

Driver_Name	Driver_P	Cab
Abelman, John	555-0020	404
Bailey, Max	555-0001	104
Bailey, Max	555-0001	108
Baker, Mary Ann	555-0002	108
Eastman, Richard	555-0012	144
Erlich, Martin	555-0011	045
French, Janice	555-0015	null
Jackson, Rafael	555-0017	null
Kolson, Jan	555-0018	null
Kowalski, Pete	555-0019	238
Lewis, John	555-0003	238
Mariott, Emily	555-0014	null
Miller, Pat	555-0005	null
Miller, Phyllis	555-0006	104
Phong, Quen	555-0007	null
Santiago, Jorge	555-0004	002
Thieu, Lin Van	555-0016	045
Wilson, Carter	555-0018	null
Wong, David	555-0008	215
Young, Leslie	555-0009	null
Zilog, Charlie	555-0010	238

Figure 8.24 SQL SELECT command—example 24

The (+) following the join condition in the WHERE clause indicates that the join should be performed as an outer join rather than as an equi-join. The result of this query can be seen in Figure 8.24.

Summary

SQL (Structured Query Language) has been accepted by the American National Standards Institute as the standard for relational database query languages. SQL, developed by IBM, is available with a wide range of relational DBMSs, from IBM's DB2, which runs only on IBM mainframes, to many microcomputer implementations.

SQL's SELECT command is used to retrieve data from existing base tables and views. Unlike the relational algebra SELECT, the SQL SELECT can:

- retrieve specific columns
- retrieve specific rows
- join tables to retrieve data from more than one table with a single command
- perform a union to combine the result of two separate queries

SQL databases support an on-line, dynamic data dictionary. The data dictionary can be queried by authorized users with the same syntax used to query data tables.

References

ANSI/X3H2 Committee. 1984. American National Standard Database Language SQL (X3H2-84-117). ANSI/X3/SPARC Project 363D. October.

Baker, Jerry. 1986. "SQL: a new standard." *Computerworld.* February 19. pp. 55-58.

Chamberlin, D. D., M. M. Astrahan, K. P. Eswaran, P. P. Griffiths, R. A. Lorie, J. W. Mehl, P. Reisner, and B. W. Wade. 1976. "SEQUEL 2: a unified approach to data definition, manipulation and control." IBM Journal of Research and Development. 20:56-574. November.

Date, C. J. 1986. *An Introduction to Database Systems,* Vol I. 4th ed. Reading, Mass.: Addison-Wesley.

Date, C. J. 1987. "Where SQL Falls Short." *Datamation.* May 1:83–84+.

Gerritson, Rob. 1991. "SQL Tutorial." *DBMS.* 4(2):44–53.

Gerritson, Rob. 1991. "Advanced SQL Queries." *DBMS.* 4(3):58–65.

Groff, James R. and Paul N. Weinberg. 1990. *Using SQL.* Osborne/McGraw-Hill.

McFayden, Ron and Vijay Kanabar. 1991. *An Introduction to Structured Query Language*. Wm. C. Brown.

Reisner, P. 1981. "Human Factor Studies of Database Query Languages: A Survey and Assessment." *Computing Surveys*. 13 (March):13-31.

Techncial Committee X3H2—Database. 1986. *Database Language SQL*. January. American National Standards Institute.

Exercises

1. Given the following relations from the Office of Margaret Holmes, D.M.D., develop the SQL syntax needed to answer the queries below.

   Patient (<u>Patient #</u>, Patient Name, Patient Address, Patient Phone,
      Bill Payer, Birth Date, Relationship to Bill Payer)
   Appointment (<u>Patient #</u>, <u>Visit Date</u>, Visit Time)
   Treatment (<u>Treatment Type</u>, Cost)
   Treatment Performed (<u>Patient #</u>, <u>Visit Date</u>, <u>Treatment Type</u>)
   Payer (<u>Bill Payer Name</u>, Payer Address, Payer Home Phone,
      Payer Work Phone, Insurance Company, Employer, $ Owed)
   Bill (<u>Statement #</u>, Bill Payer Name, Statement Date, Statement $)
   Payment (<u>Bill Payer Name</u>, Payment Source, Check #, Check $,
      Payment Date)

   a. Display the names and bill payers for all patients under 18 years of age.
   b. List the names and work phone numbers of all bill payers who owe more than $1,000.
   c. Display the dates and times of all visits made or scheduled to be made by Hilda Jones.
   d. Display the dates and times of all future visits scheduled for Hilda Jones.
   e. Display the names and birth dates of all patients for whom Martin Scola pays the bills.
   f. List the cost of all treatments received by Lincoln Dobbs in the past month.
   g. Display the names and phone numbers of all patients who haven't had their teeth cleaned in the past year.

h. Display the sum of all money owed by all bill payers.

i. For each patient, display the sum of all charges for procedures performed on that patient.

j. Display the sum of all charges for treatments performed on each patient where the sum is more than $500.

2. Given the following relations from the database of the East Coast Aquarium, develop the SQL syntax needed to answer the queries below.

Species (<u>Species Code</u>, Latin Name, English Name)
Location (<u>Location Code</u>, Place in Building, Size, Head Keeper)
Population (<u>Species Code</u>, <u>Location Code</u>, Number of Animals)
Food (<u>Type of Food</u>)
Feeding (<u>Species Code</u>, <u>Type of Food</u>, Amount of Food, Feeding Interval)
Habitats (<u>Habitat Type</u>)
Can Live (<u>Species Code</u>, <u>Habitat Type</u>)
Where Found (<u>Location Code</u>, <u>Habitat Type</u>)

Volunteer (<u>Volunteer #</u>, Vol. Name, Vol. Address, Vol. Phone)
Skill (<u>Skill Type</u>)
Can Do (<u>Volunteer #</u>, <u>Skill Type</u>)
Volunteer Schedule (<u>Volunteer #</u>, <u>Vol. Date</u>, Vol. Time, Job)

a. List the English name of all species that live in location number 101.

b. List the Latin name of all species that eat mackerel.

c. List the Latin name of all species that can live in a coral reef habitat.

d. Display the names and phone numbers of all volunteers who can conduct a dolphin show.

e. Display the names and phone numbers of all volunteers who are scheduled to work on 12/4/94.

f. Display the dates and times that Steven Schultz is scheduled to volunteer.

g. Display the type of food, amount of food, and feeding interval for all foods eaten by hammerhead sharks.

h. List the English name of all species for which Miriam Miles is the head keeper.

i. List the total number of animals that live in location 95.

j. Display the total number of animals that live in each location in the aquarium.

3. Consider again the outer join query in Figure 8.24 and answer the following questions:

   a. Why isn't the result table produced by this query a legal relation? Does it make any difference whether a result query is a legal relation? Why or why not?
   b. In an attempt to see the names and phone numbers of all drivers scheduled to drive on a given shift along with those who weren't scheduled to drive, one of FTC's clerks prepared the following query:

      SELECT DISTINCT Driver_Name, Driver_phone, Cab#
      FROM Driver, Shift_Driven
      WHERE Driver.Driver# = Shift_Driven.Driver# (+)
      AND Shift_Name = 'eve'
      AND WkDate = 11/15/94
      ORDER BY Driver_Name

      What result will this query produce? Why doesn't it work in the way the clerk thought it would? (Hint: Figure out what columns will appear in the result of the outer join and where null values will appear.) How could you fix the query to make it work?

9

SQL Data Modification

This chapter examines the SQL commands used to manipulate database structure, including creating, modifying, and deleting tables. It also looks at SQL indexes. In addition, you will be introduced to the SQL commands for adding, modifying, and deleting data.

Using SQL to Install a Third Normal Form Database

Although SQL is called a "query" language, it can do more than just retrieve data. SQL can also be used to define a relational schema (in other words, create tables) and to perform data modification. These capabilities are part of any SQL implementation, regardless of whether it is running on a PC, a minicomputer, or a mainframe.

Creating Tables

Base tables are defined with the SQL command CREATE TABLE. The general format of the command is:

        CREATE TABLE table_name
                (column_name1 type1 [NOT NULL]
                [,column_name2 type2 [NOT NULL]]...)

As you saw with the general format of the SELECT command, the preceding notation places brackets around any part of the command that is optional. An ellipsis (...) indicates that a portion of the command may be repeated.

The command below creates the Cab relation for the Federated Taxi Company (FTC) database:

        CREATE TABLE Cab
                (Cab# char (3) NOT NULL,
                Make_Model (15),
                Year char (2),
                Plate char (7),
                Condition char (35),
                Cab_Status char (15),
                Curr_Odom number (6))

Each attribute (or column) is given a unique name. The rules for column names vary from one DBMS to another. Therefore, you should consult your DBMS's documentation before deciding on column names.

The option NOT NULL is used for any columns that should not be permitted to assume a null value. Therefore, all attributes which are part of the primary key should be indicated as NOT NULL. Checks for violation of NOT NULL specifications are made when data are entered. The DBMS will not store any row that is missing data for a NOT NULL column. In other words, a SQL DBMS allows you to define entity integrity within the data dictionary and also automatically enforces it.

The name of each attribute is followed by a type designator, indicating what type of data will be stored in the column. A DBMS will display an error message if a user attempts to store data that is not compatible with a column's data type. In addition, a DBMS uses data types to determine whether the result of two SELECTs can be combined with the UNION command.

The complete set of SQL commands needed to install the FTC database appear in Figure 9.1. Although the keywords in this figure are printed in uppercase letters, SQL is not case-sensitive with keywords and the names of user-created data objects (for example, tables and views). Upper- and lowercase differences are, however, retained within the data themselves.

Deleting Tables

To completely remove a table from the database, use the command DROP TABLE:

DROP TABLE table_name

Unless you have been given database administrator privileges, you will be able to drop only those tables that you have created.

SQL Indexes

The SQL query optimizer may use an *index* to help improve query performance. An index on a relation is very much like an index in a book. The index to a book contains a list of subjects in alphabetical order. Associated with each subject are the page numbers where more information about that subject can be found. In a way, the page numbers in the index "point to" information in the rest of the book. An index on a relation is a physical entity that contains an

```
CREATE TABLE Cab (Cab# char (3) NOT NULL,
    Make_Model (15),
    Year char (2),
    Plate char (7),
    Condition char (35),
    Cab_Status char (15),
    Curr_Odom number (6))

CREATE TABLE Driver (Driver# char (2) NOT NULL,
    Driver_Name char (15),
    Driver_Address char (35),
    Driver_Phone char (8),
    License# char (6),
    Exp_Date date,
    Driver_Status char (14))

CREATE TABLE Shift (Shift_Name char (3) NOT NULL,
    WkDate date))

CREATE TABLE Shift_Driven (Shift_Name char (3) NOT NULL,
    WkDate date NOT NULL,
    Cab# char (3) NOT NULL,
    Driver# char (2),
    WkFlag char (1),
    Start_Odom number (6),
    End_Odom number (6))

CREATE TABLE Maint_Activity (Maint_Type char (15) NOT NULL)

CREATE TABLE Maint_Performed (Maint_Type char (15) NOT NULL,
    Maint_Date date NOT NULL,
    Cab# char (3) NOT NULL,
    Maint_Odom number (6))

CREATE TABLE Incident (Inci_Date date NOT NULL,
    Inci_Time char (10) NOT NULL,
    Cab# char (3) NOT NULL,
    Driver# char (2) NOT NULL,
    Inci_Type char (15),
    Inci_Details char (255))
```

Figure 9.1   SQL commands used to create the FTC database

ordered list of subjects, called *keys*, and the computer equivalent of page numbers, *pointers*, indicating where the rows that contains a given key value can be found.

How can indexes help speed up searching? Just as a list of subjects in alphabetical order can be searched faster than an unordered list by a person, an index on a relation in some known order can be searched faster by a DBMS than the unordered rows in the base table. At first blush, then, it might seem that the best strategy would be to index a relation on every column and combination of columns that might possibly be used as search criteria. However, there are two reasons to be selective about what indexes you create.

First, keep in mind that each index occupies disk space. It contains key values, duplicating data in the base tables, as well as pointers to the base tables. Second, and more importantly, indexes slow down data modification. Not only must data be entered into or changed in a relation itself, but modification must be made to every index that exists for the relation. Therefore, database designers usually compromise and create indexes for columns or combinations of columns that are used frequently as search criteria.

Once an index has been created, the DBMS automatically uses it whenever that use will facilitate performance; the user or application programmer can, in most cases, forget about it. SQL indexes can also be used to ensure that primary key values are unique. Therefore, if you are working with a SQL implementation that doesn't include extensions for primary key support, each table should be indexed at least on its primary key.

Creating Indexes

The general form of the CREATE INDEX statement is:

    CREATE [UNIQUE] INDEX index_name
            ON table_name (column_name1 [,column_name2]...)

An index for a composite key can be built by simply including more than one attribute name within the parentheses that follow the table name.

If the optional keyword UNIQUE is present, the DBMS will not permit duplicate values within the index for the columns listed in the CREATE INDEX command. For example, the SQL command to create a unique index for the Shift Driven table is:

CREATE UNIQUE INDEX shiftkey
    ON Shift_Driven (Shift_Name, WkDate, Cab#)

The effect of a unique index is to prohibit duplicate key values in the base table. However, keep in mind that although this provides a practical strategy for automatically ensuring unique primary keys, the validation is being made not on the base table, but on the index. The DBMS does not recognize whether the columns in the index key constitute a primary key. In other words, a SQL implementation that supports unique indexes does not necessarily provide support for primary keys.

Note that SQL has no trouble concatenating the column of type date (WkDate) with columns of type char (Shift_name, Cab#); no special conversion routines are required. The complete set of CREATE INDEX commands for use with the FTC database is available in Figure 9.2.

Deleting Indexes

Indexes may not be deleted automatically whenever a table is deleted with DROP TABLE. SQL also does not provide a way to modify an index once it has been created. Therefore, indexes may need to be deleted explicitly whenever the table on which they were built is deleted or if the index key must be changed.

Indexes are deleted with DROP INDEX:

DROP INDEX index_name

Modifying the Structure of a Table

The SQL standard specifies that tables can be modified in one of two ways. Either a column can be added to the table or the width of an existing column can be expanded. When adding a column, the format of the command is:

ALTER TABLE table_name
    ADD column_name type

```
CREATE UNIQUE INDEX cabkey
    ON Cab (Cab#)

CREATE UNIQUE INDEX drvkey
    ON Driver (Driver#)

CREATE UNIQUE INDEX shiftkey
    ON Shift (Shift_Name, WkDate)

CREATE UNIQUE INDEX shiftdrvkey
    ON Shift_Driven (Shift_Name, Wkdate, Cab#)

CREATE UNIQUE INDEX incikey
    ON Incident (Shift_Name, WkDate, Cab#, Inci_Time)

CREATE UNIQUE INDEX maintactkey
    ON Maint_Activity (Maint_Type)

CREATE UNIQUE INDEX maintperfkey
    ON Maint_Performed (Cab#, Maint_Date, Maint_Type)
```

Figure 9.2   SQL Commands to index the FTC database

The column name and type designation must conform to the rules for column names and data types in the CREATE TABLE command. For example, to add a column to hold the color of a cab to the Cab table:

> ALTER TABLE Cab
> > ADD Color char (8)

The syntax to expand an existing column is only slightly different:

> ALTER TABLE table_name
> > MODIFY column_name type

For example, if the 15 characters originally allocated for the *Inci_Type* attribute in the Incident relation proves too small, it can be expanded with:

> ALTER TABLE Incident
> > MODIFY Inci_Type char (25)

The MODIFY version of ALTER TABLE cannot make a column smaller. It can only increase the number of characters in a character column or change the width or number of decimal places in a number column. It also cannot be used to change the type of a column.

> **By the way:** Some SQL implementations provide extensions to the ALTER TABLE command that provide additional functionality. Consult your DBMS's documentation to discover exactly what ALTER TABLE will allow you to do.

Inserting, Modifying, and Deleting Data

SQL data modification commands affect one or more rows of a table with a single command. As you will see, however, the syntax of these commands makes them clumsy for everyday use. Although they are often embedded in application programs, many users prefer using the data entry forms supported by many DBMSs for data modification.

Inserting Data

The SQL command to enter data into a table, INSERT, comes in two formats, one to load a single row and the other to load multiple rows from some other table or view. To load a single row, the format is:

```
INSERT INTO table_name [(column_name1, column_name2...)]
        VALUES (value1, value2...)
```

If values for all attributes in the row are to be added with a single INSERT, then the names of the columns in the table are not necessary. The data values must, however, appear in the value list (in parentheses after VALUES) in the same order in which the columns were defined. For example, to insert a row into the Maintenance Performed table:

```
INSERT INTO Maint_Performed
        VALUES ('new engine',12/6/94,'002', 0)
```

Null values, for those columns that have not been defined as NOT NULL, can be entered by using the characters NULL in the value list.

If data for less than all attributes are to be loaded, then the columns must be specified:

    INSERT INTO Maint_Performed (Cab#, Maint_Type, Maint_Date)
        VALUES ('045', 'tune-up', 1/16/94)

The order of the columns need not be the same as the order in which they were defined in the table. SQL matches data in the value list by position with the attribute names.

The second INSERT format loads multiple rows of data from one relation or view to another:

    INSERT INTO table_name1 [(column_name1, column_name2...)]
        SELECT select_list
        FROM table_name2
        [WHERE predicate]
        [GROUP BY column_name [HAVING predicate]]

The rows identified by the SELECT portion of the command are loaded into the target table listed on the first line of the command. The attributes in the select list must exist in the target table. This format might be used to permanently capture a virtual table created by a SELECT. For example, assume that FTC has created a new base table to contain the average mileage driven on each day and shift:

    Averages (WkDate, Shift_Name, Avg_Miles)

The value for *Avg_Miles* is computed in a SELECT command that includes a GROUP BY clause. Periodically, the AVERAGES table can be updated with the command:

    INSERT INTO Averages
        SELECT WkDate, Shift_Name, AVG(End_Odom - Start_Odom)
            FROM Shift_Driven
            WHERE WkFlag = 'T'
            GROUP BY WkDate, Shift_Name

A unique index has been built on the primary key of this table. Its presence ensures that no duplicate rows appear in Averages, regardless of how often it is updated or how often the INSERT command is issued.

Another major use for the second version of the INSERT command is to modify the structure of tables. Because most SQL ALTER TABLE commands do not allow columns to be removed from tables or the size of columns to be changed, the quickest way to change the structure of a base table is to create a new table with the desired columns and then use INSERT to copy data from the old table to the new. Once the INSERT has been completed, the old table can be dropped.

Modifying Data

Data modification is performed with the UPDATE command:

        UPDATE table_name
                SET column_name1 = expression1
                [,column_name2 = expression2] ...
                [WHERE predicate]

For example, to change Pat Miller's address and phone number:

        UPDATE Driver
                SET Driver_Address = '12 S. 15th, Anytown 10012',
                Driver_Phone = '555-9912'
                WHERE Driver# = '05'

The WHERE clause identifies the row that is to be updated. If only a single row is to be changed then, as in the above example, the predicate includes a primary key expression. New values are assigned to columns with SET; the expression to the right of the equals sign may be constants, other attributes, or may contain arithmetic operations (for number columns only), string operations (for char and long columns only), or date operations (for date columns only).

UPDATE commands without a WHERE clause can be dangerous; they make the same change to an entire table. For example:

```
UPDATE Shift_Driven
        SET WkFlag = 'T'
```

changes the value of WkFlag to 'T' in every row in the Shift Driven table.

Deleting Data

Like UPDATE, the rows on which a DELETE command operates are specified with a WHERE clause:

```
DELETE FROM table_name
        [WHERE predicate]
```

Technically, the WHERE clause is technically optional—but, if it is left off the DELETE command removes every single row from the specified table. DELETE is therefore the potentially most destructive SQL command.

> **By the way:** SQL doesn't provide an "undo" command. Once data are deleted, they are, for all practical purposes, unrecoverable.

To delete a single row, the WHERE clause should contain a primary key expression:

```
DELETE FROM Incident
        WHERE Cab# = '104"
            AND WkDate = 11/15/94'
            AND Shift_Name = 'day'
```

Since the above command contains all three parts of the primary key, it deletes exactly one row. If, however, FTC wishes to purge all reservations from Shift Driven that occurred before a specific date, the predicate will include only the date, and not the shift or cab number:

```
DELETE FROM Shift_Driven
        WHERE WkDate < 11/16/94
```

Because SQL table definitions don't include primary key-foreign key relationships, it is possible to delete a primary key without removing all foreign key references to it. For example, if a cab is sold or otherwise removed from service and its row is deleted from Cab, all rows from Shift Driven, Incident, and Maintenance Performed that involve that cab must also be deleted. There is no way to do this deletion with a single DELETE; it requires a series of them:

```
DELETE FROM Shift_Driven
      WHERE Cab # = '144'

DELETE FROM Maint_Performed
      WHERE Cab# = '144'

DELETE FROM Incident
      WHERE Cab# = '144'

DELETE FROM Cab
      WHERE Cab# = '144'
```

By the way: The SQL standard does not support referential integrity. However, you may be working with a SQL implementation such as R:BASE 4.5, Oracle 7, or SQLBase that has extensions for referential integrity. If that is true, and you have defined referential integrity constraints, then you will be unable to delete a primary key without deleting the rows in other tables that contain foreign keys that reference it. (You will read more about SQL integrity control extensions in Chapter 11.)

Creating Views

A SQL view is a single virtual table created by selecting columns and rows from base tables and other views. Views are primarily used as security devices to restrict user access to data. As you will see in Chapter 13, when we discuss database security, it is possible to precisely tailor table and view permissions to individual users. They can also be used as a device to capture the tables produced by complex queries. In essence, the view assigns a name to a table created as the result of a SELECT. The contents of the table are not stored on disk, but the definition of how it was created is stored instead.

Views are created with the CREATE VIEW command:

```
CREATE VIEW view_name
    AS
        SELECT [DISTINCT] column_name1 [,column_name2]...
        FROM table_name
        [WHERE predicate]
        [GROUP BY column_name [HAVING predicate]]
```

Each view is given a unique name that must conform to the rules for naming tables. Once the view has been created, its name can be used in SQL commands in place of base table names. This means that views can be created from previously defined views as well as from base tables.

The contents of a view are determined by the result of a SELECT command. Remember that SELECT returns a table, and that table may be the join of other tables. For example, if FTC wished to create a view for the chief mechanic, it might include data from just the Cab and Maintenance Performed relations:

```
CREATE VIEW MrFixIt
    AS
        SELECT Cab#, Plate, Maint_Type, Maint_Date, Maint_Odom
        FROM Cab, Maint_Performed
        WHERE Cab.Cab# = Maint_Performed.Cab#
```

In this example, the WHERE clause is used to identify the primary key-foreign key relationship to be used for a join. It can also, however, be used to restrict the rows that appear in a view. The following view could simplify the job of the night shift dispatcher, since it only includes data about the night shift:

```
CREATE VIEW Nights
    AS
        SELECT Driver#, Driver_Name, Cab#, WkDate
        FROM Driver, Shift_Driven
        WHERE Driver.Driver# = Shift_Driven.Driver#
            AND Shift_Name = 'ngt'
```

Some SQL views can be used to modify data. In most cases, a DBMS will permit updating through only those views that are created from a single base table. Although any view that contains the primary key columns of the base tables from which it was created (all columns defined as NOT NULL) is theoretically updatable, most DBMSs do not yet support updating of such views.

Summary

The SQL data definition commands are used to:

- Create tables (CREATE TABLE)
- Destroy tables (DROP TABLE)
- Create indexes to speed retrieval and enforce the uniqueness of primary keys (CREATE INDEX)
- Modify tables by adding columns or increasing the width of a column (ALTER TABLE)

The data manipulation commands are used to:

- Load data into tables (INSERT)
- Modify data in tables (UPDATE)
- Delete data from tables (DELETE)

SQL supports entity integrity by permitting columns to be defined as NOT NULL. Enforcing the uniqueness of primary keys requires the use of a "unique" index; the uniqueness of the keys is enforced in the index, not directly in the base table. SQL does not, however, have provisions for specifying primary key-foreign key references and therefore does not enforce referential integrity.

SQL views are created by specifying a SELECT that retrieves the data to be stored in the view. Using the CREATE VIEW command stores the query in the data dictionary, from where it is executed when the name of the view is used in a SQL command.

References

ANSI/X3H2 Committee. 1984. American National Standard Database Language SQL (X3H2-84-117). ANSI/X3/SPARC Project 363D. October.

Baker, Jerry. 1986. "SQL: a new standard." *Computerworld.* February 19. pp. 55-58.

Cardenas, Alfonso F. 1985. *Data Base Management Systems.* 2nd ed. Boston: Allyn and Bacon.

Chamberlin, D. D., M. M. Astrahan, K. P. Eswaran, P. P. Griffiths, R. A. Lorie, J. W. Mehl, P. Reisner, and B. W. Wade. 1976. "SEQUEL 2: a unified approach to data definition, manipulation and control." IBM Journal of Research and Development. 20:56-574. November.

Date, C. J. 1986. *An Introduction to Database Systems*, Vol I. 4th ed. Reading, MA: Addison-Wesley.

Exercises

1. Given the following set of relations from the Office of Margaret Holmes, D.M.D., develop the SQL syntax to perform the operations below.

   > Patient (<u>Patient #</u>, Patient Name, Patient Address, Patient Phone, Bill Payer, Birth Date, Relationship to Bill Payer)
   > Appointment (<u>Patient #</u>, <u>Visit Date</u>, Visit Time)
   > Treatment (<u>Treatment Type</u>, Cost)
   > Treatment performed (<u>Patient #</u>, <u>Visit date</u>, <u>Treatment Type</u>)
   > Payer (<u>Bill Payer Name</u>, Payer Address, Payer Home Phone, Payer Work Phone, Insurance Company, Employer, $ Owed)
   > Bill (<u>Statement #</u>, Bill Payer Name, Statement Date, Statement $)
   > Payment (<u>Bill Payer Name</u>, Payment Source, Check #, Check $, Payment Date)

   a. Create a table for each of the relations listed. Modify table and column names wherever necessary to conform to the naming rules of the DBMS that you are using. Use the table and column names from this problem for the rest of the exercises below. Enforce entity integrity by ensuring that primary key columns are NOT NULL.

   b. Create a primary key index for each of your tables. Enforce unique primary keys if UNIQUE is available with your DBMS.

c. Make the following modifications to the structures of your existing tables:
   1. Add a column to the Treatment Performed table to hold the actual price charged the patient. (This amount might be different from the typical charge for a procedure stored in the Treatment table.)
   2. Remove the Employer column from the Payer table. If your SQL implementation cannot delete columns, what SQL command is required to copy the data from the existing table to a new table?

d. Make the following modifications to existing data:
   1. Change a patient's address
   2. Record that a patient will no longer be seen by Dr. Holmes by deleting all data about that patient from the database. How many SQL commands are needed to perform this operation?
   3. Change every appointment scheduled for 10/2/94 to 10/3/94.

2. Given the following set of relations from the East Coast Aquarium, develop the SQL syntax to perform the operations below.

Species (Species Code, Latin Name, English Name)
Location (Location Code, Place in Building, Size, Head Keeper)
Population (Species Code, Location Code, Number of Animals)
Food (Type of Food)
Feeding (Species Code, Type of Food, Amount of Food, Feeding Interval)
Habitats (Habitat Type)
Can Live (Species Code, Habitat Type)
Where Found (Location Code, Habitat Type)

Volunteer (Volunteer #, Vol. Name, Vol. Address, Vol. Phone)
Skill (Skill Type)
Can Do (Volunteer #, Skill Type)
Volunteer Schedule (Volunteer #, Vol. Date, Vol. Time, Job)

a. Create a table for each of the relations listed. Modify table and column names wherever necessary to conform to the naming rules of the DBMS that you are using. Use the table and column names from this problem for the rest of the exercises below. Enforce entity integrity by ensuring that primary key columns are NOT NULL.

b. Create a primary key index for each of your tables. Enforce unique primary keys if UNIQUE is available with your DBMS.

c. Make the following data modifications:
1. Add a row to indicate that more than three individuals of species number 5 (Bottlenose Dolphin) are now living in location number 16 (the Dolphin House).
2. Change the habitat type for Sockeye Salmon from "fresh water river" to "open ocean." (Hint: The WHERE clause in this command needs a join condition.)
3. Change the starting time at which a volunteer is scheduled to work.
4. Delete all rows from the Volunteer Schedule table. (The data have been stored on an optical disk for permanent backup.)
5. Assume that a volunteer has indicated that he or she will no longer work at the aquarium. Delete all data pertaining to that volunteer. How many DELETE commands are required?

10

Embedded SQL

Whenever SQL is used within an application program, it is known as *embedded* SQL. Unfortunately, writing embedded SQL programs is not as straightforward as simply placing SQL statements within a host language. This chapter looks at the special procedures for writing SQL application programs.

SQL can be embedded in a number of third-generation host languages, including COBOL, PL/1, FORTRAN, BASIC, and C. Only C, however, is supported by microcomputer DBMSs. At the same time, some DBMSs (for example, *dBASE IV* and *R:BASE*) recognize SQL as an integral part of their programming languages. The procedures for handling embedded SQL is somewhat different in the two types of environments. You will therefore see two versions of some of the sample programs in this chapter, one in C and one in *R:BASE*'s programming language.

SQL is typically embedded in application programs for one or two reasons. First, application programs can automate processes that are performed regularly, freeing users from repeatedly issuing the same sequence of commands. Second, it can make database use easier for technologically unsophisticated users by hiding database access commands within a user-friendly interface.

The design of database application programs is similar to the design of any other application program. The purpose of this chapter is therefore to look at those aspects of embedded SQL that are different from other types of programming.

Characteristics of Embedded SQL Programs

All embedded SQL application programs have some common characteristics that are independent of the function performed by the program. These include the grouping of SQL commands into transactions and the handling of errors produced by SQL commands.

Transaction Processing

The SQL commands issued against a database from within an application program are grouped into transactions. A *transaction* is a complete unit of work submitted to a database. Each transaction ends in one of two ways: it may be *committed*, in which case all changes made by the transaction are made permanent, or it may be *rolled back*, in which case all changes made by the transaction are undone and the database returned to the state it was in before the transaction began.

> **By the way:** Managing a database environment when multiple transactions are running against the same database at the same time is discussed in depth in Chapter 12.

A DBMS cannot determine by itself where a transaction begins or ends, nor can it decide whether a transaction should be committed or rolled back. SQL therefore contains a command that is used within a program to indicate where a transaction should begin (usually BEGIN WORK or START

TRANSACTION). It also contains commands to commit a transaction (COMMIT or COMMIT WORK) and roll back a transaction (ROLLBACK or ROLLBACK WORK).

> **By the way:** Transaction control commands differ slightly between SQL implementations.

Embedded SQL programs group logically related SQL commands into transactions. For example, when a program must issue several DELETE commands to remove a primary key row and all rows containing foreign keys that reference it, the program will group all the DELETEs into a single transaction. In this way, if one of the DELETEs happens to fail, all of them can be undone. Otherwise, a failure would leave the database in an inconsistent state, with some of the DELETEs completed and others not performed.

Embedded SQL and SQL Errors

When a SQL command is executed interactively (by typing the command directly to a SQL command processor and getting an immediate reply), an unsuccessful command generates an error message on the screen. Although the error message may frustrate the user, it has no impact on the overall state of the database. The command may be reissued or abandoned, whichever the user desires.

Application programs, however, generally do not give the user the option of reissuing a command that fails. In addition, many application programs perform more than one SQL operation. If any of the commands fail, the program must handle the problem that arises when only some of the program's actions have been performed. Embedded SQL programs must therefore contain code that checks the result of every SQL statement and takes action if a command fails. For example, a program can use the value of a SQL error code to determine whether to commit or roll back a transaction.

Basic Elements of Embedded SQL Programs

As you read earlier, SQL statements can be embedded in a general-purpose host language (in this book, C) or in a proprietary programming language supplied by a DBMS. The syntax for embedding the SQL and the procedure for making the program executable is somewhat different in each environment.

Using a General-Purpose Host Language

In Listing 10.1 you will find the C version of an embedded SQL function to create a new record in the Federated Taxi Company's Cab table. It contains the major structural elements that appear in almost every embedded SQL program that uses a high-level language as its host language.

As written, SQL statements will not be accepted by a high-level language compiler (they will generate error messages). Embedded SQL programs are therefore first processed by a *precompiler*. The precompiler turns the SQL statements into comments and inserts calls to external procedures or functions that perform the actions requested by the SQL statements. The resulting output file can then be compiled as any other program. The procedures and functions inserted by the precompiler are supplied as a run-time library. The SQL library is linked to the compiled program along with standard language run-time libraries.

SQL precompilers process any program statement that begins with EXEC SQL. A successful precompilation means that all the SQL statements were syntactically correct and that the precompiler was able to translate them into procedure or function calls. The precompiler does not, however, perform any of the syntax checking that is normally performed by a language compiler. In other words, to run an embedded SQL program you must satisfy not only the syntax rules imposed by the precompiler for SQL, but the syntax rules for host language statements imposed by the host language compiler.

The program in Listing 10.1 contains two types of SQL statements. Some are declarative (establish parameters of the SQL environment); others are executable (perform actions against the database). All SQL statements are contained completely on the lines that begin EXEC SQL. Everything else is C.

```
#include <stdio.h>
#include <ctype.h>

EXEC SQL BEGIN DECLARE SECTION;
    char Cabnum[3];
    char Make_model[15];
    char Year[2];
    char Plate[7];
    VARCHAR Condition[255];
    char Cab_status[1];
    int curodom;
EXEC SQL END DECLARE SECTION;
EXEC SQL INCLUDE SQLCA;

AddCab()
{
    EXEC SQL WHENEVER SQLERROR GOTO errexit;
    length = asks("Enter number for new cab: ",Cabnum.arr);
    while (length)
    {
        Make_model.len = asks("Make: ",Make_model.arr);
        Year.len = asks("Year: ",Year.arr);
        Plate.len = asks("License plate: ",Plate.arr);
        Condition.len = asks("Condition: ",Condition.arr);
        Cab_status.len = asks("Status (T or F): ",Cab_status.arr);
        askn("Current odometer reading: ",&curodom);
        EXEC SQL INSERT INTO Cab VALUES
            (:Cabnum,:Make_model,:Year,:Plate,:Condition,:Cab_status,:curodom);
        printf("\nNew cab inserted\n");
        length = asks("Number for new cab: ",Cabnum.arr);
    }
    EXEC SQL COMMIT WORK;
    return(1);

    errexit:
        printf("\n%.70s(%d)",sqlca.sqlerrm.sqlerrmc,-sqlca.sqlcode);
        EXEC SQL ROLLBACK WORK;
        return(0);
}
int asks(text,variable)
    char text[],variable[];
    {
    printf(text);
    return (gets(variable) == (char *) ? EOF : strlen(variable));
    }
```

Annotations:

An embedded SQL statement that defines the beginning of the section to define host language variables that will be used in SQL statements

The end of the declare section

Bring in the data structure that contains SQL statement return codes

Set the branch for error trapping

Perform the insert

Commit the transaction

Undo transaction when error occurs

Listing 10.1 An embedded SQL application to create a row for a new cab (continued on next page)

```
int askn(text,variable)
    char text[];
    int *variable;
    {
    char s[20];
    printf(text);
    if (gets(s) == (char *) 0)
        return(EOF);
    variable = atoi(s);
    return(1);
    }
```

Listing 10.1 (Continued from page 255)

Declarative Statements

Most embedded SQL programs use the following declarative statements:

- BEGIN/END DECLARE SECTION: The DECLARE SECTION defines all host variables. Host variables are all programming language variables that will be used in SQL statements. The names of host variables may be the same as columns in database tables.
- INCLUDE SQLCA: The SQLCA (SQL Communications Area) is a data structure (usually named "sqlca") into which a DBMS places messages and codes that indicate the result of executing a SQL statement. The contents of sqlca are used for handling errors that occur while a program is running. Although the exact structure of sqlca varies from one DBMS to another, in most implementations it contains:
  - sqlca.sqlcode: an integer that represents the result of executing a SQL statement. In most cases, a sqlca.sqlcode value of zero indicates that execution of the SQL command was successful. Other sqlca.sqlcode values are implementation dependent.
  - sqlcode.errml: an integer that contains the number of characters in an error message.
  - sqlcode.errmc: a string of characters of length sqlcode.errml that explains the error code in sqlca.sqlcode.
- WHENEVER: The WHENEVER statement provides traps for conditions that arise when a program is running. The conditions that can be trapped are:

- SQLERROR: a SQLERROR condition is generated when a DBMS error occurs (for example, a user attempts to access a table or view to which he or she does not have access rights). The presence of a SQLERROR generally means that the requested operation cannot be performed and that sqlca.sqlcode has a value other than zero.
- SQLWARNING: a WARNING condition is also generated by the DBMS. A warning generally means that the requested operation can be performed but may not produce expected or desired results.
- NOT FOUND: a NOT FOUND condition arises when a SELECT retrieves no rows or when an INSERT, UPDATE, or DELETE statement that is intended to affect multiple rows affects none.
- The actions that can be performed are:
  - STOP: The STOP option terminates program execution.
  - CONTINUE: The CONTINUE option instructs the program to ignore the error condition and continue processing.
  - GOTO statement_label: The GOTO option transfers control to the statement identified by statement_label.

By the way: Unfortunately, the WHENEVER traps don't allow programs to execute functions or procedures, but insist on use of the GOTO for branching. Because GOTOs can lead to unstructured code that is difficult to debug and modify, the GOTO action must be coded carefully.

A program can have up to three WHENEVER statements active at the same time, one for each condition trapped by WHENEVER. Any subsequent WHENEVER of the same type overrides the previous. For example, assume that a program contains the statements in Listing 10.2 and that there are no other branching statements (loops, GOTO, or IF statements) in the code segment. The first three WHENEVER statements set up GOTO destinations for all three types on conditions. When the fourth WHENEVER is encountered, it changes the target destination only for the SQLERROR condition. The fifth WHENEVER SQLERROR changes it once more; the other two targets aren't affected.

```
WHENEVER SQLERROR GOTO label1;
WHENEVER SQLWARNING GOTO label2;
WHENEVER NOT FOUND GOTO label3;
    :
    :
    :
WHENEVER SQLERROR GOTO label4;
    :
    :
WHENEVER SQLERROR GOTO label1;
    :
    :
```

Changes the target of the preceeding WHENEVER SQLERROR

Changes the target of the WHENEVER SQLERROR again

Listing 10.2 The function of embedded SQL WHENEVER statements

The program in Listing 10.1 includes only one WHENEVER statement. If an error of any kind occurs during program execution, program control will be transferred to the program label (errexit) that displays the text of the error message (errrpt) and stops the program. The ROLLBACK WORK statement in errexit undoes any changes that the program may have made to the database. (Note that ROLLBACK WORK is an executable statement.) The program therefore will not leave the work of the program half done.

Because it gathers data for every column in the Cab table, the DECLARE SECTION of the program in Listing 10.1 defines one host variable for every column. The DECLARE SECTION is followed immediately by the INCLUDE SQLCA statement, which makes the sqlca data structure available to the program.

Executable Statements

Executable statements include all SQL statements that can be issued interactively. In Listing 10.1 there is only one executable statement, the INSERT statement that adds the new row to Cab. There is one difference between the INSERT statement in Listing 10.1 and an interactive INSERT statement. The values that are being inserted into Cab are stored in program variables rather than entered as literals. As you can see, each variable name is preceded by a colon. This instructs SQL to use the contents of host variables. Keep in mind that only those variables that have been included in the DECLARE SECTION can be used in SQL statements.

A program that ends in an expected and/or desired manner must be terminated with a COMMIT WORK statement. The COMMIT WORK signals the DBMS that all processing is completed and that any changes made by the program should be made permanent in the database. In essence, COMMIT WORK is the opposite of ROLLBACK WORK. COMMIT WORK leaves changes in the database; ROLLBACK WORK undoes them.

Embedding SQL in a Proprietary Programming Language

Proprietary programming languages such as those supplied by *dBASE IV* and *R:BASE* are actually easier to use for embedded SQL than a general-purpose host language because the language has been written to recognize SQL statements. In other words, SQL statements aren't foreign to proprietary language processors as they are to general-purpose host language compilers. That means that you don't have to go through the precompilation step.

> **By the way:** *dBASE* programs that contain SQL statements require a special file extension. Data manipulation statements from *dBASE*'s proprietary query language cannot be used in the same program as SQL statements.

To make the difference between using a proprietary programming language and a general-purpose host language easier to understand, take a look at the program in Listing 10.3, which has been written in *R:BASE*'s programming language. As you can see, it is somewhat shorter than the C program in Listing 10.1. Part of this is the result of the more flexible I/O statements available with this language. For example, the FILLIN command displays a prompt and a place to enter a value on the screen as well as accepting that value into a variable; it takes two statements to do the same in C. In addition, the program in Listing 10.3 doesn't require EXEC SQL before SQL statements. Variables are declared to the programming language using SET VARIABLE; defining them for SQL using the DECLARE SECTION isn't required.

Because SQL statements are an integral part of a proprietary programming language, programs like that in Listing 10.3 don't need to be processed by a precompiler. Instead, they can be handled directly by the language processor, regardless of whether it is an interpreter, pseudo-compiler, or compiler.

```
SET TRANSACT ON
SET ERROR VARIABLE VError
WHENEVER SQLERROR GOTO ErrorExit

SET VARIABLE vCab# TEXT
SET VARIABLE vMake_Model TEXT
SET VARIABLE vYear TEXT
SET VARIABLE vPlate TEXT
SET VARIABLE vCondition TEXT
SET VARIABLE vStatus TEXT
SET VARIABLE vOdom INTEGER

FILLIN vCab#=3 USING 'Enter number for new cab: '
WHILE vCab# <> '' THEN
    FILLIN vMake_Model=15 USING 'Make: '
    FILLIN vYear=2 USING 'Year: '
    FILLIN vPlate=7 USING 'License plate: '
    FILLIN vCondition=255 USING 'Condition: '
    FILLIN vStatus=15 USING 'Status: '
    FILLIN vOdom=6 USING 'Current odometer reading: '
    INSERT INTO Cab VALUES
        (:vCab#,:vMake_Model,:vYear,:vPlate:,:vCondition,:vStatus,:vOdom)
    WRITE 'New cab inserted)
    FILLIN vCab#=3 USING 'Enter number for new cab: '
ENDWHILE
COMMIT
RETURN

LABEL ErrorExit
    SHOW ERROR vError
    ROLLBACK
    RETURN
```

Listing 10.3 Embedding SQL in a proprietary programming language

In general, embedding SQL in a proprietary programming language is simpler than embedding it in a general-purpose host language. However, general-purpose host languages are more commonly used. A general-purpose host language is available with many more DBMSs. In addition, code written in languages such as C or COBOL is relatively transportable (i.e., it can access more than one DBMS and/or run on more than one hardware/operating system platform). Because general-purpose host languages are used more often, the remainder of the sample programs in the chapter use C.

Queries That Retrieve One Row

Although virtually any SELECT statement can be used in an application program, using SELECT presents an interesting problem: What should SQL do with the result? An interactive SELECT displays the contents of the result table on the screen, but an application program needs to capture the output in some way.

When a SELECT will always retrieve a single row, the result can be sent directly to host variables by adding an INTO clause to the SELECT statement. The embedded SELECT therefore has the general format:

```
SELECT [DISTINCT] column_name1 [,column_name2] ...
INTO :host_variable1 [,:host_variablc2] ...
[WHERE predicate]
[ORDER BY column_name1 [,column_name2] ... ]
[GROUP BY column_name1 [,column_name2] ... ]
[HAVING predicate];
```

The program in Listing 10.4 displays data about one of FTC's drivers. The driver information is retrieved with the statement:

```
SELECT Driver_Name, Driver_Address, Driver_Phone
INTO :drvnam, :drvstr, :drvcsz, :drvphone
FROM Driver
WHERE Driver# = :drvnum
```

Because the retrieval is based on the primary key of the table (Driver#), the query will either return one row or no row. The data can therefore be sent directly to host variables with the INTO clause. Immediately after executing the SELECT, the program displays the data that have been retrieved, freezes the screen with "Hit any key to continue," and then allows the user to view data about another driver.

The possibility always exists that a user will enter a driver number that has not been stored in the Driver table. The program must therefore handle the error condition that arises when the SELECT does not return any rows. Notice that a WHENEVER NOT FOUND statement has been included in addition

```c
#include <studio.h>
#include <ctype.h>

EXEC SQL BEGIN DECLARE SECTION;
    char drvnum[4];
    VARCHAR drvname[15];
    VARCHAR drvadd[30];
    char drvphone[12];
EXEC SQL END DECLARE SECTION;
EXEC SQL INCLUDE SQLCA;

main()
{
    int length;
    int dummy;

    EXEC SQL WHENEVER SQLERROR GOTO errexit;
    length = asks("Enter driver number: ",drvnum.arr);
    EXEC SQL WHENEVER NOT FOUND GOTO NoDriver;          Error trap for
    while (length)                                      unsuccessful search
    {
        EXEC SQL SELECT Driver#, Driver_Name, Driver_Address, Driver_Phone
        INTO :drvnum, :drvnam, :drvadd, :drvphone
        FROM Driver                     Result of query goes into variables
        WHERE Driver# = :drvnum;
        printf ("information on driver #%4s(%15s):\n",drvnum, drvname);
        printf ("Address: %30s\n\n",drvadd);
        printf ("Phone: %12s\n\n",drvphone);
        printf ("Hit any key to continue:");
        scanf ("%d",&dummy);
        strlen = asks ("Enter driver number: ",drvnum.arr);
    }
    EXEC SQL COMMIT WORK;
    return(1);

NoDriver:
        printf ("There is no driver with that number in the database.");
        return(0);

errexit:
        printf("\n%.70s(%d)",sqlca.sqlerrm.sqlerrmc,-sqlca.sqlcode);
        EXEC SQL ROLLBACK WORK;
        return(0);
}
```

Listing 10.4 An embedded SQL program to display data about one driver (continued on next page)

```
int asks(text,variable)
    char text[],variable[];
    {
    printf(text);
    return (gets(variable) == (char *) ? EOF : strlen(variable));
    }
```

Listing 10.4 (Continued from page 262)

to the WHENEVER SQLERROR. If the SELECT fails, program control will be directed to the program label NoDriver. NoDriver prints an error message and then continues processing so that the user can try again.

Queries That Retrieve Multiple Rows

When a query might retrieve more than one row, the result cannot simply be stored in host variables. Host variables are no different from any other program variables; they can store only one value at a time. The solution to the problem is to define a special work area for the result of the query. This work area is known as a *cursor*.

Each cursor used by a program is defined by a SELECT. When the cursor is OPENed, SQL performs the query and positions a pointer to the first row of the result table. The data in the current row can then be moved into host variables with the FETCH statement. FETCH also moves the pointer to the next row of the result table.

The program in Listing 10.5 displays data about all cabs in the database. After connecting to the database, it declares the cursor with:

    DECLARE C1 CURSOR FOR
            SELECT Cab#, Make_Model, Year, Curr_Odom FROM Cab

C1 is the name of the cursor. The DECLARE statement also contains the SELECT that defines the result table for the data that are to be displayed. The DECLARE CURSOR statement therefore has the general format:

    DECLARE cursor_name CURSOR FOR
            SELECT_statement

```
#include <stdio.h>
#include <ctype.h>

EXEC SQL BEGIN DECLARE SECTION;
    char Cab#[3];
    char Make_Model[15];
    char Year[2];
    int Curodom;
    short cabnumi, makei, yeari, curodomi;
EXEC SQL END DECLARE SECTION;
EXEC SQL INCLUDE SQLCA;

main()
{
    EXEC SQL WHENEVER SQLERROR GOTO errprt;
    EXEC SQL DECLARE C1 CURSOR FOR
        SELECT Cab#, Make_Model, Year, Curr_Odom
        FROM Cab;
    EXEC SQL OPEN C1;
    printf ("Cab# Make/Model      Year Odometer\n");
    printf ("____ _____ ____ _____\n\n");
    EXEC SQL WHENEVER NOT FOUND GOTO finish;
    for (;;)
    {
        EXEC SQL FETCH C1 INTO
            :Cab#:cabnumi,:Make_Model:makei,:Year:yeari,:Curodom:curodomi;
        if (makei) Make_Model = "unknown";
        if (yeari) Year = "?";
        if (curodomi) Curodom = 0;
        printf ("%4s %15s %4s %8d\n",Cab#,Make_Model,Year,Curodom);
    }

    finish:
        printf (\nSelect completed.\n");
        EXEC SQL CLOSE C1;
        EXEC SQL COMMIT WORK;
        exit(0);

    errprt:
        printf ("\n %.70s\n",sqlca.sqlerrm.sqlerrmc);
        EXEC SQL WHENEVER SQLERROR CONTINUE;
        EXEC SQL ROLLBACK WORK;
        exit(1);
}
```

Cursor is defined as a SELECT that might return more than one row

Opening the cursor performs the select and initializes as pointer to the first row in the result table

One row from the result table is copied into host language variables

Listing 10.5 An embedded SQL program to list data about all cabs

The DECLARE CURSOR statement does not actually perform the query. The statement:

OPEN cursor_name;

instructs the DBMS to execute the SELECT and position the pointer to the first row in the result table. The FETCH statement retrieves one row of data and moves the cursor's pointer. It has the general format:

FETCH cursor_name INTO :host_variable1 [,host_variable2 ...]

Once the FETCH has been executed, the contents of the host variables can be handled by the program as needed. If you look at the FETCH statement in Listing 10.5, you will notice that the host variables are listed as:

:variable_name:variable_namei

The second variable (its name ends in "i") is an *indicator variable*. Indicator variables are optional but can be handy for determining if the contents of a host variable is null or if the value placed in the host variable has been truncated because the size of the host variable was smaller than the size of the data. The cab listing program tests the contents of the indicator variables and substitutes appropriate values when null is encountered.

Embedded SQL programs that use cursors should close their cursors before terminating the program with:

CLOSE cursor_name

The CLOSE statement releases the work area.

If needed, application programs can use more than one cursor. The weekly driver summary report (look back at Figure 2.15 for a sample) is actually a listing within a listing. For each driver, the report must select all rows in the Shifts table for the time period of the report. A program to prepare that report can be found in Listing 10.6.

The cursor that holds a listing of all drivers (C1) is defined by a SELECT that retrieves just the driver number and driver name. The cursor that holds the shifts driven by a given driver (C2) uses the value of the driver number to restrict rows. This means that the query that defines C2 must be re-executed

```
#include <stdio.h>
#include <ctype.h>

EXEC SQL BEGIN DECLARE SECTION;
    char drvnum[4];
    VARCHAR drvname[15];
    char shift[3];
    char wkdate[8];
    char cab#[3];
    int start_odom;
    int end_odom;
EXEC SQL END DECLARE SECTION;
EXEC SQL INCLUDE SQLCA;

main()
{
    int strlen;
    int miles;
    int totalmiles;
    char start[8];
    char end[8];

    EXEC SQL WHENEVER SQLERROR GOTO errexit;
    printf ("Starting date for report: ");
    scanf ("%8s",start);
    printf ("\nEnding date for report: ");
    scanf ("%8s",end);

    EXEC SQL DECLARE C1 CURSOR FOR
        SELECT Driver#, Driver_Name
        FROM Driver
        ORDER BY Driver#;
    EXEC SQL OPEN C1;
    EXEC SQL DECLARE C2 CURSOR FOR
        SELECT WkDate, Shift_Name, Cab#, (End_Odom - Start_Odom)
        FROM Shift_Driven
        WHERE Driver# = :drvnum AND
            WkDate BETWEEN :start AND :end
        ORDER BY WkDate, Shift_Name;

    printf ("               Driver Summary Report\n");
    printf ("                    for\n");
    printf ("               %8s through %9s",start,end\n\n");
```

This cursor creates a table containing all driver names; it is created once and used throughout the program.

This cursor creates a table of shift info for one driver; it is recreated for every driver.

Listing 10.6 An embedded SQL program to create the weekly driver summary report
(continued on next page)

```
for (;;)
{
    EXEC SQL WHENEVER NOT FOUND GOTO end_of_report;
    EXEC SQL FETCH C1 INTO :drvnum, :drvname;
    EXEC SQL OPEN C2;
    printf ("%4s %15s\n",drvnum,drvname);
    totalmiles = 0;
    EXEC SQL WHENEVER NOT FOUND GOTO end_of_driver;
    printf ("  Shift Date    Cab# Miles\n");
    printf ("  _____ _____ ____ _____\n");

    for
    {
        EXEC SQL FETCH C2 INTO :wkdate,:wkshift,:cab#,:miles;
        totalmiles = totalmiles + miles;
        printf ("  %5s %8s %3s %5d\n",wkshift,wkdate,cabnum,miles);
    }
    printf (  Total: %6d\n\n",totalmiles);
}

end_of_driver:
    EXEC SQL CLOSE C2;
    break;

end_of_report:
    EXEC SQL CLOSE C1;
    EXEC SQL COMMIT WORK;
    exit(0);

errexit:
    printf ("\n %.70s\n",sqlca.sqlerrm.sqlerrmc);
    EXEC SQL WHENEVER SQLERROR CONTINUE;
    EXEC SQL ROLLBACK WORK;
    exit(1);
}
```

Opening this cursor creates a table containing data for one driver; notice that it is inside a "for" loop.

Closing the cursor removes the table containing data for one driver from memory; the table containing the names and numbers of all drivers is unaffected.

Listing 10.6 (Continued from page 266)

for each driver. C2 is opened immediately after FETCHing a row from C1. This ensures that the query that defines C2 will use the correct value for driver number. C2 is closed by the end_of_driver module that is triggered by the WHENEVER NOT FOUND that is placed just before the loop that displays shift information.

The WHENEVER NOT FOUND statements in Listing 10.6 play an important part in the program's logic. The nested "for" loops that print the drivers and the shifts driven are actually infinite loops. They are terminated when a FETCH discovers that the cursor's row pointer has moved below the last row in the result table and the WHENEVER NOT FOUND is triggered. The modules to which the program branches on the NOT FOUND condition contain a "break" statement that stops the loop and continues processing with the statement below the closing brace (}) that defines the bottom of the loop.

Summary

SQL statements can be embedded in application programs written in high-level language, although C is the only general-purpose language supported by microcomputer DBMSs. (DBMSs that have proprietary programming languages, such as *dBASE* and *R:BASE*, also permit embedding of SQL within those languages.) Embedded SQL programs are first precompiled, a process during which SQL commands are replaced with calls to external subroutines or functions. The external subroutines and functions are supplied in a run-time library that is linked to the compiled program.

Before SQL can be used within an application program, all host variables (program variables used in SQL statements) must be declared in an SQL DECLARE SECTION. A data structure known as the SQL Communications Area (SQLCA) is also included to hold information about the result of SQL command execution. Information from the SQLCA is used to identify and process errors and conditions (e.g., no rows found) that arise while the program is running. Errors are trapped by the WHENEVER statement. WHENEVER can be used to stop the program, continue the program, or branch to a program module that handles the error in some way.

Queries that retrieve a single row can be executed directly. The data are stored in host variables by adding an INTO clause to the SELECT statement. However, the result of a query that may return more than one row must be stored in a work area known as a cursor. Once a cursor is defined, it is opened. Opening the cursor executes the query and initializes a pointer to the first row of the result table. The FETCH statement stores data from the current row in host variables and moves the cursor to the next row.

References

Ageloff, Roy. 1988. *A Primer on SQL*. Times Mirror/Mosby.

Gerritson, Rob. 1991. "SQL for Programmers." *DBMS*. 4(5):66–72.

Exercises

Note: Many of these exercises ask you to write embedded SQL programs. Because the details of embedded SQL programming vary from one DBMS to another, be sure to consult the documentation that came with your DBMS to determine specific program requirements. Consider things such as:

- Do you need a precompiler? If so, how is it used?
- What statements, if any, must precede or follow embedded SQL statements?
- How are the beginning and end of transactions indicated?
- Does the DBMS use SQLCA to report errors? If so, what are the component parts of the SQLCA data structure? If not, what mechanism is used to report errors?
- Where can you find a table of SQL error codes?
- Does your implementation support indicator variables?
- What syntax is required in SQL statements to differentiate between SQL column names and host language variables?

1. Examine the DBMS you are using for this course to answer the following questions:
   a. Does the DBMS support transaction processing? If so, what command indicates the beginning of a transaction? What commands are used to commit and roll back transactions?
   b. What host languages does the DBMS support?
   c. What are the procedures for processing a source file containing embedded SQL statements to make it an executable program?

2. Using the following relations from the Office of Margaret Holmes, D.M.D., write the programs below.

   Patient (<u>Patient #</u>, Patient Name, Patient Address, Patient Phone, Bill Payer, Birth Date, Relationship to Bill Payer)
   Appointment (<u>Patient #</u>, <u>Visit Date</u>, Visit Time)
   Treatment (<u>Treatment Type</u>, Cost)
   Treatment Performed (<u>Patient #</u>, <u>Visit Date</u>, <u>Treatment Type</u>)
   Payer (<u>Bill Payer Name</u>, Payer Address, Payer Home Phone, Payer Work Phone, Insurance Company, Employer, $Owed)

Bill (<u>Statement #</u>, Bill Payer Name, Statement Date, Statement $)
Payment (<u>Bill Payer Name</u>, Payment Source, Check #, Check $,
  Payment Date)

a. Write an embedded SQL program that enters a new patient into the database.
b. Write an embedded SQL program that changes a patient's address and phone number.
c. Write an embedded SQL program that enters into the database the procedures performed during one appointment.
d. Write an embedded SQL program that processes a payment received by the dentist's office. (Hint: This program must enter a row into the Payment table and then modify *$ Owed* column in the Payer table.)
e. Write an embedded SQL program that lists all patients.
f. Write an embedded SQL program that lists all patients and their last appointment date. (Hint: this program requires only one cursor using a SELECT that performs a join; the last appointment date can be retrieved with the MAX grouping function.)
g. Write an embedded SQL program that prepares monthly bills to send to patients. Each bill should include the name of the payer, the name of each patient, the procedures performed on each patient, the cost of each procedure, and the total cost for all procedures on the bill. (Hint: This program requires three cursors and an additional SELECT to compute the total.)

3. Using the following relations from the East Coast Aquarium, write the programs below:

Species (<u>Species Code</u>, Latin Name, English Name)
Location (<u>Location Code</u>, Place in Building, Size, Head Keeper)
Population (<u>Species Code</u>, <u>Location Code</u>, Number of Animals)
Food (<u>Type of Food</u>)
Feeding (<u>Species Code</u>, <u>Type of Food</u>, Amount of Food,
  Feeding Interval)
Habitats (<u>Habitat Type</u>)
Can Live (<u>Species Code</u>, <u>Habitat Type</u>)
Where Found (<u>Location Code</u>, <u>Habitat Type</u>)

Volunteer (<u>Volunteer #</u>, Vol. Name, Vol. Address, Vol. Phone)
Skill (<u>Skill Type</u>)
Can Do (<u>Volunteer #</u>, <u>Skill Type</u>)
Volunteer Schedule (<u>Volunteer #</u>, <u>Vol. Date</u>, Vol. Time, Job)

a. Write an embedded SQL program that enters data about a new volunteer.
b. Write an embedded SQL program that enters feeding instructions for an animal. Make sure that the program can enter more than one type of food.
c. Write an embedded SQL program that shows the feeding instructions for one species when the program's user knows only the species's English name. (Hint: The SELECT for this program must use a join.)
d. Write an embedded SQL program that displays the Latin name and population of all species that live in one location in the aquarium. (Hint: This program requires one cursor with a SELECT that contains a join.)
e. Write an embedded SQL program for East Coast Aquarium that summarizes volunteer activity for one month. Show the name of each volunteer that worked during the month and the shifts worked by that volunteer. Show the volunteers in alphabetical order by name. (Hint: This program requires two cursors.)
f. Write an embedded SQL that collects information about a new species, including its Latin and English names, the habitats in which it can live, and its feeding instructions. (Hint: You must enter rows into multiple tables.)

11

Database Integrity

As discussed earlier in this book, database integrity (also often called *data validation*) involves ensuring that primary keys are unique and nonnull and that foreign key values reference existing primary key values. In addition, a given database system may have additional integrity rules that help to maintain accurate, consistent data. For example, if a given article of clothing comes in sizes small, medium, and large, the company marketing that clothing can add to the integrity of its database by defining an integrity rule that describes the acceptable values for size.

This chapter looks at techniques for enforcing database integrity. Some SQL implementations include extensions for primary key support and referential integrity. Database integrity rules can therefore be stored in the data dictionary and enforced automatically by the DBMS. Others, however, adhere only to the SQL standard and therefore require application programming to ensure data integrity.

Ideally, a DBMS should support the definition of integrity rules that are stored in the data dictionary. The DBMS will then automatically enforce those rules during data modification. The alternative is to code integrity control into application programs. However, relying on application programs introduces the risk that some programs won't be written to perform the required integrity validation. Whenever possible, data integrity should by cnforced by the DBMS. Resort to an application program only when the DBMS can't handle data integrity by itself.

Using SQL Data Definition Facilities to Enforce Integrity Rules

As you saw in Chapter 9, the SQL standard includes minimal support for data integrity. The NOT NULL clause in the CREATE TABLE command can be used to ensure that primary key columns have values (entity integrity). SQL indexes can be used to enforce unique primary keys. Nonetheless, the SQL standard does not fully support primary keys: There is no requirement that a table have a primary key. In addition, it has no provisions for referential integrity control.

To answer these deficiencies in the SQL standard, DBMSs such as *Oracle 7, SQLBase, R:BASE 4.5*, and *DB2* have added extensions for integrity constraint support; many other DBMSs will be supporting these extensions in the near future. Integrity constraint extensions are added to the CREATE TABLE and ALTER TABLE commands. The constraints themselves are stored in the data dictionary and enforced by the DBMS whenever data are entered, modified or deleted.

Defining Primary Keys

The SQL integrity extensions include support for unique nonnull primary keys. When a table has a single-column primary key, the primary key can be defined along with the primary key column. For example, to define a primary key for the Cab table:

CREATE TABLE Cab
    (Cab# char (3) CONSTRAINT cab_key PRIMARY KEY,
    Make_Model (15),
    Year char (2),
    Plate char (7),
    Condition char (25),
    Cab_Status char (1),
    Curr_Odom number (6))

The keyword CONSTRAINT alerts SQL that what follows is some kind of integrity constraint. The constraint is given a name (cab_key) and defined as a primary key.

> **By the way:** The precise syntax used to express primary and foreign key relationships varies somewhat from one DBMS to another. If your DBMS supports these SQL extensions, consult your product documentation for the exact syntax.

When a table has a concatenated primary key, the primary key constraint is added to the table as a whole rather than to a single column. For example, the primary key of the Shift_Driven table is defined as:

CREATE TABLE Shift_Driven (Shift_Name char (3),
    WkDate date,
    Cab# char (3),
    Driver# char(3) NOT NULL,
    WkFlag char (1),
    Start_Odom number (6),
    End_Odom number (6),
    CONSTRAINT sd_key PRIMARY KEY (Shift_Name, WkDate, Cab#)

Notice that when a primary key is defined as a constraint, the NOT NULL clause may not be required on the primary key columns. (This varies from one DBMS to another.) However, the Shift_Driven table includes NOT NULL for the Driver# column. Although Driver# isn't part of the primary key, the Federated Taxi Company nonetheless wants to ensure that no row is ever entered without a driver number.

> **By the way:** As powerful as the extension you have just seen may be, it doesn't provide complete primary key support: it is still possible to create a table without a primary key.

Defining Foreign Keys

The SQL integrity constraint extensions also include provisions for foreign keys. Foreign key definitions specify which column or columns reference the primary key of another table and can include instructions about what to do when the primary key the foreign key references is deleted.

When a foreign key is a single column, a referential integrity constraint can be added to the column definition. For example, the Cab# and Driver# foreign keys can be added to the Shift_Driven table with:

```
CREATE TABLE Shift_Driven (Shift_Name char (3),
     WkDate date,
     Cab# char (3)
     CONSTRAINT fk_cab REFERENCES Cab(Cab#),
     Driver# char(3) NOT NULL
     CONSTRAINT fk_driver REFERENCES Driver(Driver#),
     WkFlag char (1),
     Start_Odom number (6),
     End_Odom number (6),
     CONSTRAINT sd_key PRIMARY KEY (Shift_Name, WkDate, Cab#)
```

Each foreign key is given a name that is used to identify the constraint when it is enabled. Notice also that the foreign key need not have the same column name as the primary key it references, even though tables are usually defined with matching column names.

When a table contains a concatenated foreign key, the foreign key reference is applied to the table as a whole. For example, the complete definition of the Shift_Driven table becomes:

```
CREATE TABLE Shift_Driven (Shift_Name char (3),
    WkDate date,
    Cab# char (3)
    CONSTRAINT fk_cab REFERENCES Cab(Cab#),
    Driver# char(3) NOT NULL
    CONSTRAINT fk_driver REFERENCES Driver(Driver#),
    WkFlag char (1),
    Start_Odom number (6),
    End_Odom number (6),
    CONSTRAINT sd_key PRIMARY KEY (Shift_Name, WkDate, Cab#)
    CONSTRAINT sd_fk FOREIGN KEY (Shift_Name,WkDate)
            REFERENCES Shift (Shift_Name, WkDate)
```

Unless you indicate otherwise, the DBMS will prevent the deletion of primary keys that have existing foreign key references. However, if the ON DELETE CASCADE is added to the clause defining the foreign key, the DBMS will delete all foreign key references whenever a primary key is deleted. For example, if ON DELETE CASCADE is added to the Cab# foreign key in Shift_Driven, deleting a cab from the Cab table will also delete rows that reference the cab from Shift_Driven. Keep in mind, however, that if other foreign keys reference the Cab table without the ON DELETE CASCADE option, a deletion of a cab will still be prevented.

Using Application Programs to Enforce Data Integrity

As you read earlier, people developing database applications using a microcomputer DBMS that doesn't provide internal data integrity control must use application programs to enforce data integrity. This can be done for a SQL-based DBMS or a DBMS that supports only a proprietary programming language.

Enforcing Referential Integrity in a SQL Environment

In most cases, SQL DBMS can store rules about nonnull and unique primary keys in their data dictionaries. An application developer is therefore left with the problem of enforcing referential integrity. One way to do so is to use an application program written in a high-level language.

The C function in Listing 11.1 has been written to create shift reservations for the Federated Taxi Company. As you will remember, there are two foreign keys in the Shift_Driven table: the cab number and the driver number. The program must therefore explicitly perform lookups to ensure that the cab number exists in Cab and the driver number in Driver.

The program first asks the user for the driver number. A SELECT is then used in an attempt to retrieve a row from Driver that matches the driver number that has been entered from the keyboard. If the row is found (in other words, the WHENEVER NOT FOUND is not triggered), the program continues by requesting the cab number. The program then continues the integrity checking by searching for the cab number in Cab. If the row is found (in other words, the WHENEVER NOT FOUND is not triggered), the program gathers the remainder of the data for the record and then performs the INSERT. (The work flag and odometer readings are given default values; the user is therefore not prompted to enter them.)

If you have studied structured programming techniques, then the structure of the program in Listing 11.1 may bother you. The WHENEVER NOT FOUND statements use GOTOs to branch to program modules that print appropriate error messages. It then uses GOTOs to reach the portion of the program that lets the user indicate that he or she wants to try again. (The assumption is that this function is called by a main program inside a loop.) In terms of structure, the use of the GOTOs is not the most desirable way to write the program. However, the WHENEVER statement does not support calls to functions but instead relies on GOTOs. The careful use GOTOs for branching is therefore the cleanest way to structure this type of program.

Enforcing Integrity Constraints in a Non-SQL Environment

Some DBMSs that do not support SQL have no ability to support data integrity constraints. People developing database applications using such DBMSs have no choice but to include both primary key constraints and referential integrity in application programs.

The sample programs that follow demonstrate how application programs can be used in an environment where the DBMS provides no integrity controls. The language used follows the xBase standard, a database access language used by DBMSs such as *dBASE IV* and *FoxPro*.

```
#include <stdio.h>
#include <ctype.h>
EXEC SQL BEGIN DECLARE SECTION;
     char Shift_Name[3],WkDate[9],Cab#[3],Driver#[2],WkFlag = 'F';
     int Start_Odom = 0,End_Odom = 0;
EXEC SQL END DECLARE SECTION;
EXEC SQL INCLUDE SQLCA;

int MakeReservation()
{
     EXEC SQL WHENEVER SQLERROR GOTO errexit;
     length = asks("Shift: ",Shift_Name.arr);
     while (length)
          {
          EXEC SQL WHENEVER NOT FOUND GOTO NoDriver;
          Shift_Name.len = length;
          wkdate.len = asks("Date: ",wkdate.arr);
          Driver#.len = asks("Driver number: ",Driver#.arr);
          EXEC SQL SELECT Driver#
               INTO :Driver#
               FROM Driver
               WHERE Driver# = :Driver#;
          EXEC SQL WHENEVER NOT FOUND GOTO NoCab;
          Cab#.len = asks("Cab number: ",Cab#.arr);
          EXEC SQL SELECT Cab#
               INTO :Cab#
               FROM Cab
               WHERE Cab# = :Cab#;
          EXEC SQL INSERT INTO Shift_Driven VALUES
               (:Shift_Name,:WkDate,:Cab#,:Driver#,:WkFlag,:Start_Odom,:End_Odom);
          printf ("\nShift reservation created successfully\n");
          EXEC SQL COMMIT WORK;

     AnotherShift:
          length = asks("Shift: ",Shift_Name.arr);
          }
     return(1);

     NoCab:
          printf ("\nThere is no cab with that number in the database.");
          EXEC SQL ROLLBACK WORK;
          goto AnotherShift;
```

This GOTO is triggered when the SELECT that searches for a driver number fails

This SELECT checks to see if a matching driver number exists in the Driver table

This resets the GOTO target so that it branches properly when the SELECT that searches for a cab number fails

This SELECT check to see if a matching cab number exists in the Cab table

Listing 11.1   An embedded SQL program that verifies referential integrity (continued on next page)

```
    NoDriver:
        printf ("\nThere is no driver with that number in the database")
        EXEC SQL ROLLBACK WORK;
        goto AnotherShift;

    errexit:
        printf ("\n%.70s \n",sqlca.sqlerrm.sqlerrmc)
        EXEC SQL ROLLBACK WORK;
        return(0);
}

int asks(text, variable)
    char text[], variable[];
    {
    printf (text);
    return (gets(variable) == (char *) ? EOF : strlen(variable));
    }
```

Listing 11.1 (Continued from page 279)

Enforcing Primary Key Constraints

The strategy for enforcing entity integrity (nonnull primary key values) is to accept data from the keyboard into variables so that the values in the variables can be verified before the data are actually stored in the database. Consider, for example, the sample code in Listing 11.2.

The module uses a custom screen form (invoked with SET FORMAT TO) to gather data into variables (triggered by the READ command). It then proceeds to explicitly check entity integrity. The program verifies that mCABNUM actually contains some value other than blanks; if mCABNUM does contain blanks, the row will not be added to the Cab table. Note that this check means that the DO WHILE loop that controls the data entry cannot be stopped by a simple carriage return. The user must enter a specific end-of-data flag ("quit").

To determine whether the cab number represents a unique primary key, the program issues a command to determine if the cab number is already present in the database file (FIND &mCABNUM). A no-find condition (FOUND() returns true) indicates that the cab number stored in mCABNUM is not currently present in Cab. However, if the DBMS was able to find the mCABNUM value, FOUND() will be false. In that case, the program prints a message indicating that the cab number already exists; the record is not added to the file.

```
USE CABS INDEX CABNUM
mCABNUM = SPACE(3)
mMAKE_MODEL = SPACE(15)
mYEAR = SPACE(2)
mLICNUM = SPACE(7)
mCONDITN = SPACE(25)
mCABSTAT = SPACE(1)
mCURODOM = 0
SET FORMAT TO CABENTRY &&CABENTRY is a form that accepts data into variables
READ
DO WHILE mCABNUM <> LCASE("quit")
    IF mCABNUM = ""
        CLOSE FORMAT
        CLEAR
        @ 5,5 SAY "You must enter a cab number"
    ELSE
        FIND &mCABNUM          ⟵──────────── Search for the cab by cab number
        IF FOUND()   ⟵───────────── Trap a successful search (a duplicate
            CLOSE FORMAT                  primary key value)
            CLEAR
            @ 5,5 SAY "That cab number already exists"
            WAIT                          Handle an unsuccessful search for
        ELSE   ⟵──────────────────────── cab number (primary key of new row
            APPEND BLANK                  is unique)
            REPLACE CABNUM WITH mCABNUM
            REPLACE MAKE_MODEL WITH mMAKE_MODEL
            REPLACE YEAR WITH mYEAR
            REPLACE CONDITN WITH mCONDITN  ⟵
            REPLACE CABSTAT WITH mCABSTAT
            REPLACE CURODOM WITH mCURODOM        Add the record to
        ENDIF                                    the relation
    ENDIF
    mCABNUM = SPACE(3)
    mMAKE = SPACE(15)
    mMODEL = SPACE(15)
    mYEAR = SPACE(2)
    mPURDATE = SPACE(8)
    mLICNUM = SPACE(7)
    mCONDITN = SPACE(25)
    mCABSTAT = SPACE(1)
    mCURODOM = 0
    SET FORMAT TO CABENTRY
    READ
ENDDO
RETURN
```

Listing 11.2   Verfiying primary key constraints for the Cabs relation

Enforcing Referential Integrity

Code that enforces referential integrity must not only verify that primary key references exist whenever a foreign key is added to a database file or modified, but it must also delete all foreign key records whenever the primary key is deleted from its database file.

Listing 11.3 contains a module that adds records to Shift Driven. The module first verifies that values have been entered for cab, date, and shift (in other words, it verifies entity integrity) and then ensures that no reservation with those values already exists (in other words, it verifies that the primary key is unique). The variable *flag* is set to one if a reservation is already present; a nonzero value for *flag* prevents a record from being appended to Shift_Driven.

If the reservation is not present, then the program module attempts to find the cab number in Cab (SEEK mCABNUM). A FOUND( ) value of false indicates that the cab number is not present. At that point, the user is given two choices—enter a record in Cab corresponding to the cab number or abort the attempt to make a reservation (*flag* is set to one).

If the cab number exists in Cab (in other words, *flag* still has a value of 0), the module attempts to find the driver number in Driver (SEEK mDRV-NUM). A no-find presents the user with the same choice he or she had for a missing cab number: Add the driver to Driver or abort the reservation attempt.

The record is appended to Shift Driven only if the data entered by the user passes all four tests: values are present for cab, date, and shift; the record has a unique primary key; a record for the cab number exists in Cab; and a record for the driver number exists in Driver. WkFlag is given a default value of F (false), since a shift hasn't been driven at the time the reservation is made. The starting and ending odometer readings (S_ODOM and E_ODOM) are initialized to zero.

When a record is deleted from a table that has foreign keys that reference its primary key, all foreign key references must be deleted from their tables as well. If this does not happen, then deleting the primary key row will leave the database in a state that violates referential integrity (in other words, foreign keys will exist that reference nonexistent primary keys).

Listing 11.4 contains a module that deletes a cab from the FTC database. This module would be used, for example, if a cab were sold or if a cab were destroyed in a traffic accident. In either situation, all reservations (past and future) that exist for the cab should be removed. Maintenance and incident records should also be purged.

```
USE CAB INDEX CABNUM
SELECT B
USE DRIVER INDEX DRVNUM
SELECT C
USE SFT_DRV INDEX SHFTKEY
SET RELATION TO drvnum INTO DRIVER
mCABNUM = SPACE(3)
mDRVNUM = SPACE(4)
mWKDATE = SPACE(8)
mWKSHIFT = SPACE(3)
flag = 0
choice = 0
SET FORMAT TO SHFTFMT &&SHFTFMT is a data entry screen for SHIFTS
READ
DO WHILE mCABNUM <> LCASE("quit")
    IF mCABNUM = "".OR. mWKDATE = "" .OR. mWKSHIFT = ""          ←——— Verify entity
        CLOSE FORMAT                                                     integrity
        CLEAR
        @ 5,5 SAY "You must enter a cab number, date, and shift"
    ELSE
        Lookup = mWKDATE + mWKSHIFT + mCABNUM
        SEEK Lookup     ←——— Search for an existing row with the same primary key
        IF FOUND()  ←——— 
            flag = 1                ——— Handle a successful search for an existing primary key
            CLOSE FORMAT            (primary key of new row isn't unique; row can't be
            CLEAR                   added)
            @ 5,5 SAY mCABNUM + "Is already reserved for " + mWKSHIFT + " on ";
                + mWKDATE
            WAIT
        ELSE
            SELECT CAB          ——— Check to see if cab exists in the Cab table
            SEEK mCABNUM    ←———
            IF .NOT. FOUND()            Handle an unsuccessful search for a
                CLOSE FORMAT            matching cab (violation of referential
                CLEAR               ←—— integrity)
                @ 5,5 SAY mCABNUM + " isn't in the database."
                @ 7,5 SAY "You may 1) Add the cab or 2) Abort the shift reservation"
                @ 9,5 SAY "Which one? " GET choice
                READ
                IF choice = 1
                    DO ADDCAB && Run a module to add the cab
                ELSE
                    flag = 1
                ENDIF
            ENDIF
```

Listing 11.3   A program module to add a shift reservation (continued on next page)

```
            IF flag = 0
                SELECT DRIVER        ←————————  Check to see if a driver exists in the driver table
                SEEK mDRIVER                    Handle an unsuccessful search for a
                IF .NOT. FOUND()                driver (violation of referential integrity)
                    CLOSE FORMAT
                    CLEAR
                    @ 5,5 SAY mDRVNUM + " isn't in the database."
                    @ 7,5 SAY "You may 1) Add the driver or 2) Abort the shift reservation"
                    @ 9,5 SAY "Which one? " GET choice
                    READ
                    IF choice = 1
                        DO ADDDRVR && Run a module to add a driver
                    ELSE
                        flag = 1
                    ENDIF
                ENDIF
            ENDIF
            SELECT SHIFTS
            IF flag = 0
                APPEND BLANK
                REPLACE WKDATE WITH CTOD(mWKDATE)
                REPLACE WKSHIFT WITH mWKSHIFT
                REPLACE CABNUM WITH mCABNUM
                REPLACE DRVNUM WITH mDRVNUM
                REPLACE WKFLAG WITH "F"          ←——  All tests have been passed;
                REPLACE S_ODOM WITH 0                 the new row can be added.
                REPLACE E_ODOM WITH 0
            ENDIF
        ENDIF
        mCABNUM = SPACE(3)
        mDRVNUM = SPACE(4)
        mWKDATE = SPACE(8)
        mWKSHIFT = SPACE(3)
        flag = 0
        SET FORMAT TO SHFTFMT
        READ
ENDDO
RETURN
```

Listing 11.3 (Continued from page 283)

The module first locates the record for the cab in the relation Cab. If the record is present, it is flagged for deletion (DELETE). The module must then search each table that might contain foreign key references. Because an index-based search only finds the first occurrence of an index key value, neither FIND or SEEK can be used to locate the foreign key references. The solution to this

```
USE CAB INDEX CABNUM
SELECT B
USE SFT_DRV INDEX SHIFTKEY
SELECT C
USE INCIDENT INDEX INCIKEY
SELECT D
USE MAINTAIN INDEX MAINKEY
mCABNUM = SPACE(3)
SELECT CAB
CLEAR
@ 5,5 SAY "Cab number to delete: " GET mCABNUM
READ
DO WHILE mCABNUM <> " "
    SEEK mCABNUM         ←──────────── Find the cab in the Cab table
    IF .NOT. FOUND()
        @ 5,7 SAY "That cab isn't in the database."
        WAIT                ─ Delete the cab
    ELSE                 ╱
        DELETE  ╱
        SELECT SHIFTS                   Find the first row in Shift Driven
        LOCATE FOR CABNUM = mCABNUM ╱   with the number of the cab being
        DO WHILE .NOT. EOF()            deleted
            DELETE          ←────────── Delete the row in Shift Driven and search
            CONTINUE                    for the next match
        ENDDO
        SELECT MAINTAIN                  Find the first row in Maintenance
        LOCATE FOR CABNUM = mCABNUM ←─── Performed with the number of
        DO WHILE .NOT. EOF()            the cab being deleted
            DELETE
            CONTINUE  ←──────── Delete the row in Maintenance Performed
        ENDDO                 and search for the next match
        SELECT INCIDENT                  Find the first row in Incident with
        LOCATE FOR CABNUM = mCABNUM ←─── the number of the cab being deleted
        DO WHILE .NOT. EOF()
            DELETE
            CONTINUE  ↖
        ENDDO            Delete the row in Incident and search for the
    ENDIF                next match
    SELECT CAB
    CLEAR
    mCABNUM = SPACE(3)
    @ 5,5 SAY "Cab number to delete: " GET CABNUM
    READ
ENDDO
choice = ""
@ 5,15 SAY "Pack the database files? " GET choice
```

Listing 11.4   A module to delete a cab (continued on next page)

```
READ
IF UPPER(choice) = "Y"
    PACK
    SELECT SHIFTS
    PACK
    SELECT INCIDENT
    PACK
    SELECT MAINTAIN
    PACK
ENDIF
RETURN
```

Pack the files to physically remove deleted
rows and compress the files. (Whether this
step is required depends on the DBMS.)

Listing 11.4 (Continued from page 285)

dilemna is to perform a sequential search using LOCATE FOR to find the first
occurrence of CABNUM and then CONTINUE to locate all the others.
Because the delete command merely flags records for deletion, the module finishes by giving the user the chance to pack the database files to physically
remove the delete records.

Summary

There are three major types of integrity rules that should be enforced in a relational database:

- Unique primary keys: The primary key of each table must be unique.
- Entity integrity: No part of a primary key can be null.
- Referential integrity: Every nonnull foreign key must reference an
  existing primary key value.

In an ideal world, database integrity rules should be stored in the data
dictionary and enforced automatically by a DBMS. However, most DBMSs do
not support such a wide range of integrity checking. Integrity checking varies
greatly from one DBMS to another:

- Any type of integrity rule can be defined, stored in the data dictionary,
  and enforced automatically. Such capability is available with SQL
  DBMSs that include extensions to the SQL language standard. It is also
  available with some proprietary microcomputer DBMSs.
- Integrity rules can be defined for single field keys only.

- Entity integrity and unique primary keys are supported but referential integrity is not. SQL DBMSs that have not extended the SQL language standard automatically handle both entity integrity and unique primary keys. However, referential integrity must be defined from within an application program.
- No integrity rules are available. All integrity rules must be enforced from within an application program.

References

Brown, R. 1988. "Data Integrity and SQL." *Database Programming and Design.* 2(5):60–69.

Fernandez, E. B., R. C. Summers, and C. Wood. 1981. *Database Security and Integrity.* Reading, MA: Addison-Wesley.

Vassilov, Y. 1981. "Functional Dependencies and Incomplete Information." *Proceedings of the 6th International Conference on Very Large Data Bases.* Montreal, Canada. 260–269.

Things to Think About

1. Throughout this book, a great deal of emphasis has been placed on enforcing database integrity. Is this emphasis justified? Why or why not?

2. Many DBMSs provide tools that can be used to define data entry forms. A great deal of integrity checking can be performed from those forms.
   a. What does a database developer gain by being able to enforce data integrity from a data entry form?
   b. Why might it not be a good idea to rely on data entry forms to enforce integrity? (Hint: Think about the kinds of things a knowledgeable user [as opposed to a naïve or unsophisticated user] can do with a DBMS.)

3. One of the SQL standard's greatest failings is its inability to define and enforce referential integrity. What advantages do the data integrity extensions to that language bring to a database environment? How would the presence or absence of these extensions affect your decision as to what DBMS to purchase?

Exercises

The complete database for the office of Margaret Holmes, D.M.D. is comprised of the following set of third normal form relations:

> Patient (<u>Patient#</u>, P_Name, P_Address, P_Phone, SSN, Bill_Payer,
>   Rel-To-Who-Pays, Payment Source)
> Bill_Payer (<u>Bill_Payer</u>, BP_Address, BP_Home_Phone, BP_Employer,
>   BP_Work_Phone, Insurance_Carrier, $Owed)
> Appointment (<u>Patient#</u>, <u>Appt_Date</u>, Appt_Time, Appt_Flag)
> Visits (<u>Patient#</u>, <u>Appt_Date</u>, <u>Procedure</u>, Comments, $Charged)
> Costs (<u>Procedure</u>, Usual$)
> Income (<u>Bill_Payer</u>, <u>Payment_Date</u>, <u>Source</u>, Payment$)
> Supply Item (<u>Item#</u>, Item_Desc, Reorder_Point, Reorder_Qty,
>   #On_Hand)
> Order (<u>PO#</u>, PO_Date, V_Name, PO_Total$)
> Vendors (<u>V_Name</u>, V_Address, V_Phone, V_Contact_Person,
>   Balance_Due)
> Line_Item (<u>PO#</u>, <u>Item#</u>, Order_Qty, Unit$, Total$)
> Payment (<u>Check#</u>, Check_Date, V_Name, $Paid)

1. Consider the DBMS that you are using for this course. If that DBMS provides complete integrity control, answer the following questions:
   a. Consider the 3NF relations listed above. What extra attributes must be added to which relations so that a complete set of integrity rules can be specified?
   b. Write a set of integrity rules for the database. The complete set of rules should verify that primary keys are nonnull, that primary keys are unique, and that all foreign key values reference existing primary keys.
   c. What additional integrity rules are needed to help ensure consistent, clean data?

2. Consider the DBMS that you are using for this course. If it follows the xBase standard, do the following:
   a. Consider the 3NF relations for Margaret Holmes' dental practice. What integrity rules can be defined as part of the database structure? What types of integrity checking must be performed from within an application program?

b. Write and test application programs that will perform the functions listed below. The programs should include all necessary integrity checking.

- Insert a new patient.
- Make an appointment.
- Receive a payment against a bill.
- Change a patient's address.
- Delete a patient.
- Record all data about a purchase order.

3. Assume that you are working with a SQL DBMS.
   a. Considering the 3NF relations above, what integrity rules can be defined as part of the database structure? What types of integrity checking must be performed from within an application program?
   b. If you have a SQL DBMS available, write and test application programs that will perform the functions listed below. If you do not have a SQL DBMS, develop the logic for such applications using pseudo-code or flowcharts. Include all integrity checking that will not be performed by the DBMS itself.

- Make an appointment.
- Delete a patient.
- Record all data about a purchase order.
- Delete all data about a vendor.
- Delete all data about a purchase order.

4. If the DBMS you are using for this course does not meet any of the criteria for exercises 1, 2 or 3, do the following for your DBMS:
   a. Describe the technique needed to ensure unique primary keys for the Appointment and Visit tables. Implement your strategy to make sure that it works.
   b. Describe the technique needed to ensure referential integrity for the Visit and Income tables. Implement your strategy to make sure that it works.

12

Going Multiuser

One of the most important reasons that businesses install database systems is to make it easy to share data. In most cases, this means that more than one person will be using the database at the same time. Access to a database by more than one person at a time is known as *concurrent access*, which introduces a whole new set of problems to database implementation.

This chapter looks at the special issues that arise when databases are used over a network and by more than one user at the same. Because so many organizations are replacing mainframes and minicomputers with networks of microcomputers (*downsizing*), database management over a local area network (LAN) has become one of the focal points in systems development today.

Multiuser Versus Client/Server DBMSs

In today's business environment there are two ways in which a database management system can allow more than one user access to the same database. A DBMS may be *multiuser* or it may be *client/server*. Although a client/server DBMS does allow more than one user to access the same database at the same time, it does so in a different way than a simply "multiuser" DBMS.

> **By the way:** A client/server DBMS is often called a *database server.* As you will see, the term is certainly correct but can be confusing because the same term is often used for a computer that stores a database on a LAN.

Multiuser DBMSs

A multiuser DBMS provides a single, *centralized* database that many users can access. (The database is "centralized" because the entire database is stored on one computer.) Users access the database over a local area network to query the database and run application programs against the database. All users use the same DBMS; all application programs must be written for that specific DBMS.

A multiuser DBMS is appropriate for the Federated Taxi Company. As you can see in Figure 12.1, FTC's local area network includes a high-end microcomputer dedicated as the server and four PCs used as workstations. Because this is a very small network that has no communications with the outside world, a single server can act as both a network server and a database server.

> **By the way:** FTC's network would not necessarily be a workable configuration for a larger network or a network that supports electronic mail, bridges to other local area networks, and/or gateways to wide area networks. The database traffic and data communications traffic would overwhelm a single server, significantly degrading network performance.

The database server stores the DBMS, the database, and all the application programs that have been written to manipulate data stored in the database. Each workstation logs onto the DBMS across the network. The multiuser DBMS is configured to allow only the number of users for which FTC has paid. For example, if FTC has purchased three multiuser licenses, then only

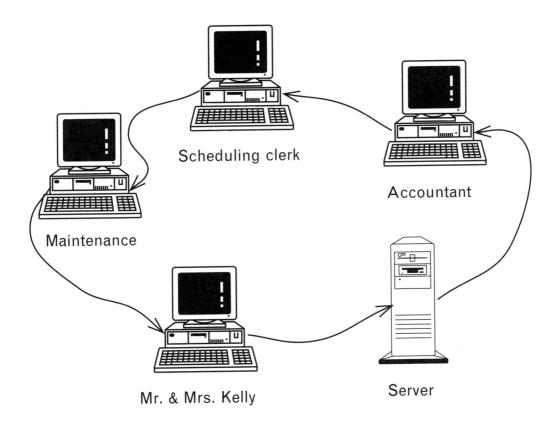

Figure 12.1 Local area network configuration for the FTC database

three users can work with the database at the same time; a user at the fourth workstation will have to wait until someone signs off before he or she can use the database.

> **By the way:** Deciding on the exact configuration of a local area network for database use requires knowledge of both database management and data communications. If it is not already part of your academic program, seriously consider taking a course in data communications. The move to database systems on local area networks is so important that it is difficult to do an effective database development project without significant consideration of networking issues.

Client/Server DBMSs

On the surface, a client/server DBMS looks very similar to a multiuser DBMS. However, a client/server DBMS can accept data manipulation requests from more than one type of application program. Most client/server DBMSs are based on SQL. An end user uses his or her software to formulate a query. That query is then translated by a program (known as *middleware*) into the SQL required by the client/server database.

Each client/server DBMS is designed accept queries from a specific group of end user applications (*front ends*). A client/server front end is usually a single-user version of a DBMS such as *dBASE, Paradox, R:BASE*, or *4th Dimension*. However, it might also be a spreadsheet, a programming language, or an application program written specifically as a front end.

A client/server DBMS may also provide gateways to other databases. Such gateways let the client/server DBMS query minicomputer and mainframe DBMSs such as *DB2* and *Oracle*. In other words, a client/server DBMS can not only accept incoming queries from single-user DBMSs, but can send outgoing queries to other DBMSs.

A single client/server DBMS maintains a centralized database. However, when multiple client/server DBMSs residing on separate computers are used to handle a single database, they provide what is known as a *distributed database*. A distributed database is a database in which the data themselves are stored on more than one computer. The computers on which the database is stored are linked by telecommunications lines.

Small Bank, for example, might be a good candidate for a distributed database. A possible architecture for that system can be found in Figure 12.2. Each branch has two high-end microcomputers acting as servers. One server manages the database; the other handles the local area network and communications between the local area networks at the other branches. A portion of the overall Small Bank database is stored at each branch; the complete Small Bank database is therefore the sum of all the database parts.

> **By the way:** A distributed database introduces some additional complexity to a multiuser environment. More about distributed databases and their advantages and disadvantages can be found later in this chapter.

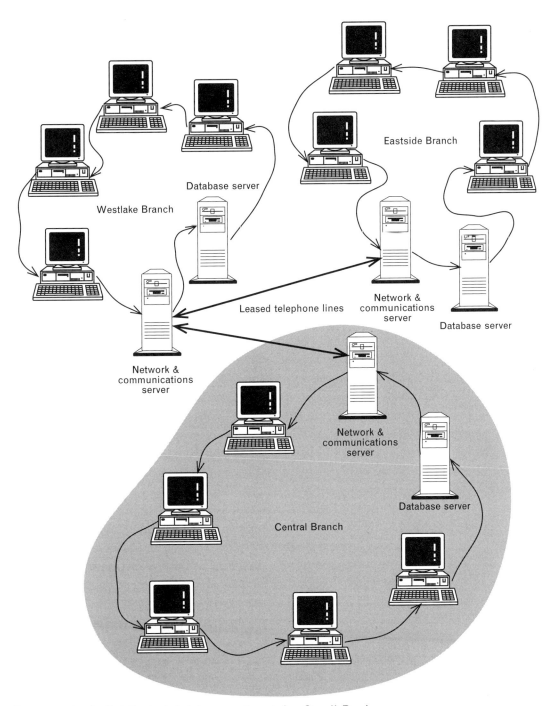

Westlake Branch

Database server

Network &
communications
server

Leased telephone lines

Eastside Branch

Network &
communications
server

Database server

Network &
communications
server

Central Branch

Database server

Figure 12.2 A distributed database network for Small Bank

Client/server DBMSs are particularly attractive to businesses for two reasons. Most importantly, because they run on microcomputers, they are generally cheaper to run and upgrade than a single, larger computer system. (They are not necessarily cheaper to develop and install than a minicomputer or mainframe database system.) Second, client/server DBMSs provide great flexibility in end-user and development tools. An organization using a client/server DBMS can give each user the query tool best suited to the user's individual needs, rather than being locked into a single tool as the organization would be with a multiuser DBMS.

Transaction Control

Most multiuser DBMSs group activities against a database into transactions. A transaction, as discussed in Chapter 10, is a unit of work. It may be as small as a single retrieval command, or it may include an entire group of changes made to the database at one time.

A transaction can end in one of two ways. If it is successful, if it ends in a desired manner, it will be *committed* (all changes to the database are made permanent). If it ends unsuccessfully, in an undesirable manner, the database will be *rolled back*; all changes will be undone and the database will be restored to the state it was in before the transaction began.

To effect transaction roll-back, a DBMS must somehow keep track of every action a transaction takes while it is in progress (a transaction *log*). This log of the data can then be used to restore the database if a transaction fails. The data saved to be used in case of roll-back are known as a *before-image* and are written to a *before-image file*.

Most of today's DBMSs maintain a single before-image file. It is usually a direct-access file to which a record is written each time any transaction performs any activity against the database. The records for any one transaction are identified by a transaction number assigned to the transaction by the DBMS.

A record in a before-image file contains two types of data. First, it contains the command issued by the user. Second, it contains an image of the data affected by the command *before* the command is performed. This is the "before image." A portion of a before-image file can be found in Figure 12.3. In it you can see the commands issued by several transactions. (The before-images have been omitted to make the sequence of actions easier to follow.)

Record #	Trans. #	Action taken by transaction	Next record for transaction
0	105	Start transaction	NULL
1	190	Start transaction	NULL
2	105	SELECT ...	0
3		*Unused record will hold the next before image*	
4	355	Start transaction	NULL
5	355	DELETE ...	3
6	190	SELECT ...	1
7	210	Start transaction	NULL
8	105	INSERT ...	2
9	105	INSERT ...	7
10	190	SELECT ...	5
11	210	SELECT ...	6
12	230	Start transaction	NULL
13	105	INSERT ...	8
14	230	UPDATE ...	11
15	230	UPDATE ...	13
16	230	UPDATE ...	14
:	*(Remainder of before-image file)*		
Directory of available records: 3, 25, 109, ...			

Figure 12.3 A portion of a before-image file

Each record in the before-image file contains a pointer to the location of the "preceding" record for the transaction. As you can see in Figure 12.3, you follow the pointers from the end of the file to the beginning of the file. The first record for each transaction (the one with the null pointer) contains the "Start transaction" action. Once a transaction has begun, it can then perform any number of actions against the database. The number of actions that make up a transaction are under user and/or application program control.

All of the transactions in Figure 12.3 are in progress (sometimes called *in flight*). Once a transaction is completed (regardless of whether it is rolled back or committed), its records are removed from the before-image file. Notice in Figure 12.3, for example, that record 3 is empty. This represents space that has been reclaimed from a completed transaction. Subsequent transactions can then reuse that space. A before-image file therefore also maintains a directory of unused records so that it knows where it can write before-images. The sample in Figure 12.3 uses the end of the file for the directory of available records.

Notice in Figure 12.3 that the actions for several transactions alternate with one another. This interweaving of actions is typical of concurrent use of a database. Although multiple users are working with the database at the same time, the server still has only one CPU and can therefore only do one thing at a time. The actions from transactions that are running concurrently must take turns accessing the database.

When the actions of many transactions are interwoven in the way you have just seen, they are said to be *interleaved*. Unfortunately, interleaved transaction execution creates problems that do not arise when transactions are not interleaved.

Problems with Concurrent Use

If you have been investigating the price of DBMSs, then you will have discovered that the multiuser version of a DBMS costs significantly more than the single-user version. It also requires more main memory. Why this price and main memory difference? Multiuser DBMSs contain extra program code that isn't needed in single-user DBMSs. The extra code is there to deal with the problems created by interleaved transaction execution.

When two or more transactions are interleaved, the goal of a DBMS is to provide each transaction with the same result that would have been produced had the transactions not been interleaved (in other words, as if they had run in a series, one after the other). Interleaved transactions that produce the correct result when executing in this manner are said to be *serializeable*. To achieve serializeability, a multiuser DBMS must have some form of *concurrency control*, a mechanism for controlling and managing interleaved transaction execution.

Lost Updates

To better understand the kind of problems that can occur when interleaved transactions aren't controlled, consider the following situation: Two travel agents, one located in Boston and the other in Philadelphia, are both using the same airline reservations database. A customer calls the Boston travel agent and, as part of a cross-country trip, needs three seats from Chicago to Denver on a specific date and at a specific time. The travel agent queries the database and discovers that exactly three seats are available on a flight that meets the customer's criteria. She reports that fact to the customer who is waiting on the phone.

Meanwhile, a customer calls the travel agent in Philadelphia. This customer also needs three seats from Chicago to Denver, on the same date and at the same time as the customer in Boston. The travel agent checks the database and discovers that there are exactly three seats available. These are the same three seats that the Boston travel agent just saw.

While the Philadelphia travel agent is talking to his customer, the Boston travel agent receives an OK from her customer to book the seats. She does so. The number of available seats on the flight is modified from three to zero.

The Philadelphia travel agent has also received an OK to book the reservations. When he issues the command, another three seats are reserved. The problem, however, is that the Philadelphia travel agent is working from old information. There may have been three seats available when he queried the database, but they are no longer available at the time he makes the reservations. As a result, the flight is now over-booked by three seats (the seats-available attribute will contain a -3).

This problem is known as the *lost update* problem. It occurs when the actions of one user (in this example, the Philadelphia travel agent) cause an update made by another concurrent user (the Boston travel agent) to be lost. Figure 12.4 contains a time line that shows exactly how the Philadelphia travel agent accidentally ended up overbooking the flight.

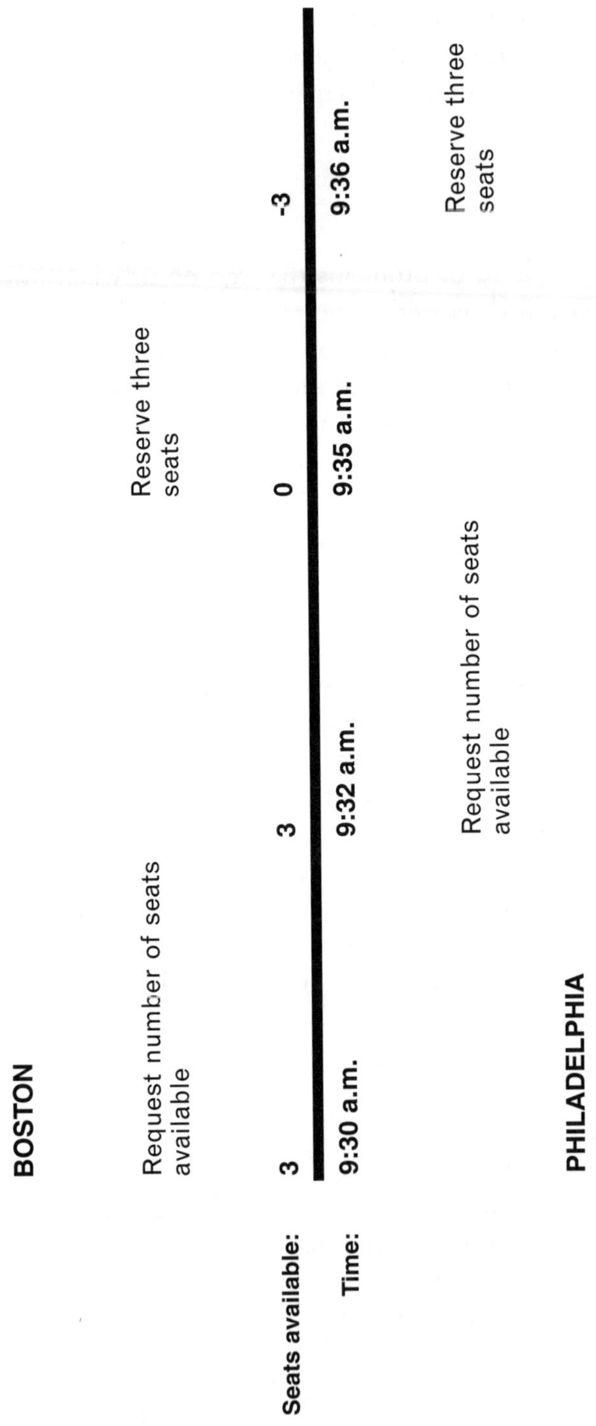

Figure 12.4   A lost update resulting in an overbooked airline flight

Inconsistent Analysis

In addition to a lost update, a transaction may be the victim of *inconsistent analysis*. As an example, consider a retrieval transaction originating in Boston. Its purpose is to add up the number of seats sold on flights 125 and 309 for a daily report of seats sold. At the time the transaction begins, flight 125 has 185 seats sold and flight 309 has 212 seats sold.

A travel agent in Philadelphia, however, wants to book three seats on each of the same two flights, bringing the total sold on flight 125 to 188 and the total sold on flight 309 to 215. If the Boston transaction runs by itself first, the correct result is 397. If the Philadelphia transaction runs first, followed by the Boston transaction, then the correct result from the Boston transaction is 403. Either 397 or 403 is correct because these are the results that would be produced if the transactions were to run one after the other; the order in which they run doesn't matter. Therefore, when the two transactions run interleaved, the goal is to produce either total.

Unfortunately, the interleaving of the transactions occurs as in Figure 12.5. After the Boston transaction retrieves the number of seats sold on flight 125 (185 seats), the Philadelphia transaction books three seats on flight 125 and three seats on flight 309. The Boston transaction then retrieves the number of seats sold on flight 309 (215 after the modification made by the Philadelphia transaction). Finally, the Boston transaction adds the two previously retrieved values, producing the incorrect result of 400. The inconsistent analysis occurred because data modification was performed before the Boston transaction had retrieved all the data it needed for its work.

Locking

The scheme most commonly used to handle concurrency control problems is *locking*. Locking permits each user to limit the access other concurrent users will have to the parts of the database with which he or she is working. For example, if the Boston travel agent had been able to prevent the Philadelphia travel agent from looking at the seats-available data until she had finished with it, then the Philadelphia travel agent would have seen that there were no seats available and would not have attempted to make the reservations. Locks can either be *implicit*, in which case they are placed automatically as needed by the DBMS, or they can be *explicit*, where they are placed by a command issued by the user.

9:30 a.m.:: 185 seats sold on flight 125, 212 seats sold on flight 309

BOSTON

# of Seats:	MA125: 185	MA125: 185	MA125: 188	MA309: 212	MA309: 215	MA309: 215	400
Time:	9:31 a.m.	9:32 a.m.	9:33 a.m.	9:34 a.m.	9:35 a.m.	9:36 a.m.	9:36 a.m.

Retrieve seats sold on flight MA125

Request number of seats available on flight MA125

Reserve three seats

Request number of seats available on flight MA309

Reserve three seats

Retrieve seats sold on flight MA309

Add seats sold

Incorrect answer (if transactions were serializeable, answer would be 397 or 403)

PHILADELPHIA

Figure 12.5   An inconsistent analysis

Many different data objects within a database can be locked. Locks can be placed on entire relations, on specific rows within a relation, or on specific columns within specific rows within a relation. The size of the object being locked is known as the *granularity* of the lock. The larger the object being locked, the easier the locking scheme is to incorporate into a DBMS. However, locking large objects, such as entire relations or disk pages, cuts down on the amount of concurrency the DBMS will support. Users who cannot access part of the database because another user has it locked will have to wait until the lock is released. Therefore, the more specific the objects being locked, the more opportunities for concurrent use that will exist.

> **By the way:** A disk page is the unit of data transferred from disk to main memory at one time.

Some multiuser microcomputer DBMSs support locking at the row level; this almost always provides an acceptable amount of concurrency for most database environments. In particular, row locking is used when an application program retrieves data using a cursor. Each row in a result table is locked as the cursor points to the row. DBMSs also lock tables and occasionally the entire database. The latter occurs in some microcomputer DBMSs whenever someone is making changes to the structure of the database.

The most primitive and powerful type of lock is the *exclusive lock*. If a user obtains an exclusive lock on a data object, then no other user can modify or view that data until the lock is released. In other words, only one user can obtain an exclusive lock on any given data object at a given time. To see how an exclusive locking scheme would solve the travel agency lost update problem, take a look at Figure 12.6.

In this case, the Boston travel agent receives an exclusive lock on the row describing the flight in question. When the Philadelphia travel agent attempts to retrieve the same tuple, his request is put in a wait state, where it remains until the Boston travel agent releases the lock. At that point, the Philadelphia request is honored and retrieves data based on the update made in Boston.

For locking to be effective, all locks must be held until the end of a transaction. This has a major impact on the amount of concurrent use that can occur in a database. The more of a database that is locked, the less shared use that can occur. Therefore, to promote the highest level of concurrent use, transactions should be kept relatively short.

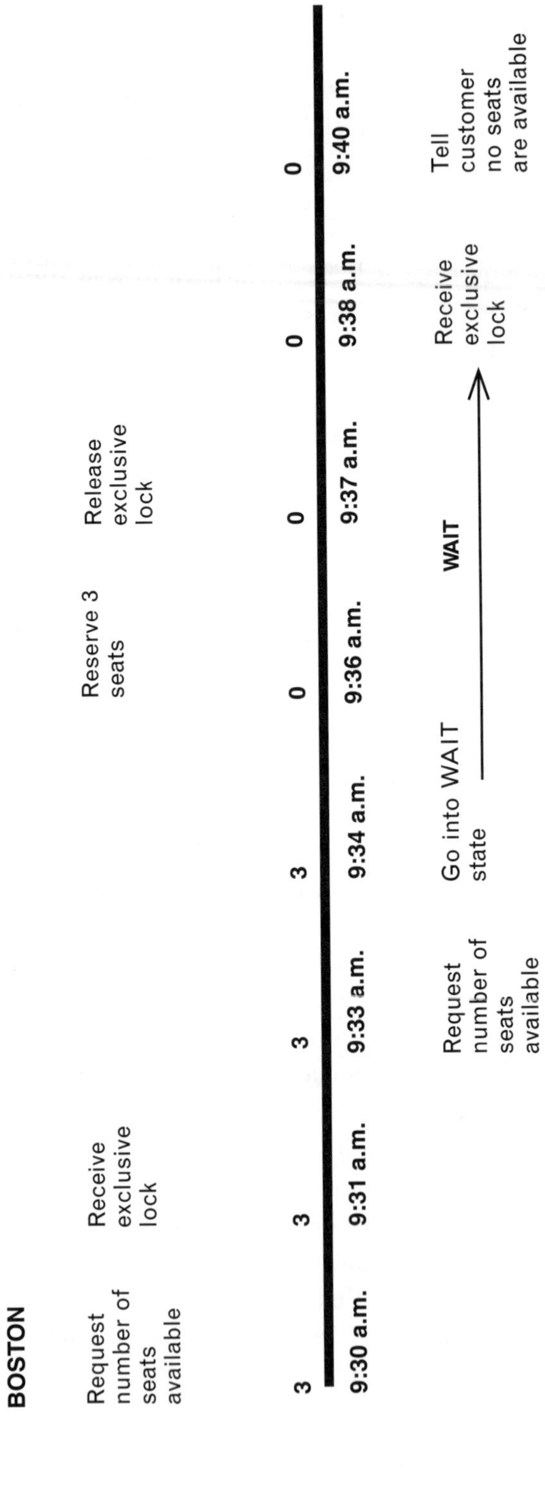

BOSTON

9:30 a.m.	9:31 a.m.	9:33 a.m.	9:34 a.m.	9:36 a.m.	9:37 a.m.	9:38 a.m.	9:40 a.m.
3	3	3	3	0	0	0	0

Request number of seats available — Receive exclusive lock — — Reserve 3 seats — Release exclusive lock

Request number of seats available — Go into WAIT state — — WAIT — Receive exclusive lock — Tell customer no seats are available

PHILADELPHIA

Figure 12.6   Using exclusive locks to solve the lost update problem

> **By the way:** Transactions should also be kept short because whenever a transaction must be rolled-back, the entire transaction must be rolled back.

Shared Locks

While exclusive locks solve the lost update problem, the use of exclusive locks does cut down on the amount of concurrent use a DBMS can provide. Problems such as inconsistent analysis, however, can be solved by simply preventing other users from changing data, but not necessarily from viewing it. Therefore, most DBMSs support a second, less restrictive, type of lock known as a *shared lock*.

A shared lock permits the user to retrieve a data object, but not to modify it. A data object that is locked with a shared lock can be retrieved by users other than the one initially placing the lock. These other users also receive a shared lock on that same data object. However, no user can modify the data item (in other words, receive an exclusive lock on it) until all shared locks on it are released.

A shared lock is sufficient to solve the travel agency's inconsistent analysis problem. In Figure 12.7, for example, when the Philadelphia transaction requests an exclusive lock on the number of seats sold for flight 125, the lock cannot be placed; the transaction is blocked by the shared lock held by the Boston transaction. However, should any other transaction attempt to place a shared lock on the same data, the shared lock will be granted. The Philadelphia transaction will be unable to proceed until all shared locks have been released.

> **By the way:** Microcomputer DBMSs provide many variations on exclusive and shared locks. In fact, some provide no exclusive locks at all, but instead handle the lost update problem by updating all data viewed by users whenever that data changes, so that no transaction ever has old data. The drawback to this approach is that it significantly increases the amount of data traveling over the network, slowing down overall performance.

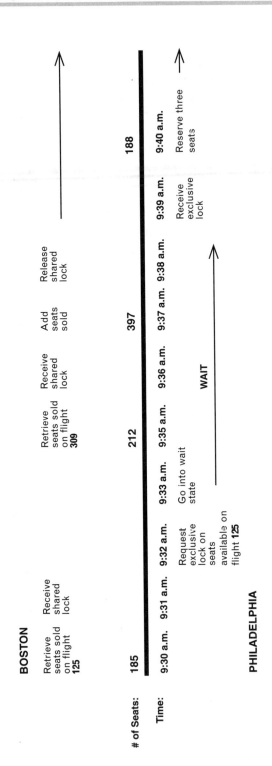

Figure 12.7 Using shared locks to prevent an inconsistent analysis

Deadlock

While locks can solve concurrency control problems, they do spawn a problem all of their own. Assume now that the Boston and Philadelphia travel agents are working with two new customers. The customer calling the Boston travel agent wants to book flights from Boston to Philadelphia and back; the customer calling the Philadelphia travel agent wants to go from Philadelphia to Boston and back. Both customers want to travel on the same day and wish to leave and return at approximately the same time.

The Boston travel agent queries the database about a Boston to Philadelphia flight and receives an exclusive lock on the tuple. While she is looking at the result on her screen, the Philadelphia travel agent places a request for data about a Philadelphia to Boston flight. He receives an exclusive lock on the tuple.

The Boston travel agent then requests data about a return flight for her customer (Philadelphia to Boston). However, the Philadelphia travel agent already has an exclusive lock on the tuple. The Boston request goes into a wait state. The Philadelphia travel agent asks for data about a return flight (Boston to Philadelphia). The Boston to Philadelphia flight, though, is locked by the Boston travel agent. The Philadelphia request also goes into the wait state. Now both travel agents are waiting for tuples on which the other has a lock. Neither can proceed until one of them releases a lock. This situation (diagrammed in Figure 12.8) is known as *deadlock*, or a *deadly embrace*.

There are two main ways that a DBMS can handle deadlock, by avoiding it or by breaking it when it occurs. Both methods are used by today's DBMSs.

DBMSs detect deadlock by keeping a list of who is waiting for whom (technically, a *directed graph*). When a cycle appears in the list (a user is waiting for someone before him or her in the list), then a deadlock has occurred. The only way to break the deadlock is to force one user in the list to release his or her locks. A DBMS will have rules by which it selects the "victim." It may, for example, choose the last transaction that entered the list or the transaction that has been running the shortest amount of time. The victim is rolled back, which in turn releases all the victim's locks. In a "detect and break" deadlock control scheme, every transaction begins execution, but not all run to completion.

Deadlock avoidance means that a transaction must obtain all the locks it needs before it begins (a *pre-declaration of locks*). Any transaction that begins will run to completion, but fewer transactions actually start than with a detect

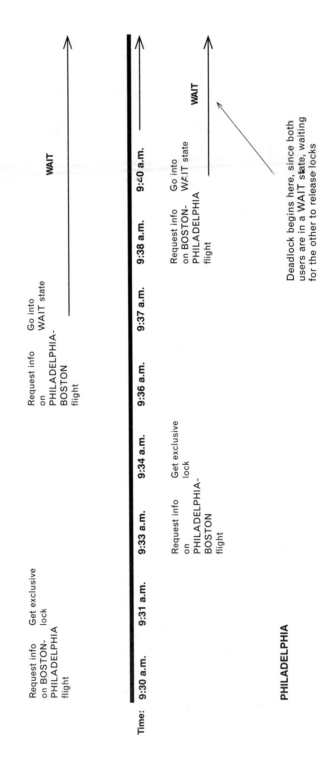

Figure 12.8   Deadlock

and break scheme. It is also often difficult for a transaction to predict exactly what data it will access before it starts. Deadlock avoidance is therefore more difficult to implement than allowing deadlock to occur and breaking it.

SQL Concurrency Control

SQL DBMSs work in a transaction-based environment. If a user is issuing SQL queries from a terminal, each transaction is automatically defined as a single SQL command. If an embedded SQL program contains no statements to mark transaction boundaries, it, too, is treated as a single transaction. However, it is often desirable to have explicit control of when a transaction is committed and when it is rolled back. For that reason, SQL contains statements that mark transaction boundaries and that commit and roll back transactions. In addition, most SQL implementations provide statements that explicitly lock and unlock data objects. These locking statements override any implicit locking scheme that the DBMS might provide.

Marking Transaction Boundaries

The SQL DBMSs indicate the start of a transaction in a variety of ways. Some use the commands BEGIN TRANSACTION or BEGIN WORK. Others assume that a new transaction begins immediately after the end of the previous transaction. In all cases, the beginning of a transaction initiates before-imaging.

> **By the way:** This is the way in which the programs in Chapter 10 were written.

All of the SQL DBMSs have statements to either commit or roll back a transaction. Although the syntax varies slightly (for example, END TRANS-ACTION/ROLLBACK, COMMIT WORK/ROLLBACK WORK, END TRANSACTION/ABORT, or COMMIT/ROLLBACK WORK), the effect is the same. If a transaction is committed, its changes are left in the database (in other words, made permanent). If a transaction is rolled back, its changes are undone, using the transaction log information stored in the before-image file.

Types of Locks

Although exclusive and shared locks are the two basic types of locks, some SQL DBMSs have implemented a number of variations on those types. For example, some DBMSs place no exclusive locks. Instead, all data can be viewed by all transactions. However, an action that modifies the database places a lock on the data being modified. Although other transactions can still view the data, no other transaction can modify the data until the lock is released. This type of locking scheme (a "shared update" lock) increases the amount of concurrent access, but also increases the risk that a retrieval-only transaction may be viewing old data (data that have been changed by a subsequent transaction).

Alternatively, some SQL DBMSs place only exclusive locks. The benefit of such a scheme is that users never view old data. However, it does significantly cut down on the amount of concurrent use of the database. Still others support all three types of locks: shared, exclusive, and shared update.

Distributed Databases

As you read earlier in this chapter, a distributed database is a database in which the data themselves reside on more than one computer. The computers are linked by some form of telecommunications. Each location that is part of a distributed database has its own hardware, its own DBMS and application programs, and a portion of the database's data.

The goal of a distributed database is to appear to users as a centralized database. (This is Codd's rule 11—distribution independence.) Users should be able to query the database and write application programs without regard to where data are stored. The DBMS should keep track of the location of data and automatically provide it, regardless of storage location, whenever requested. The DBMS that provides distribution independence makes it easy to move data from one place to another without requiring rewriting of application programs.

In most cases, each site in a distributed database system has a copy of the portion of the database that it uses most often. The result is often a significant amount of duplicated data. A distributed DBMS must therefore deal with the problem of data consistency.

Advantages of a Distributed Database

An organization can gain a number of advantages by moving from a centralized to a distributed database:

- Because each site has the data it uses most often stored locally, most database tasks can be performed more quickly than they can be when every piece of data must be accessed over a data communications network.
- A distributed database gives local users more control over their data and application programs. Each site can tailor its procedures and programs to its own specific needs.
- Because most data access is local, a distributed database requires only a small portion of the data communications required by a centralized database. This provides the bulk of the financial savings that an organization can realize through a distributed database. In fact, most organizations decide to move from a centralized to a distributed database when the telecommunications costs for a centralized database outweigh the costs of placing hardware and software at each site.
- Because local users are more familiar with their data, data entry is more accurate.
- Hardware and software can be tailored to the needs of each individual location. An organization doesn't need to invest in large computers when smaller ones will do. Each site can be upgraded as needed, rather than upgrading a large central facility. In general, this scheme (known as *incremental growth*) will save an organization money over time.

Problems with Distributed Databases

As attractive as distributed databases may sound, there are many problems associated with their use:

- Although performance of data manipulation using local data is very fast, data manipulation requiring data not stored locally can be very slow. The computer accepting the request for data stored elsewhere must initiate a data communications call to the site containing the data.

It must then wait for the data to be transferred over the telecommunications lines. Both actions significantly slow down the performance of the local machine.

• The distributed database must maintain a data dictionary that indicates where data are stored. How, then, should the data dictionary be maintained? If it is kept in a single, central location, then each site must use a data communications call to determine the location of any data not stored locally. If a copy of the data dictionary is kept at each location, then the database system is faced with updating each of those copies every time anyone at any site makes a change to the structure of the database.

• Distributing data means that control of data and application programs is removed from central control. It is more difficult to enforce standards for data integrity and for application programming when those working with the data are located at multiple, remote sites. In addition, distribution makes it more difficult to provide technical support to users.

• Because a distributed database stores the data used most frequently at each site, it contains a great deal of duplicated data. A distributed database is therefore vulnerable to all of the data integrity problems associated with duplicated data.

Distributed Concurrency Control

The presence of duplicated data in a distributed database presents significant concurrency control problems. If locking is used for concurrency control, then every copy of a data object must be locked before an update can take place. Placing the locks requires data communications activity, but the performance slowdown the locking causes is the least of the problems. The major problem occurs during the commit process.

Assume, for example, that there are three copies of a personnel table at three different sites that are part of a distributed database. An application program at site A initiates a transaction that updates several rows in the personnel table. Before beginning, the transaction locks the tables at all three sites. Upon commit, the DBMS commits at site A and then places a data communications call to commit at site B. However, when the DBMS attempts to contact site C to commit the changes to the third copy, the data communications call can't be completed. What can the DBMS do? Two copies exist with committed changes; the third copy of the table is locked and contains uncommitted changes. The database has been left in an inconsistent and inaccurate state. One solution might be to roll back the two copies that were committed. However, by definition, a committed transaction is never rolled back. (In fact, the commit process probably erased the before-images of the transactions at sites A and B, making rollback impossible.)

Most client/server DBMSs therefore use a *two-phase* commit. As the transaction is executing, the DBMS locks all copies of data that will be modified by the transaction. When the transaction issues a COMMIT, the DBMS uses the first phase to poll each locked site to determine whether it is ready and able to commit. Once the DBMS has received a "ready to commit" signal from each site, the DBMS uses the second phase to send the final instruction to execute the COMMIT and release the locks on the data.

If the second phase fails, the DBMS places the transaction in an "in doubt" state and does not commit the changes to the database. It is then up to local database administrators to manually check which transactions are in doubt and decide which should be manually committed. This is certainly not an ideal solution; manually forcing a commit could introduce inconsistent data. However, it does represent the current state of the art in distributed concurrent control.

The problems with concurrency control have limited the implementation of distributed databases. At this time, good DBMSs exist for retrieval from distributed systems. Such DBMSs usually use SQL as their query language. Most allow the DBMSs at local sites to be any DBMS that recognizes SQL. However, there is little distributed database software that supports on-line, real-time updates.

Summary

Multiuser DBMSs permit more than one user to use the data at any given time (concurrent use). Concurrent use brings with it a problem known as a "lost update." A lost update occurs when a user makes a change to the database based on incorrect data; another user has changed the data since the first user viewed the data. Lost updates may cause invalid data to be stored in the database.

Most multiuser databases use locking to handle the lost update problem. Users who intend to update data obtain an exclusive lock on that data, preventing any other user from even viewing the data until the lock is released.

Exclusive locks can create a problem of their own—deadlock. Deadlock occurs when a user locks a data object needed by another user and another user has a lock on a data object needed by the first user. A DBMS can either take measures to prevent deadlock or can wait for deadlock to occur and then break it. Most microcomputer DBMSs choose to do the latter. Breaking deadlock usually involves selecting one user as the victim. The victim's transaction is aborted, forcing the release of all of its locks.

Exclusive locks, because they prevent other users from even viewing data, cut down on the amount of concurrent activity a DBMS can support. Many DBMSs therefore use a second type of lock, the shared lock, to allow multiple users to view the same data. A shared lock prevents modification of the data until all locks on it are released (no one can obtain an exclusive lock). However, many users can hold a shared lock on the same data object.

References

Bernstein, P. A., N. Goodman, E. Wong, C. L. Reeve, and J. B. Rothnie, Jr. 1981. "Query Processing in a System for Distributed Databases (SDD-1)." *ACM Transactions of Database Systems.* 6(Dec.):602–625.

Bernstein, P. A., V. Hadzilacos, N. Goodman. 1987. *Concurrency Control and Recovery in Database Systems.* Reading, Mass.: Addison-Wesley.

Casanova, M. A. 1981. The Concurrency Control Problem of Database Systems. Lecture Notes in Computer Science. Berlin: Springer-Verlag.

Champine, G. A. 1977. "Six Approaches to Distributed Data Bases." *Datamation.* 23(May):69–72.

Darling, Charles B. 1991. "Waiting for Distributed Database." *DBMS.* 4(10):46–51.

Groff, James R. and Paul N. Weinberg. 1990. "Transaction Processing." *DBMS.* 3(13):44–60.

Haerder, T. and A. Reuter. 1988. "Principles of Transaction-Oriented Database Recovery." *ACM Computing Surveys.* 15(4):287–318.

Kedem, Z. M. 1983. "Locking protocols: from exclusive to shared locks." Journal of the ACM. 30(4):787-804. October.

McGoveran, David and Colin White. 1990. "Clarifying Client-Server." *DBMS*. 3(12):78–89.

Papdimitrious, Christos. 1986. *Database Concurrency Control*. New York: Computer Science Press.

Traiger, I., J. Gray, C. Galtiteri, and B. Lindsay. 1982. "Transactions and Consistency in Distributed Database Systems." *ACM Transactions on Database Systems*. 7(3):323–342.

Van Name, Mark L. and Bill Catchings. 1993. "Follow a rightsizing map on road to client/server." *PC WEEK*. March 8: 86–111.

Wiorkowski, G. and D. Kull. 1989. "Distributed DB2." *Database Programming and Design*. 2(4):52–57.

Things to Think About

1. Multiuser databases cause problems that aren't present with single-user databases. What are some of these problems? Though these problems exist, why might an organization choose to go to a multiuser DBMS?

2. Your best friend is writing a multiuser DBMS. Though your friend has a lot of experience with single-user DBMSs, he's never worked with a multiuser DBMS. You've spent three days now trying to convince your friend that he needs to use record locking, but a discussion of the theory hasn't gotten through. What you need is a concrete example.
    a. Describe an actual situation where a multiuser database will suffer from a lost update problem if record locking isn't used.
    b. Show how exclusive locks might be used to solve the problem.
    c. Extend your example to show how deadlock might occur.

3. Can shared locks ever be responsible for deadlock? If so, give an example of how it might occur. If not, why not?

4. In some circumstances, DBMSs lock entire tables rather than just rows within a table. Since this cuts down on the amount of concurrency a database will support, why do you think system designers chose to do it this way?

5. The general trend in computing today is away from centralized systems toward distributed systems. What advantages can you see to having a distributed database? What disadvantages might there be?

13

Managing a Database System

Even the best designed and programmed database system must be managed once it has been put into everyday use. Good management ensures that the database system continues to meet an organization's needs and that procedures for enforcing data integrity and security are followed.

The activity of managing a database system is known as *database administration*. The person who performs database administration functions is a *database administrator*. This chapter looks at many of the issues surrounding database administration, beginning with an overview of the responsibilities of a database administrator. It then finishes with a discussion of database security.

Database Administration

As mentioned in Chapter 1, a database administrator (DBA) is someone who is responsible for managing a database installation. Though the DBA function is most commonly referred to as if it were performed by a single individual, the job may be shared by more than one person, especially in large database environments.

The job description also varies widely from business to business. It generally, however, includes some or all of the following areas of responsibility:

- System planning and design
- Application program development (this includes employee supervision)
- Design (data dictionary) maintenance
- Security
- Public relations

System Planning and Design

If a business is going to "do it right," a database administrator will be the first person hired after the organization makes the commitment to install a database system. The DBA will work closely with a systems analyst to evaluate the business's information needs and will often have the responsibility of designing the schema for the database. This aspect of the job has implications for the kind of educational background and/or experience a DBA should have.

To design an effective schema, a DBA must have technical database knowledge and experience. In the past, this has meant that some database administrators were promoted into that position from the data processing department. They followed the career path of programmer → programmer analyst → analyst → database administrator.

However, if a database system is to serve an organization for more than a short time, its design must be based on more than just immediate needs; it must allow for growth and change. In other words, the DBA needs to know something about upper-level management's plans for the future. Upper-level management has, in some cases, been most comfortable sharing that sort of information with an individual who has management experience. Therefore, some database administrators have been middle managers who made a lateral move from another department.

Both middle managers without technical expertise and data processing specialists without management experience tend to find a DBA's job difficult. Ideally, a database administrator should have education and/or experience in both data processing (including systems analysis techniques) and management. During the past decade, undergraduate and graduate programs have been developed that provide exactly that combination of studies. These programs are often called Computer Information Systems, or just Information Systems.

Application Development

A DBA may have supervisory responsibility for programmers and programmer/analysts who develop applications programs for the database system. This aspect of the job is more than just a managerial responsibility; the DBA must be concerned with program standards as well.

Standards for applications programs are essential. These standards include:

- Performance: the speed at which a program responds to the user
- User interface: the type of interface (for example, menu vs. command driven)
- Programming style: how the program should be structured
- Testing procedures: how new programs should be tested and who will verify the tests

Performance

How long are you willing to wait for a computer to respond to a command you type? Not very long. When you're staring at a CRT, 30 seconds is an eternity. To force programmers to design and code efficient applications programs, a DBA will often establish standards which specify the maximum amount of time that may be permitted to elapse between whatever action terminates user input, sending a request to the DBMS, and the display of a response on the screen.

User Interface

Left alone, many programmers will create command-driven programs that provide little or no information to the user. That kind of interface is adequate if the program is only going to be used by highly trained, technologically sophisticated individuals. However, in most database environments, the majority of users are not computer professionals. Rather, they are people trained in other areas who are using computers to help them do their jobs.

User interface standards will therefore often prescribe when menu-driven systems are required and describe data entry screen formats. They may also require programmers to make an effort to make their programs easy to use by placing the bulk of the work on the program rather than on the user.

For example, assume that an applications programmer is writing a data entry program. There are two ways to control the program loop that allows the user to enter repeated sets of data. The first way is to ask the user how many sets of data he or she plans to enter and to then have the program code count, stopping the program when the requested number of records have been entered. This, however, places too great a burden on the user. The second technique for controlling the loop—using an end-of-data flag—is far better in terms of user interface. The user doesn't have to know how many sets of data are to be entered. When the user has finished, he or she simply enters the end-of-data flag or makes an appropriate choice from a menu and exits the program.

Programming Style

Database administrators may establish standards that regulate how programs will be logically structured and in what style they should be written. While at first this might seem to take away a programmer's creativity and freedom, it is essential if programs are to be easy to maintain. In fact, in environments where a database system has been implemented for a period of time, more than 80 percent of the programming activity that takes place involves maintaining existing programs rather than creating new ones.

Often, the person maintaining the program will not be the same as the person who originally wrote it. If all programs have a consistent structure and style, it will be significantly easier for someone who wasn't the original author to understand and therefore modify a program.

Testing Procedures

As mentioned earlier in this chapter, one of the prime sources for accidental destruction of data in a database is the testing of new applications programs that have not been thoroughly debugged against "real" data. The problem is easily solved by establishing a separate database for testing. This test database contains a subset of the real database and can be easily regenerated if an application program destroys any data.

Who, then, should decide when an application program is ready to be run on actual data? Generally, it's not wise to let programmers decide for themselves. The author of a program knows the code very well; he or she may inadvertently continue to interact with the program in such a manner that hidden bugs never appear. A better test is to let someone completely unfamiliar with the program source code interact with it. It is the DBA's responsibility to establish standards as to who will do the testing and the levels of performance a program must achieve before it can be run against the database.

There are two important implications of all these standards. First of all, they must be documented. If a new programmer is hired, some sort of document must exist that can be given to the new employee to read; you can't expect someone to adhere to standards if they don't know what they are. Secondly, standards must be enforced. It is the DBA's responsibility to monitor programmer performance and determine if established standards are being met. As a manager, the DBA must also take corrective measures if variation from the standards is beyond a tolerable level.

Design Maintenance

Regardless of how thorough the needs assessment that leads to a database design, the time will come when the database no longer adequately meets the needs of an organization. Perhaps the users have become more sophisticated and are making requests for information that was not captured in the original design. Perhaps the activities of the organization have changed, bringing different requirements for data analysis. Whatever the cause, a database must change with the needs of its users. It is therefore the responsibility of the DBA to set procedures for and manage changes in the design of the database.

Making a change in a database schema is not always a simple matter. For example, suppose that Small Bank does decide to go from five-digit to nine-digit zip codes. Who will the change affect? Which applications are affected?

For Small Bank, any applications programs that print materials for mailing as well as CRT data entry forms will feel the impact of the change. How much will it cost to implement the change? How much reprogramming is involved? If it will cost a great deal in programmer time to change output formats to accommodate the longer zip code, savings in postage may be overridden by programmer salaries.

In large database environments, where many different departments share the same database, requests for changes to the database schema are made in writing to the DBA. The DBA then circulates the proposed change to all those who are potentially affected by the change, asking for their opinion. Generally, the DBA reviews the responses and makes a decision whether or not to allow the modification. If the modification is allowed, the DBA or an authorized person on the DBA's staff will make the change in the data dictionary.

This procedure for managing design changes has given database administrators a reputation for always saying "NO." It has also given rise to one of the worst "light bulb" jokes of all times (included here so you can have at least one database joke to tell your friends):

QUESTION: How many database people does is take to change a light bulb?

ANSWER: Three. One to write the insertion program, one to write the removal program, and a database administrator to make sure that no one else changes it while the first two are working.

Security

A database administrator has the responsibility for establishing and monitoring security standards and procedures. This includes not only the security measures that are discussed later in this chapter, but deciding who has access to what data. Making decisions as to which users will be permitted to access which data is not a trivial problem. Humans as a rule are very possessive of their privileges; anything which makes a person feel that he or she is less privileged than another is a possible source of contention.

Consider this not-so-farfetched scenario: You are hired as a database administrator for a small college. After performing your needs assessment, you determine (in concert with the systems analyst and management) that the first department to be handled by the new database system will be Personnel.

Currently, personnel files are kept in a set of three filing cabinets. While the cabinets lock, a physical lack of space has forced them to be kept in the main reception area. The receptionist has always kept the key; she unlocks the cabinets whenever anyone needs a file. No one has ever had much trouble with the arrangement, though it is apparently well-known among the clerical staff that the receptionist "peeks." She always has juicy gossip to share over coffee.

Once the database system is installed and tested, the paper personnel files are removed to storage. It makes more room in the reception area, but the receptionist is furious. The only access she's been given to the personnel portion of the database is the schedule for on-campus interviews. She has no rights to look at any individual's data. Now she's in your office, standing in front of your desk, demanding to know why she can't get to the data, since she's always been able to before.

As a manager, you've made the correct decision not to give the receptionist rights to personal data. Her job includes answering the phone, making appointments, and verifying that people show up for scheduled appointments. It in no way involves data stored about current employees. However, you must still deal with the interpersonal problem that has arisen because someone feels offended that her "privileges" have been unfairly reduced.

No matter how good a DBA's interpersonal skills, situations like the one just described do occur. They can't always be resolved just between the DBA and the individual making the complaint. Many organizations will therefore have a committee whose sole purpose is to evaluate access requests and either grant or deny them. Rather than taking authority away from the DBA, such a committee more often than not supports the DBA by giving him or her a place to turn for arbitration.

Public Relations

A database administrator often functions as a liaison between the database staff and the rest of the world. The DBA must interact with system users, management, and people outside the organization. In this role, he or she walks a very fine line, since the wishes of the data processing staff must be balanced against the demands of users and top-level management.

As an interface between top-level management and the database staff, the DBA must ensure that management doesn't set unrealistic goals for systems development projects. This function has serious implications as to where the DBA should be placed in the organizational hierarchy.

In some businesses, DBAs are placed on project development teams at the same organizational level as the programmers and analysts. However, DBAs who are part of the data processing staff tend to have a difficult time getting management to listen to them. If a DBA is going to be effective as a management-DP liaison, then he or she has to be someone with some managerial clout. Not only must a DBA be able to enforce standards, but he or she must also be comfortable, if not in the board room, at least in the CEO's office. A DBA should therefore report directly to someone at the vice presidential level (preferably a vice president for data processing) or, in a smaller organization, directly to the CEO.

The DBA's responsibility as the interface between management and data processing personnel goes two ways. While the DBA protects the DP staff from unreasonable management demands, he or she must also realize that the DP staff may be capable of producing more work in a shorter amount of time than they claim. Once system development goals have been established, it is the DBA's responsibility to supervise the process and make sure the goals are met.

The DBA must also act as an interface between users and the database. End users require training. Sometimes they may want to understand why a particular type of output that they requested cannot be produced. They need someone to whom they should direct their suggestions for system modifications. The DBA and his or her staff will therefore be responsible for designing and conducting user training sessions as well as fielding any queries users might have.

In some organizations, the database administrator is expected to act as a spokesperson for his or her employer. The DBA may be asked to speak about the organization's database system at professional meetings, or to describe the system for other businesses considering the installation of a similar system.

Database Security

Security wasn't much of an issue when it was possible to put your data on a single floppy disk and carry it away to lock safely in a drawer. However, the introduction of large-capacity hard disks and multi-user microcomputer DBMSs has raised the question of how sensitive data can be protected. If you are administering a database system you must be concerned with both intentional and unintentional unauthorized modification and disclosure of data.

Unintentional Data Damage

Unintentional modification or destruction of data can happen in a number of ways. It may be the result of a hardware problem, either media failure (for example, a disk head crash) or a power loss. It may also be caused by the misbehavior of applications programs that have not been properly debugged. In addition, the past few years have seen an increase in the threat from viruses, insidious programs that destroy data.

Backup

The best insurance against hardware problems is to keep backup copies of data along with paper documents for all activity against the database that has occurred since the backup was made. These can be used to restore the database once the hardware problem has been corrected. The generally accepted practice is to keep three sets, or generations, of backups (this is known as a *grandparent-parent-child* scheme). Having three generations of backups helps to ensure that a failure while attempting to restore the database from a backup isn't catastrophic.

How often should backups be taken? That depends on how active a database is. In very active environments, databases are backed up every day. However, most microcomputer databases must be idle (in other words, no activity in process) while the backup is being taken. For a single-user database, that presents no problem, but scheduling of backups for multi-user databases does take some care.

> **By the way:** Some minicomputer and mainframe DBMSs do support "live" backups, backups that can be performed while users are working with the database.

On the whole, backing up a database is a time-consuming, bothersome procedure. Unless someone insists, system operators may simply "forget" to take backups. This, however, is a potentially dangerous (read "costly") situation. Consider what happened to a lazy independent contractor back in 1982.

This contractor was using an old Apple II+ with a 10 Mb Bernoulli Box (a high capacity floppy disk drive with changeable media cartridges) to maintain a mailing list of over 5,000 names. The database stored on the Bernoulli Box cartridge would fill up eight standard Apple II+ floppy disks. Backing up the file required manually splitting the database into floppy-sized chunks and then downloading the data to floppies. The entire process took about two hours.

Like many people, the contractor was lazy and decided to take a chance. No backup of the database was taken for over a year. Then the worst happened. While printing a set of mailing labels, the cartridge failed (a Bernoulli Box's high-density floppy disk is more susceptible to damage than a hard disk). The contractor had two choices—re-enter all 5,000 names from hard copy or attempt to recover the data. So, the cartridge was mailed to the manufacturer of the disk drive in the hope that the database could be recovered.

You can decide for yourself if the contractor was lucky. The drive manufacturer was able to recover all but three of the 5,000 records. However, the price tag for the recovery process (labor and the cost of a new cartridge) was over $250. (Remember, this occurred in 1982, when $250 was a lot more money than it is today!) As you might guess, the first thing the contractor did when the recovered cartridge arrived was to make a backup copy.

An alternative to off-line backups that is being used more widely today as the cost of magnetic media goes down is *disk mirroring*. In a mirrored system, the server maintains a second hard disk identical to the hard disk on which the database is stored. Mirroring software automatically transfers all modifications made to the database to the second disk, ensuring that the copy on the second disk is a mirror image of the database actually being used. If the primary hard disk fails, the server can switch immediately to the other hard disk. Disk mirroring is more costly than using tapes for backup and does have some impact on performance (the server's CPU must take time to copy changes to the second hard disk). However, restoration after media failure is faster and easier with a mirrored system, since replacement media are always available.

Application Programs

Damage caused by bugs in application programs cannot always be avoided. Even the most carefully tested program may contain code that will behave unexpectedly in rare circumstances. However, application development should not take place using actual data. To protect the database from errors caused by programs not yet completed, all testing should occur against a special test database set aside for that purpose. The test database is usually a subset of the real database which can be regenerated from the real database at any time.

The Virus Threat

A *virus* is an unauthorized, destructive program that gets in to a computer system. (The name virus comes from the program's ability to create copies of itself and transmit those copies so that other computers become infected.) The intent of most virus programmers is malicious; viruses are designed to destroy data stored on a hard disk or, at the very least, disrupt normal data processing.

There are two major sources of viruses. The first is over telecommunications lines. One of the most widely publicized virus attacks occurred in 1988, when a virus was embedded in a program that sent electronic mail over the Internet network. Each time electronic mail was sent, the virus was sent as well, infecting each new system on the network that received mail from an already infected system. Although this particular virus did not destroy anything on infected systems, it did tie up the infected computers so that they were unable to perform their own work. It cost hundreds of thousands of dollars in machine and technician time to clear the virus from the network.

Viruses can also enter a computer system when software is installed from a floppy disk. Public domain software (software that is not copyrighted and often distributed by user groups) is particularly vulnerable because its transmittal is not controlled in the same way commercial software is controlled.

Although there is no guaranteed way to secure a system against virus attack, it is prudent to control the installation of software from unknown sources. Public domain software, regardless of whether it comes on a disk or was downloaded from an information service, should be run the first time on a computer without a hard disk. It should not be installed on a hard disk until it has been shown to run as expected, without any unusual behaviors.

Because viruses can enter a system over telecommunications lines, external telecommunications (in other words, those that use standard telephone lines for communication with the outside world) should be supported by its own hard disk. In other words, if at all possible, don't allow a database and telecommunications to share the same hard disk. Uploading of software (transmitting software from a remote computer to the local computer) should be permitted only to the telecommunications disk. Once on the system, it should be subject to the same testing procedures as new software supplied on floppy disk.

Intentional Data Damage and Disclosure

The simplest way to secure a database system against willful tampering is to restrict physical access to the computer. Placing a computer in a locked room and keeping tight control over who has the keys, for example, can be an effective way to control who has access to a database. However, if the computer handles remote users (either over telephone lines or through a network) or if the computer is shared by many different applications, then physical security is not enough. Security measures must be implemented while the user is on-line.

Identifying the User

The first step in on-line security is to identify the user. In multiuser environments, this is handled by the operating system. When a user attempts to log on to the system, he or she must enter a user name and an associated password. Anyone who cannot supply a recognizable user name/password combination is not permitted access to the computer. Once the user is on the system, the computer must assume that the user is the individual for whom the user name and password were created. To ensure the integrity of a password system, users must be encouraged not to share their passwords, not to write them down, and to change them frequently.

Single-user microcomputer operating systems generally do not have individual user accounts or work areas. The computer assumes that anyone who has access to the keyboard is authorized to use the machine. Security must therefore be handled at a lower level—by the DBMS itself.

Internal DBMS Security

A fully relational DBMS handles security through what is known as an authorization matrix. Conceptually, an authorization matrix is a table that records which users can perform which kinds of activity against which data objects. Figure 13.1 contains a portion of a sample authorization matrix for the Federated Taxi Company database. Rights are granted to a specific user by relation and by operation. For example, the Kellys have all rights to every relation in the database. However, the chief mechanic can only view the cab reservation data; he cannot change it. By the same token, the scheduling clerk can view the names of available shifts but can't change them.

USER	Cab	Driver	Shift	Shift_Driven	Incident
Accountant	SELECT	SELECT	SELECT	SELECT	SELECT
AKelly	ALL	ALL	ALL	ALL	ALL
Clerk	MODIFY	MODIFY	SELECT	MODIFY	MODIFY
ChiefMechanic	MODIFY	SELECT	SELECT	SELECT	SELECT
Dispatcher1	SELECT	SELECT	NONE	SELECT	MODIFY
Dispatcher2	SELECT	SELECT	SELECT	SELECT	MODIFY
Dispatcher3	SELECT	SELECT	SELECT	SELECT	MODIFY
Dispatcher4	SELECT	SELECT	SELECT	SELECT	MODIFY
Dispatcher5	SELECT	SELECT	SELECT	SELECT	MODIFY
Dispatcher6	SELECT	SELECT	SELECT	SELECT	MODIFY
OtherMechanics	SELECT	NONE	NONE	NONE	SELECT
QKelly	ALL	ALL	ALL	ALL	ALL

Notes:
1. MODIFY rights imply SELECT rights.
2. ALL rights include the right to change the rights of another user.

Figure 13.1 A portion of an authorization matrix for the FTC database

A DBMS uses an authorization matrix in the following way: When a user makes a request for data retrieval or modification, the DBMS checks the user name against the relation name in the matrix. If the user has the appropriate access rights, then the operation is allowed to proceed. If not, the user request is denied. A DBMS that works in this way is said to be *data dictionary driven.*

Securing a SQL Database

SQL databases often implement security at two levels. First, a user must be identified to the DBMS by a matching user name and password. Only then can access to tables and views be keyed to user names through an authorization matrix. The first step is therefore to establish user names and passwords, a process which varies from one DBMS to another. If a DBMS does not maintain its own user names and passwords, the DBMS identifies the user by the name under which the user logged into the operating system.

Managing Users

If a SQL DBMS issues its own user names and passwords, the function of the GRANT and REVOKE commands is often extended to handle user management tasks. (As you will see, these commands are also used to assign access rights to tables and views.) When a DBMS of this type is first installed, it has only one authorized user name/password (for example, SYSTEM/MANAGER. The SYSTEM user has DBA (database administrator) privileges. Any user with DBA privileges can:

- Establish other user name/password combinations
- Create and modify tables and their contents without restriction
- Retrieve data without restriction
- Grant and revoke the rights of other users

> **By the way:** Before attempting to use GRANT and REVOKE in this way, consult your DBMS's documentation to determine whether it maintains its own user names or uses those under which a user logged into the operating system.

While any user with DBA privileges can grant DBA privileges to any other user, in practice you may not wish to do so. In most installations, there is only one user with DBA privileges and its user name/password are guarded carefully.

To log on to a DBMS that maintains its own user names, a user must at least have CONNECT rights. A DBA can issue those rights with the command:

GRANT CONNECT TO NewUser IDENTIFIED BY MyPassword

The above command establishes a user name of "NewUser" and an associated password of "MyPassword." NewUser can now log on to the database, but can neither create tables nor access existing tables or views.

Alternatively, a user who must not only be able to CONNECT to the database, but who must be able to create and drop tables and views as well is granted RESOURCE rights:

GRANT RESOURCE TO NewUser IDENTIFIED BY MyPassword

Users with RESOURCE rights can drop only tables and views that they have created themselves.

It is also possible, though not necessarily desirable, to create another user with DBA privileges:

GRANT DBA TO NewUser IDENTIFIED BY MyPassword

The command:

REVOKE CONNECT
FROM NewUser

removes NewUser from the database system entirely. When this occurs, all rights granted by NewUser are also automatically revoked.

Controlling Access to Tables and Views

Once a user name and password have been installed for a user, other rights are granted to give the user access to needed data objects. By default, a user has all rights to all tables and views that he or she has created; other users have no access to those tables or views. Additional access must be granted explicitly with the GRANT command; access is removed with the REVOKE command.

The types of rights that can be assigned are:

- ALL (all of the rights below)
- SELECT (retrieval only)
- INSERT (add data)
- UPDATE (modify data)
- DELETE (delete data)
- ALTER (add or expand columns)
- INDEX (create indexes)

Any of these rights can be applied to a single table for a single user. SELECT, INSERT, UPDATE, and DELETE rights can be applied to views. The general syntax for granting rights on data objects is:

GRANT right1 [,right2...]
ON table-name/view-name
TO user-name1 [,user-name2...]
[WITH GRANT OPTION]

For example, to give NewUser the right to query the CAB relation:

GRANT SELECT
ON Cab
TO NewUser

If the WITH GRANT OPTION is included, then NewUser will be able to grant his or her rights to other users. However, if NewUser did not create the table to which he or she is granting rights, then the table name must be preceded by the creator's user name. For example, assume that NewUser wishes to grant SELECT rights to Cab to OldUser:

GRANT SELECT
ON system.Cab
TO OldUser

The name of the user who created a table is separated from the table name by a period. In this case, Cab was created by "system."

In some cases you may wish to grant a particular kind of right to all users. In that case, replace the name of the user following TO with the keyword PUBLIC. For example, to let all of FTC's users see the Driver table:

GRANT SELECT
ON Driver
TO PUBLIC

More than one type of access right can be granted with a single GRANT command. To give NewUser the right to retrieve from and add data to Cab:

GRANT SELECT, INSERT
ON Cab
TO NewUser
WITH GRANT OPTION

The above command also gives NewUser the right to grant SELECT and INSERT rights to CAB to other users.

Rights can be taken away from users by using REVOKE to reverse the grant process. In general, the REVOKE command appears as:

REVOKE right1 [,right2...]
ON table-name/view-name
FROM user-name1 [,user-name2...]

This same syntax can be used to revoke rights to data objects or to revoke rights to the Oracle system. To prevent NewUser from inserting records into Cab:

REVOKE INSERT
ON Cab
FROM NewUser

NewUser will keep his or her SELECT rights to Cab, but loses INSERT rights. Rights can be revoked only by the user who granted them.

An Alternative Security Scheme

In addition to the SQL authorization matrix, there are other security schemes in use in microcomputer DBMSs. One commonly used security method assigns security classification levels to data objects and then grants users access rights based on the classification level of their user name.

> **By the way:** This type of security is used by *dBASE IV*.

In a DBMS that uses security classification levels, a user name is assigned to one access level. (The access levels are really arbitrary; consistency must be maintained by the database administrator.) Access levels are then assigned to objects within the database environment. Separate access levels are assigned to read, insert, modify, and delete operations to a data object. To access an operation on a data object, a user must have an access level that is less than or equal to the access level on that file. However, to modify a data object, a user must have the same access level as the data object being modified. This latter restriction is required because modifying a data object assigns it the security classification level of the user doing the modification. Data objects with low security levels might inadvertently be promoted to higher security levels after a modification.

The classification level security scheme presents at least one major problem. Because users can modify only data that have the same classification level, users who need to modify data at more than one classification level need one user name for each level at which they must modify data. Such users must therefore keep track of multiple user names and passwords. When a user has many user names and passwords, it becomes very tempting to write them down rather than making the effort to keep them memorized, thus compromising the security of the database.

Summary

Data stored in databases must be secured against both intentional and unintentional disclosure, alteration or destruction.

Unintentional damage disclosure can be caused by hardware failures (e.g., media failure or a power outage) or by application programs that contain errors. There are two major strategies for securing a database against those kinds of damage:

- Keeping backup copies of the database (if the database is damaged, it can be restored from the backup copy).
- Establishing procedures for testing new application programs (new programs are run against a sample database until they are free of errors).

Databases are secured against willful tampering by restricting access to the computer. Merely restricting physical access to the machine is sufficient only if the machine cannot be used via telecommunications lines (i.e., it supports dial-up access over telephone lines and/or is multiuser). In that case, the first line of defense lies with the computer operating system. Before a user gains access to the computer he or she must supply a user name and matching password.

This type of security is not generally available with single-user microcomputers. Security must therefore be handled by the DBMS itself. Relational databases use authorization matrices to record the rights of individual users to data objects. Generally, relational databases are secured at the table level. The term "database administration" refers to the activities involved with managing a database environment. The "database administrator" (DBA) may be a single individual or a group of individuals.

While the duties of the DBA vary considerably from organization to organization, in its fullest sense the job involves the following areas of responsibility:

- Coordinating system planning and design (The DBA serves on the system design team and works closely with systems analysts to develop an effective database schema.)
- Supervision of application development (The DBA establishes standards for application program performance, for the user interface, for programming style, and for program testing procedures.)
- Coordinating design maintenance (The DBA supervises and authorizes changes to the schema.)
- Security (The DBA establishes and maintains security standards and procedures.)
- Public Relations (The DBA functions as a liaison between the database staff and the rest of the world.)

References

Auerbach Publishers, Inc. 1981. *Practical Database Management*. Englewood Cliffs, N.J.: Prentice-Hall.

Beyer, Trine D. "Designing an Application Backup and Recovery Plan." *370/390 Data Base Management*. 1(11):22–28.

Bloombecker, J. J. 1989. "Short-Circuiting Computer Crime." *Datamation*. 55(19):71–72.

Gerritson, Rob. 1991. "SQL for Database Administrators." *DBMS*. 4(4):64–72.

Jaqua, D. J. 1988. "SQL Database Security." *Database Programming and Design*. 1(7):25–35.

King, Julia. "Demand for Database Managers Intensifies." *Computerworld.* 25(43):81.

La Plante, Alice. "RIM Positions Require Broader IS Skills." *Computerworld.* 25(43):93.

Martin, E. W., D. W. DeHayes, J. A. Hoffer, and W. C. Perkins. 1991. *Managing Information Technology: What Managers Need to Know.* New York: Macmillan.

Things to Think About

1. One way to secure a database system against damage from power failures is to install a stand-by power supply that provides enough battery power for a computer operator to save all activity to disk and perform an orderly shut down. Is this a sufficient hedge against power failure? Why or why not? If not, what else should be done?

2. It takes three hours for the Quality Mail Order Company to back up its order-entry database. However, the backup procedure means that the database can't be used while the backup is being made. QMOC advertises that it will accept orders 24 hours a day, seven days a week except for national holidays. The manager has therefore scheduled backups on holidays. Is this enough? Why or why not? If not, when should the manager schedule the backups? Is there going to be an optimal time to do it?

3. You are working for a small but exclusive investment firm. Data about client portfolios are kept on a single microcomputer which has a hard disk. Your boss thinks that the best way to secure the data is to put the computer in a small, windowless room and keep track of who has the keys. Is this a good idea? Why or why not?

4. You are a software reviewer who has been assigned the evaluation of a new DBMS. As you read the documentation, you find that it uses an authorization matrix to secure tables. The people who comprise the audience for your review won't understand the term "authorization matrix," much less how one works. Write the portion of the review that will explain the technique for your readers.

5. List the skills and personality traits, that, in your opinion, characterize the ideal database administrator. Is this a job you would like to have? Why or why not?

6. A database administrator can be placed at many levels in an organization's job hierarchy. A DBA might be assigned to each systems development team, or the DBA might be a staff position that reports to a corporate vice president. What are the advantages to each approach? What are the disadvantages? Formulate your answer in terms of the responsibilities of the DBA job.

7. Imagine that you are the DBA for a good-sized grocery chain (there are over 100 stores in a three-county area). The board of directors wants to install UPC scanners in all of the stores. The software that will handle the cash registers and the inventory is to be written by the chain's in-house DP staff. Management says that the scanners can be delivered and installed in the stores in four weeks. They want you to make sure the software is ready at the same time. However, your experience tells you that you have more than six months of programming time ahead of you. What will you tell the board of directors? Should the installation of the scanners be delayed? If so, what arguments can you make to persuade them to accept the delay?

8. You are the DBA for a mail-order company that specializes in sporting goods, camping equipment, and above-ground swimming pools. The manager of the swimming pool division wants to change the domain for the shipping weight of merchandise (currently the domain is numbers from 0.1 pounds to 99.9 pounds). As DBA, how will you proceed with this request for change? What criteria will you use to make the decision about whether or not to allow the change?

9. You are still the DBA for the mail-order company in question 8 above. In response to a request from the sporting goods division manager, you have assigned a team of programmers to create an application program that will categorize and summarize sales for each quarter. Three weeks later, the lead programmer appears in your office, grinning from ear to ear. "All done," he says, "two weeks ahead of schedule. We've put it on the system for that sporting goods fellow." After hearing this, you get very upset.

a. What's wrong with what the programming team did? What problems might their activities cause?

b. Outline some procedures that might be used to avoid the potential problems created by your programming team.

10. Imagine that you are the DBA for a county library system. Every library employee has the right to retrieve data from the database that has replaced the card catalog. However, only the technical services librarians have the right to make changes. This restriction angers some of the library service technicians, who had formerly made changes themselves to the card catalog. How will you answer their demands for the right to modify the database?

The Office of Margaret Holmes, D.M.D.

1.   Transcript of a conversation between Dr. Margaret Holmes and a systems analyst:

> **Dr. Holmes:** Thanks for coming. I know it's late, but I really need your help. The paperwork around this place is really getting out of hand.

> **Analyst:** How do you mean?

> **Dr. Holmes:** I started my practice three years ago—from scratch, mind you! I'm a good dentist; I really take good care of my patients, but nobody at dental school ever talked about how you manage a practice. We sure could have used a class in keeping patient records, hiring staff, firing staff, billing, inventory, patient scheduling—you name it. I seem to be swimming in paper in this office.

> **Analyst:** Let's see if we can narrow down your problems a bit. First of all, how many employees do you have?

> **Dr. Holmes:** Just two—a Receptionist, clerk-type person and a Dental Assistant.

> **Analyst:** Who's responsible for the paperwork?

> **Dr. Holmes:** The Receptionist. She makes appointments and is supposed to keep track of patient records.

> **Analyst:** What about the financial end of things?

> **Dr. Holmes:** I have an accountant.

> **Analyst:** Does the accountant do the billing?

> **Dr. Holmes:** Yeah. Actually, she's my sister. She comes in once a week and picks up all the payments we've received. Then she balances the checkbook, pays all the bills, and does whatever-accountants-do with the ledger sheets. Once a month she comes up with a summary of patient charges and amounts people owe. Then she makes a listing for the Receptionist, who does the typing and mailing of the statements.

> **Analyst:** Do you pay your sister?

> **Dr. Holmes:** As much as I can. Considering all the work she's doing, it's really not enough.

Analyst: So you can either pay her more, cut down on the amount of work you ask her to do, or both.

Dr. Holmes (laughing): Well, if you can help me, I can cut down on her workload. If we can also get more accurate billing information, then I can make more money and pay her more, too.

Analyst: More accurate billing? What's the problem there?

Dr. Holmes: I suppose it's the fault of the way I record patient charges. I keep a history card for each patient. Whenever I see a patient, I write down whatever I did and note the charge. I give the card back to the Receptionist, who's supposed to log the fact that I saw the patient in a notebook. Then the card gets filed.

Analyst: The notebook you just mentioned—is that what your sister uses to figure out the billing?

Dr. Holmes: That and the history cards themselves. You see, when a patient makes a payment or when we get a payment from an insurance company for a patient, the Receptionist pulls the patient's card and marks the payment on the card. The log tells my sister who's been in the office, but the history card actually records what the patient still owes.

Analyst: Since you say there's a problem with billing, the system obviously isn't working.

Dr. Holmes: All sorts of things go wrong. Sometimes the patient history cards get misfiled. My sister can't find them when she needs to see how much someone really owes us. Then we're faced with either letting it go and hoping the patient has insurance to cover the cost, or running the risk of angering a patient by billing them for something that's already been paid. Other things go wrong, too. Sometimes payments aren't recorded, or they get credited to the wrong patient.

Analyst: How do you organize the patient files?

Dr. Holmes: By name.

Analyst: Hmm. What happens if you have two patients by the same name?

Dr. Holmes: Then the Receptionist is supposed to look at the address.

Analyst: Well, here's a simple suggestion—something you can do right now, even before we get to installing a computer system for you. Why not assign each patient a number? Put that number on the statements as they go out and ask your patients to write the number on their check. That should make cross-referencing payments and patients much easier.

Dr. Holmes: Now, why didn't I think of that?

Analyst (smiling): I hope it helps. Now, does your sister also handle payroll?

Dr. Holmes: Yes. It's not difficult, considering that there's only the two employees. I pay her as a consultant.

Analyst: And you get whatever's left over?

Dr. Holmes: More or less. Some of the profit goes back into the business, for equipment and the like.

Analyst: Let me summarize just a bit here, so I can be sure that I understand everything we've talked about so far. You're having trouble with patient billing, but the major underlying cause of that trouble is the system you use to keep records about patients. Both patient history and patient billing records are kept on the same card. If the cards are misfiled or lost, then the patient billing data may be inaccurate.

Dr. Holmes: Exactly. Can a computer help?

Analyst: In both cases, yes. I think you need to consider keeping patient history data and patient billing data separate—not on two computers or in two different programs, but logically separate. If you request a copy of a patient's dental history, for example, you needn't see the financial history as well.

Dr. Holmes: You mean I should have one system to record financial information and one to record medical information?

Analyst: They can be the same system, but they are two distinct functions that share some data. I think part of what has gotten you into trouble up to this point is mixing the two.

Dr. Holmes: I think I see what you mean.

Analyst: What about patient scheduling? Is that a problem?

Dr. Holmes: Not at all. The Receptionist has one of those oversized scheduling books. She just writes a patient's name in the right spot when an appointment is made. A liberal application of white-out is enough to cancel an appointment. If we've got to choose something that doesn't need to be computerized, it can be patient scheduling.

Analyst: OK. There's one more thing you mentioned—inventory.

Dr. Holmes: I haven't got one. I mean, I order supplies and drugs, but I haven't any written record of what there is.

Analyst: How do you decide when to re-order?

Dr. Holmes: My Dental Assistant and I just look at the shelves in the storeroom; if we see that something is low, we put it on the list for the Receptionist to order.

Analyst: Is that a satisfactory procedure?

Dr. Holmes: Are you kidding? We always seem to be running out of one thing or the other.

Analyst: Well, a computer can help you keep track of inventory levels, but you'll have to determine your own re-order point.

Dr. Holmes: Re-order point?

Analyst: The minimum quantity of an item that you will accept before placing an order for more.

Dr. Holmes: You're telling me that this computer won't be much more than a record-keeping device, that it won't make decisions.

Analyst: That's more or less true. It can make decisions of a sort, if the rules are laid out clearly. For example, if you let the computer know the re-order point for items in your inventory, it can decide whether or not an item needs to be re-ordered by comparing the quantity on hand to the re-order point you've established.

Dr. Holmes: I see. I guess I should have had a computer course as well as an office management course.

Analyst: An introductory course at a community college, or through the continuing education department of a college or university, wouldn't hurt. In fact, you might want to send your employees as well, since they'll be using whatever system we install for you.

Dr. Holmes: If nothing else, it'll make us less afraid of the machine.

Analyst: That's exactly it... .

2. Transcript of a conversation between the Analyst and the Receptionist for Dr. Margaret Holmes:

Analyst: Dr. Holmes tells me that you're in charge of most of the paperwork in this office.

Receptionist: And answering the phone, and opening the mail, and calming frightened kids, and calling people to remind them about appointments...

Analyst: I'm afraid I can't help you with answering the phone, or the frightened kids, but Dr. Holmes has asked me to see what can be done to clean up the record keeping.

Receptionist: First of all, we need to do something about those patient record cards. I mean, I try really hard to make sure that they get put back in the right place, but I'm only human. Sometimes I make mistakes. And it gets so busy in here. I'll have two dozen of those stupid cards on my desk, three people with six noisy kids waiting out here, the phone'll be ringing, and then the mailman'll come in and dump a sack of letters on top of everything. Man, those cards have got to go. I mean, once one gets lost, then we're dead.

Analyst: I'm hoping that we can come up with some solution, but in order to find one, I need to get some information from you about how you do things.

Receptionist: Like what?

Analyst: Why don't you pretend that a patient has just walked through the door? Tell me, step by step, exactly what you do until the time that patient leaves.

Receptionist: OK. First, I get the person's name. Then I check him off in the appointment book, just so I know that he's come in. I've already pulled his card from the file—I pull the cards for all the day's patients first thing in the morning—so all I have to do is find it in the pile on my desk. When she's ready, Karen—that's the Dental Assistant—comes out and calls the patient. After that, I don't do anything until both Dr. Holmes and Karen are through. Whichever one was the last to see the patient gives the card back to me. They've written down what they've done. I use my chart here to figure out how much to charge the patient, and I write the numbers on the back of the card. See—here's charges and payments for the patient all right here on the cards. Sometimes, if the charge isn't the regular fee, Dr. Holmes writes me a little note, so I have to look carefully. Before the patient leaves I make another appointment, either for more work or a six-month check-up. At the end of the day, I write the name of every patient that we saw in this notebook; that's so Susan knows who might need to be billed. Then I file all the cards.

Analyst: What happens, then, when the mail comes in?

Receptionist: I separate it. I set aside bills we have to pay for Susan, the accountant. I take the checks that have come in and pull the cards for each person who sent a payment. Then I write down the payment, and subtract that amount from what the person owes. Dr. Holmes got me a calculator so my figures would be right. Insurance companies sometimes send us one big check for several patients; then I have to read the letter that comes with the check very carefully, to make sure that I credit the right patients with the right amount. Oh, yeah, I have to leave out all the cards that have recorded payments for Susan; otherwise, she won't know who's paid. It can get pretty tricky.

Analyst: I bet it can. I think I've got a pretty good feeling for how the record keeping part of your job works. Now that I think of it—don't you also take care of ordering supplies?

Receptionist: Yeah. I just write down everything that Dr. Holmes and Karen tell me to order. Then once a month I type up purchase orders and mail them out.

Analyst: How do you figure out how much to order?

Receptionist: If it's something I haven't ordered before, I ask Dr. Holmes. Otherwise, I just order the same amount I did last time, unless Karen or Dr. Holmes tells me exactly how much they want.

Analyst: How do you figure out where to order from?

Receptionist: If it's something new, Dr. Holmes or Karen will tell me. Otherwise, I order from the same place as I did before, unless, of course, I'm told to do it differently.

Analyst: OK. I want to thank you very much for talking with me.

Receptionist: What's going to happen next?

Analyst: I'm not sure. I need to talk to Karen and Susan. Then I'll make a report to Dr. Holmes and see what she wants to do from there.

3. Transcript of a conversation between the Analyst and Dr. Holmes' Dental Assistant:

Analyst: I'd like you to tell me about your part in keeping patient records, and in working with the supply and drug inventory.

Dental Assistant: Well, I write on the patient history cards, just like Margaret does.

Analyst: Where do you get the cards?

Dental Assistant: From the corner of the Receptionist's desk. I'm the one who gets the patient from the waiting room. I get them settled in a chair and then either leave them for Margaret, or go ahead and do whatever work I have to do. Like, if they need a cleaning or X-rays, I'll do that before Margaret sees them. As soon as I'm done, I write down whatever I did on the card; I leave it on the counter for Margaret.

Analyst: Does every patient see Dr. Holmes?

Dental Assistant: Actually, no. Sometimes we do have people who just come in for a cleaning. For example, if they're taking a drug like tetracycline that precipitates stains on the teeth, they might need to be cleaned once a month or so.

Analyst: What happens to the card in that case?

Dental Assistant: Then I take it back to the Receptionist. Even if I forget, I get all cards back to her by the end of the day. I always make a check of the treatment rooms before I go home.

Analyst: What if the Receptionist goes home before you do?

Dental Assistant: Then I leave the cards on her desk anyway. She takes care of it in the morning.

Analyst: OK. I think I understand how it works. So, let's talk about the supplies.

Dental Assistant: There's not much to say. We've got that storage room you saw when Margaret gave you the tour. If we need anything, we just go in and get it.

Analyst: What do you do when things run low?

Dental Assistant: Tell the Receptionist. She keeps a list. Once a month, she sends out orders.

Analyst: Do you have any problems with having too much of something or too little?

Dental Assistant: Oh, every so often we run out of something, but it's not a big problem. I'll tell you—I think the problem with those patient history cards and the screwy billing system is far more serious than running out of cotton wadding.

Analyst: I hear you.

4.   Transcript of a conversation between the Analyst and Susan Holmes, Margaret Holmes' sister and accountant:

Susan Holmes: Did you know that it was my idea that Margaret call you in?

Analyst: No.

Susan Holmes: Well, it was. She didn't have any idea how bad things were. She wasn't working with the figures! I've been trying to keep her books, but this crazy system she's come up with for recording patient charges and payments is a major problem. If she'd ever had a course in basic bookkeeping she'd know what she's doing to me.

Analyst: What sort of system are you using right now?

Susan Holmes: A one-write system. I've got a checkbook and cash-disbursements journal, and a cash-receipts journal. I also have a very small payroll system and an accounts payable system that's based on ledger cards. But accounts receivable? Arg—it's all on those stupid cards. I haven't been able to convince her that she needs to keep separate records about patient finances.

Analyst: Let's start with accounts payable. How do you manage that part of the business?

Susan Holmes: I get copies of purchase orders from the Receptionist. I use those to create accounts payable entries. The Receptionist gives me all the bills as they come in. I write the checks and post the payment on the ledger cards. I have complete control over accounts payable entries, so it works quite well. The same is true, by the way, for payroll. Margaret tells me how much to pay everyone. I write the checks, pay the IRS, etc. Since there's so few people, I also do the W-2 forms at the end of the year. What I really want to talk about, though, is accounts receivable. Jeez—my sister doesn't even know what that term means!

Analyst: Why don't you tell me how it works, then.

Susan Holmes: Well, when a payment comes in, the Receptionist records the amount credited to a patient's account on the patient history card. Then she sticks the card in a pile that's supposed to be given to me once a week, so I know who's paid what. But there are so many of those stupid cards laying around the outer office that they go astray. I really wish Margaret would realize that she needs a separate set of accounts receivable records. Then the checks could come straight to me. I wouldn't mind keeping track of what people owe her...

Analyst: What about the billing?

Susan Holmes: Talk about clumsy systems. Once a month, I get a list of all the patients who have been seen. That list is people who might be billed. I have to check each person in that list against their cards to see exactly what they owe. But who knows where the card is? It might be in the file, it might be in the pile of cards that have posted payments that week, it might be lost somewhere. Who knows? At any rate, once I decide what people really owe, I make up a billing sheet. The Receptionist actually types the statements and sends them out.

Analyst: There's something that's eluding me here. How do you catch overdue bills?

Susan Holmes: It's very difficult. The only way to figure out whose account isn't up to date is to go through all those history cards. When Margaret's practice was small, it wasn't a problem. The Receptionist did it during slack times. But now, she's too busy with just keeping the office going. We're losing revenue there, for sure. Look, I've told my sister that if she doesn't put in a computer system to keep patient records and do accounting, I'm going to quit. I think you're going to get this contract, because she certainly won't find another accountant who'll work as cheap as I do!

Analyst: I don't think I'd better comment on that... .

B

East Coast Aquarium

East Coast Aquarium is a nonprofit marine aquarium in a major northeastern city. The aquarium, which has ocean frontage, is supported by donation, memberships, charges for private functions, and the small admission fees it charges to the public. The aquarium grounds consist of three buildings: the main facility, a dolphin house, and a marina where the aquarium's research barge is docked.

1. Transcript of a conversation between a systems analyst and the aquarium director:

> **Analyst:** Wow! What an exciting place you've got here. I really like that center tank. It must be three stories tall.

> **Director:** Yes, it reaches the full three stories. It lets us simulate the way in which habitats change as the ocean depths change. We have species that dwell on the ocean floor, coral reef fish, and sand bar dwellers, all in the same tank. When you have more time, you can walk the spiral walkway that loops around the tank. We've placed glass windows in the sides at just about every level, so you can see the changes in species as the depth changes. And don't forget to look in the top; we've got some surface-dwelling species living there.

> **Analyst:** I also like some of the smaller tanks around the outside walls.

> **Director:** They're useful because they let us house species that have special habitat requirements or that don't coexist well with other species. I mean, I'd hate to bring in an endangered reef fish and have it eaten by some other species in the main tank!

> **Analyst:** There seems to be a lot to manage here: the animals, where they can live, what they need to eat.

> **Director:** We also need to track shipments of animals. We need to know where we can get species if we need them and what happens to shipments after they arrive at the aquarium. Oh, and to make things more complicated, we have all those volunteers who work with us. We need to keep track of what they do and when they're scheduled to do it.

> **Analyst:** Then we might be talking about two databases, one for the animals and one for the volunteers.

Director: That makes sense. There isn't any sharing of information between the two. Can you help us pull this all together?

Analyst: I'm certainly going to try. First, I need to talk to some of your staff members, to see what data they store and how they use it.

2. Transcript of a conversation between a systems analyst and the head keeper:

Analyst: Your job is to oversee the care of the animals?

Keeper: That's right. I have four full-time keepers working for me.

Analyst: Only four?

Keeper: I know that doesn't sound like a lot of people for an installation this size, but don't forget that we use a lot of volunteers. We train them to clean tanks and feed animals. Some of the more experienced ones can also help us medicate sick animals.

Analyst: What kind of records are you keeping now?

Keeper: A lot, in these file boxes. See, there's a separate section for each tank in the aquarium. This first card describes the size of a tank and its location in the building. The card also lists the tank's habitats.

Analyst: A tank can have multiple habitats?

Keeper: Certainly. In particular, the main tank has about fifteen different habitats. And a few of the smaller tanks have two or three.

Analyst: What else do you have in that box?

Keeper: A list of each species that lives in each tank. The same species might be housed in more than one location and each tank obviously can house many species.

Analyst: Do you keep track of how many of each species live in a given tank?

Keeper: Yes, but we don't always count every individual. I mean, it's easy to know how many dolphins and seals you have, but when it comes to something like the coral reef fish that swim in schools in the main tank, we can only approximate.

Analyst: Anything else in that box?

Keeper: Uh-huh—the problems that occur in a tank. A problem might be something like the salinity rising too high. We jot down every problem that occurs, when it happened, what we did to fix it, and when it was resolved.

Analyst: Does this arrangement work well?

Keeper: Not particularly. It's rather clumsy, especially if we need to find something like where all the animals of a given species are housed. Or even worse, if we need to locate all the species of the same genus.

Analyst: Oh, you've got the Latin names of the species?

Keeper: Yes, we keep both the Latin name and the English name. But finding things by the Latin name is hard. The box that describes the tanks only lists the English names; the Latin names are in this other box, the one that has information about the species. What we really need is a way to get all this information together, so that we aren't restricted in the way we can find info.

Analyst: That's exactly what a database system can do for you. So tell me, what do you have stored in that box about the animals?

Keeper (showing a card to the analyst): The English name, the Latin name—I mentioned those before—and a list of the habitats in which the species can live. We also have a list of the foods the animal eats, how often it gets fed each type of food, and the amount of food it gets each time it is fed.

Analyst: Can I assume that many species can eat the same type of food?

Keeper: Yes, but each species might not get the same quantity of that food or be fed it at the same time.

Analyst: Who uses all this information?

Keeper: Myself, my staff, and the volunteers. It needs to be accessible to everyone who might be trying to find out where to place a new animal, how to feed an animal, or how to fix a problem that has come up. You see, we use that problem history to help us figure out what to do when new problems arise. It lets us figure out what worked and what didn't. Oh, yes, the volunteers often use it to find out where a specific species is housed, especially when they're putting together a tour for a special group.

Analyst: Well, I think the database system we're planning can make things easier for you. It'll put all the data in one place, where it can be accessed in many different ways.

Keeper: I look forward to it.

3. Transcript of a conversation between the systems analyst and the animal procurement manager:

Analyst: As I understand it, your job is to obtain animals for the aquarium and to manage their arrival here.

Procurement Manager: That's right. When someone comes to me and asks that we get some critters, I find out where we can get them. Then I call up the supplier and get a price. Sometimes I place the order right over the phone; if we aren't in a hurry, we send the order through the mail. We always send confirming purchase orders for phone orders, though.

Analyst: So you keep track of not only orders, but where you *might* be able to get an animal if you needed it?

Procurement Manager: Yup. I've got a couple of Rolodexes right here. This one has all the suppliers we use. I can look up a supplier's name and find out all the types of critters they can sell us. This other one has the critters in it. See, I've got all the suppliers that the animals come from.

Analyst: Do you always buy animals?

Procurement Manager*:* No. Sometimes critters are donated. Other times we trade them with other aquariums or zoos. But even so, we handle them just like suppliers that we purchase from.

Analyst: How would you like to be rid of those Rolodexes and use a computer instead?

Procurement Manager: Sounds good to me. Can you get rid of all this order paperwork, too?

Analyst: We can sure try. Why don't you show me how you track orders.

Procurement Manager: Well, once we figure out where we want to order an animal, one of the office clerks types up a purchase order. Like I said earlier, even if we phoned in the order, we send a paper copy. Oh, here's one. See, it has a purchase order number and information like the order date and the company it's being sent to. Then, below that header info, we have all the animals that are being ordered—the species, the quantity, and the price. Can that computer of yours handle all this?

Analyst: Oh, I think so. This is a pretty typical way to handle purchasing. What do you do when a shipment comes in?

Procurement Manager: *That* might be different from other purchase orders. You see, before we put new animals in their permanent homes, we keep them in holding tanks in the back. That's so we can watch for illness. We don't want to put animals that carry disease into tanks with healthy animals!

Analyst: How long do you hold them?

Procurement Manager: It depends on the type of critter. When the quarantine period is over, then we put the animals out into the aquarium.

Analyst: Do all the animals of one species on one shipment go to the same tank?

Procurement Manager: Always. That way, if something goes wrong with the critters later, we can look back and find out where they came from. I mean, if we consistently get critters that aren't healthy from one supplier, well, we aren't going to order from that source any more.

Analyst: I guess you wouldn't want to, at that. Well, I think everything you've told me can be handled by the computer system that my co-workers and I are going to design for you. You'll be able to cut down on the amount of paper you have to keep.

Procurement Manager: I'm all for that!

4. Transcript of a conversation between the systems analyst and the volunteer coordinator:

Analyst: I understand that a lot of the work in the aquarium is performed by volunteers.

Volunteer Coordinator: That's true. We couldn't operate without them.

Analyst: How do you keep track of them and what they do?

Volunteer Coordinator: First, I use a card file to store each volunteer's name, address, and phone number. The card also lists all the skills that the volunteer has.

Analyst: Skills?

Volunteer Coordinator: Oh, things like "feed the dolphins" or "lead a high-school tour group" or "adjust the salinity of a tank of less than 100 gallons." The problem, of course, is that if I need to find someone who can do a specific job, I have to leaf through all of these cards, in order. It's a good thing I know the pool of volunteers pretty well. It can be a real problem if I'm sick or on vacation and someone else has to do it.

Analyst: Hopefully, the computer database system we're developing will help with that. So, once you know the name of a volunteer who can do a job, how do you schedule that person?

Volunteer Coordinator: I have a notebook right here. There's a page for each day. I write in the name and phone number of the volunteer, the time he or she will start, and the time he or she will finish. I also write in the job the person will be doing. Every morning I give the page for the day to the receptionist; she lets the full-time staff know who to expect to help them. Then, the volunteers check in with her when they arrive. She calls any that are more than a half hour late.

Analyst: What happens to the daily schedule at the end of the day?

Volunteer Coordinator: It gets filed. We use it for a number of things, including reports on the number of volunteer hours, rewards for the best volunteers, and identifying volunteers who never show up and who shouldn't be scheduled for work.

Glossary

Ad hoc query: An ad hoc query is a request for data from a database that cannot be predicted, that arises at the spur of the moment, and may never be repeated.

All key: A relation is all key if it contains no non-key attributes. In other words, every attribute in the relation is required to make a unique primary key.

Anomaly: An anomaly is a problem that occurs in a relation because of poor relational design. See also **deletion anomaly, insertion anomaly**, and **modification** anomaly.

Application program: An application program is a computer program that does useful business work. Application programs are often contrasted with systems programs, which work to make the computer more efficient.

Attribute: An attribute is a data item that describes an entity about which data are to be stored in a database; an attribute is a column in a relation.

Authorization matrix: An authorization matrix is a table that contains information about user access rights to data. The columns in the table correspond to objects within the database; the rows correspond to users.

Backup: Backup is the act of making a copy of a database as a hedge against some sort of system failure.

Base table: Base tables are tables whose contents are physically stored on disk by a relational DBMS. See also **virtual table**.

Batch processing: A technique for processing data that groups together activities against a file for execution at one time. The group of activities is referred to as a *batch*.

Candidate key: A candidate key is any set of attributes that meet the criteria to be a primary key. Every relation has at least one candidate key (the one selected as the primary key); some have more than one candidate key.

Catalog: A catalog is a data dictionary for a relational database.

Centralized database: A database is centralized if the entire database resides on one computer.

Client/server DBMS: A client/server DBMS is a multiuser DBMS that accepts data manipulation requests from more than one type of program, including other DBMSs and programs specifically written to function as front ends to the server.

Composite entity: A composite entity is an entity than stands for the relationship between two or more other entities. The most common use of a composite entity in a relational database is to provide a way to model many-to-many relationships.

Concatenated key: A concatenated key is a primary or foreign key that is made up of the data stored in more than one column. The DBMS manipulates the entire concatenated key as if the data were all in a single column; nonetheless, the data are stored in separate columns.

Conceptual schema: In the three-schema architecture model of a database, the conceptual schema represents the overall, logical plan of a database.

Concurrent use: A DBMS permits concurrent use if more than one user can simultaneously interact with the same database. This does not imply, however, that concurrent users can simultaneously use the same piece of data.

Constraint: Generally, a constraint is a rule to which data must adhere. More specifically, a constraint is a strict rule that governs some aspect of the behavior of data in a relational database.

Data consistency: A database system exhibits data consistency when data that represent the same thing are stored in the same way through the entire database system.

Data dictionary: A data dictionary is the place where the definition of a database schema is recorded.

Data disintegrity: Data disintegrity occurs when multiple copies of what should be exactly the same piece of data are no longer the same.

Data file: In a file management system, a data file is the physical file in which data are stored.

Data flow diagram: A data-flow diagram is a graphic tool used to show the flow of information through an organization. Typically, data flow diagrams use three different symbols: a square for sources of data, a circle or round-cornered rectangle for processes applied to data, and a rectangle for places where data are stored.

Data inconsistency: Data inconsistency occurs when data that represent the same thing are not stored in the same way throughout a file management or database system.

Data independence: A database with data independence is implemented in such a way that changes to physical data storage have no affect on the logical way that users and application programs view the data.

Data model: A data model is a framework used to describe the logical relationships between data in a database.

Database: A database is a collection of data stored in physical files along with the definitions of the relationships between the data in those files such that the data are perceived as a unified, logical whole, without regard for the physical storage structures.

Database administration: Database administration is the function within an organization that manages and supervises a database installation.

Database administrator: A database administrator is one or more individuals whose responsibility it is to manage a database installation.

Database design: Database design is the process of identifying the data relationships within a database environment and modeling those relationships into a database schema.

Database management: Database management is a technique for storing, organizing, and retrieving data stored in a database.

Database management system: A database management system is software that acts as an interface between a user and the physical storage of data in a database. The user issues a request to the database management system, which in turn takes care of storing and retrieving the data.

Database server: A database server is either a client/server DBMS or a computer that runs a client/server DBMS.

DBA: DBA is an abbreviation for Database administrator.

DBMS: DBMS is an abbreviation for Database management system.

Deadlock: Deadlock, or a deadly embrace, is a condition within a multiuser database in which one ore more transactions are frozen because (1) the data each needs are locked by another transaction, and (2) each holds locks on data needed by another transaction. The most common way to break deadlock is to force one transaction to release all its locks.

Deletion anomaly: A relation has a deletion anomaly if, when a row is deleted, data that should be retained are inadvertently lost.

Determinant: A determinant is an attribute for which at any given time there is only one value of each of a group of other attributes associated with it. See also **functional dependency.**

Distributed database: A database is distributed if the database resides on multiple computers linked by data communications lines.

Domain: A domain is the set of possible values for an attribute.

Domain constraint: A domain constraint is a rule that verifies that the values stored for an attribute come from that attribute's domain.

Entity: An entity is a person, place, object, or event about which data are stored in a database.

Entity integrity: Entity integrity is a constraint on a relation that states that no part of a primary key can be null.

Entity-relationship diagram: An entity-relationship diagram is a DBMS-independent way of graphically representing the relationships between entities in a database environment.

Entity-relationship model: The entity-relationship model is a method for identifying and documenting the relationships between entities in a database environment.

ER: ER is an abbreviation for entity relationship.

Exclusive lock: A transaction in a multiuser database is given an exclusive lock on a data object after indicating an intent to update that object. Once an exclusive lock is placed on a data object, no other transaction can update or even view that data until the exclusive lock is released.

Field: In a file processing system, a field is a piece of data that describes the single entity about which data are stored.

File: A file is a physical entity generally located on a magnetic or optical disk. (Files are also often placed on magnetic tape for backup purposes.) A file has a name and may contain the text of a document, the code for a computer program, or data organized in some known structure.

File management: File management is a technique for storing, organizing, and retrieving data that are stored in individual, isolated physical files. There is no logical pooling of the data. Each file supports its own group of application programs.

First normal form: A relation is in first normal form if it is represented as a two-dimensional table with columns and rows and no repeating groups. All relations are therefore in first normal form.

Foreign key: A foreign key is one or more attributes that reference (are the same as) the primary key in another relation. See also **referential integrity**.

Full functional dependency: A full functional dependency exists between two attributes or groups of attributes, A and B, if a functional dependence exists (in other words, A determines B) and the determinant is composed of the smallest number of attributes necessary to establish the determinance.

Functional dependency: A functional dependency exists between two attributes or groups of attributes, A and B, if, at any given time, only one value of B is associated with any given value of A. B is determined by A, or B is functionally dependent on A.

Impossible output: Output from a database system is impossible if it simply cannot be generated from the database, regardless of resources expended.

Index: An index is an implementation technique that is used to speed up the searching of relations.

Inconsistent analysis: Inconsistent analysis occurs in a multiuser database when a transaction modifies data that another transaction is using for data analysis, causing the result of the data analysis transaction to be incorrect.

Infeasible output: Output from a database system is infeasible if it would consume amounts of resources disproportionate to its value.

Input-process-output: Input-process-output is a systems development model that first looks at the output required by a system, then figures out what input data are required to produce the needed output, and finally considers the process to transform the input into the output.

Insertion anomaly: A relation has an insertion anomaly if data cannot be added to the relation when needed because the data to form a complete primary key are not available.

Instance (of a relation): An instance of a relation is the relation itself (the definition of the columns that make up the relation) and data stored in that relation.

Interleaved: Transactions in a multiuser database are interleaved if their actions take turns accessing the database.

IPO: IPO is the abbreviation for input-process-output.

Locking: Locking is a technique to prevent problems in a multiuser database. A transaction is given a lock on a data object to prevent other transactions from modifying (and perhaps viewing) the data object while the transaction holding the lock is working it.

Logical-physical data independence: See **Data independence**.

Logical schema: In the three-schema architecture, the logical schema is the portion of the conceptual schema used by an application program or a user.

Lost update: A lost update occurs when two transactions update the same data item in a multiuser database one after the other. The second update, based on the value of the data item before the first update, erases the first update (in other words, it is lost) and may introduce bad data into the database.

Many-to-many relationship: A many-to-many relationship exists between two entities, A and B, if A can be related to zero, one, or more occurrences of B and B can be related to zero, one, or more occurrences of A.

Modification anomaly: A relation has a modification anomaly if it contains unnecessary duplicated data that may become inconsistent during data modification.

Multiuser: A DBMS is multiuser if it permits more than one user to have simultaneous access to the data in a database. See also **Concurrent use, Client/server.**

Multivalued: An attribute is multivalued if there is more than one value for that attribute for a single occurrence of an entity.

Needs assessment: A needs assessment is the part of the systems development cycle that identifies the data processing needs of an organization.

Normal form: A normal form is a set of rules that governs the way attributes are assigned to a relation.

Normalization: Normalization is the process of designing relations so that they adhere to the rules for higher normal forms to avoid relational design problems.

Null: Null is a value that means "unknown." It is not the same as a zero or a blank.

Occurrence (of an entity): An occurrence of an entity is the collection of actual data values that describe one real-world entity.

One-to-many relationship: A one-to-many relationship exists between two attributes, A and B, if A can be related to zero, one, or more occurrences of attribute B but B can be related to only zero or one occurrence of A.

One-to-one relationship: A one-to-one relationship exists between two attributes, A and B, if A can be related to zero or one occurrence of attribute B and B can be related to zero or one occurrence of attribute A.

Parallel implementation: Parallel implementation is a technique for introducing a new computer system into an organization. Both the old system and the new system are run together, in parallel, through at least one business cycle. This helps to verify that the new system is working properly and provides an up-to-date alternative should the new system have to be shut down.

Physical schema: In the three-schema architecture, the physical schema represents the physical data storage structures.

Plunge implementation: Plunge implementation is a technique for introducing a new computer system into an organization. The old system is discontinued in favor of the new.

Primary key: A primary key is comprised of one or more attributes whose values uniquely identify each row in a relation.

QBE: QBE is the abbreviation for Query-By-Example.

Query-By-Example: Query-By-Example is a graphic database query language.

Query language: A query language is a special-purpose computer language used to manipulate data in a database either interactively by an end user or by embedding it an a host programming language.

Record: In a data file used by a file management system, a record is a collection of data that describes one occurence of an entity.

Redundant data: Redundant data occurs within a computer system when the same data about the same entity is stored more than once; multiple copies exist of the same data.

Referential integrity: Referential integrity is a constraint on a relation that states that all non-null foreign key values must reference existing primary key values. No foreign key value can exist in the database unless the primary key it references is also present.

Relation: A relation is the definition of a two-dimensional table made up of columns and rows. The term comes from mathematical set theory.

Relational algebra: The relational algebra is a set of operations for manipulating relations use by DBMSs. Each operation performs a single function. It is therefore often necessary for a DBMS to use a sequence of operations from the relational algebra to complete an information request. The eight basic operations of the relational algebra are select, project, join, union, difference, intersect, product, and divide.

Relational calculus: The relational calculus is a way to express multiple relational algebra operations in a single statement. Most relational query languages are based on the relational calculus, although the user rarely has to deal with a query language's mathematical roots.

Relational database: A relational database is a database that contains only one data structure: two-dimensional tables.

Relationally complete: A DBMS is relationally complete if it supports five operations from the relational algebra: select, project, join, union, and difference.

Requirements document: A requirements document is the end product of the needs assessment phase of a systems development project. The document contains, in detail, the requirements of a new or improved information system. It may contain data-flow diagrams, lists of data items, and/or samples of required system output.

SQL: SQL (Structured Query Language) is the U.S. national standard for a relational database query language.

Schema: A schema is the overall, global logical organization of a database. It contains definitions of all data items that the database will contain as well as the relationships between the entities described by those data.

Serializeable: In a multiuser database, two transactions are serializeable if the result of running them in an interleaved fashion produces the same result as running them in a series (one after the other).

Second normal form: A relation is in second normal form if it is in first normal form and all non-key attributes are fully functionally dependent on the primary key.

Shared lock: A shared lock is used in a multiuser database to prevent a transaction from changing data while another transaction is viewing it. Many transactions can hold a shared lock on the same data object. However, no transaction can obtain an exclusive lock until all shared locks are released.

Systems analysis: Systems analysis is the process of evaluating an existing information system and then assessing user needs to determine where the system should be modified to better meet user needs. A systems analysis will often end with proposals for new and/or improved systems.

Systems analyst: A systems analyst is a person who is trained to evaluate information systems and propose alternatives for changing them so they will better meet user needs.

Systems development cycle: The systems development cycle is a sequence of activities used to develop computer information systems. The steps in the cycle include performing a needs assessment to define needs, formulating and evaluating alternative solutions, designing the new system, and implementing the new system.

Subschema: A subschema is a logical subset of a database schema for use by a specific application; it is a user's logical view of a database.

Third normal form: A relation is in third normal form if it is in second normal form and there are no transitive dependencies.

Three-schema architecture: The three-schema architecture is a way of viewing the organization of a database from the user's view, the database designer's view, and the systems programmer's view.

Transaction: A transaction is a unit of work submitted to a database for processing. Interactive query languages usually define a transaction as a single command; application programs can control the length of a transaction.

Transitive dependency: A transitive dependency exists in a relation with three attributes A, B, and C when A determines B, B determines C, A determines C, and A is the primary key of the relation. Relations with transitive dependencies will have insertion and deletion anomalies as well as update problems.

Tuple: A tuple is a row in a relation.

Update anomaly: See **Modification anomaly.**

View: A view is a subset of a relational database for use by a specific user or application program. It is represented in the data dictionary as a query statement that is executed to produce a view table whenever a user wants to work with the view.

Virtual table: A virtual table is a temporary table created in main memory by a relational DBMS as the result a relational operation.

Index